"I have to poop!"

Dedicated to the world's 7.6 billion native speakers, all of whom (we're sorry to say) we'll probably offend at least once in this book.

Our sincere apologies in advance—and our thorough admiration at the remarkable languages you've mastered.

BUSHEL & PECK BOOKS

Published by Bushel & Peck Books, a family-run publishing house in Fresno, California, that believes in uplifting children with the highest standards of art, music, literature, and ideas. Find beautiful books for gifted young minds at www.bushelandpeckbooks.com.

Type set in Josefin Sans, Times New Roman, Arial Unicode MS, Nirmala UI, Abyssinica SIL, Padauk, and Khmer MN.

Designed by David Miles.

Bushel & Peck Books is dedicated to fighting illiteracy all over the world. For every book we sell, we donate one to a child in need—book for book. To nominate a school or organization to receive free books, please visit www.bushelandpeckbooks.com.

ISBN: 9781952239649

First Edition

Printed in the United States

10 9 8 7 6 5 4 3 2 1

"I have to poop!"

AND OTHER IMPORTANT PHRASES IN OVER 85 LANGUAGES

PUBLISHER'S NOTE

Dear reader,

At the onset, let us frankly admit a few things this book is not. It is not a travel guide—unless you regularly find yourself breaking toilet plungers and walking to Mordor on your travels. And though we've done our best, we can't claim it's especially accurate. Translation is a ticklish business even at the best of times, so be generous as you peruse the pages and remember that this particular bookish experience is more about breadth than it is linguistic depth.

But with that in mind, there are several other things this book is. It's quirky. It's fat. And it's a thoroughly entertaining introduction to the many languages spoken around the world. Observant readers will find parallels among different language families and, if nothing else, a fun reminder that this blue marble we live on is at once so much more complex and simple than we often realize.

We hope you'll find a window to that complex simplicity in these pages. But if not, when you're in a pinch on the Dubai Metro, you'll at least know how to shout:

"I HAVE TO POOP!"

Most sincerely,

Bushel & Peck Books

WHERE CAN YOU HEAR THESE LANGUAGES?

Language doesn't stop at border crossings, and indeed, thanks to travel and emigration, most of these languages might be heard in one form or another anywhere in the world. In the chart below, we've noted the places you're *most* likely to hear them. Some of these languages are considered vulnerable or endangered (we've marked these with a *), while others are just one of many spoken in one country alone. This list is just a fraction of the hundreds of languages spoken worldwide.

Afrikaans	South Africa, Namibia
Albanian	Albania, Kosovo
Amharic	Ethiopia
Arabic	Middle East, Northern Africa
Armenian	Armenia
Azerbaijani	Azerbaijan
Basque*	Spain and France
Belarusian	Belarus
Bosnian	Bosnia-Herzegovina
Bulgarian	Bulgaria
Burmese	Myanmar
Catalan	Spain, Andorra
Cebuano	Philippines
Mandarin Chinese	Mainland China, Taiwan
Corsican*	Corsica (France)
Croatian	Croatia
Czech	Czech Republic
Danish	Denmark

Dutch	The Netherlands
Esperanto*	Europe
Estonian	Estonia
Filipino	Philippines
Finnish	Finland
French	France, Canada, Belgium, Switzerland, parts of Africa
Galician*	Spain
Georgian	Georgia
German	Germany, Austria, Belgium, Luxembourg
Greek	Greece, Cyprus
Haitian Creole	Haiti
Hausa	Niger, Nigeria
Hawaiian	Hawaii
Hindi	India
Hmong	Thailand, Laos, Myanmar, China, Vietnam
Hungarian	Hungary
Icelandic	Iceland

Igbo	Nigeria
Indonesian	Indonesia
Irish*	Ireland
Italian	Italy, Vatican City
Japanese	Japan
Javanese	Java (Indonesia)
Kannada	Karnataka (India)
Kazakh	Kazakhstan
Kinyarwanda	Rwanda
Korean	South Korea, North Korea
Kurdish	Turkey, Syria, Iraq, Iran
Kyrgyz	Kyrgyzstan
Latvian	Latvia
Lithuanian	Lithuania
Luxembourgish	Luxembourg
Macedonian	North Macedonia
Malagasy	Madagascar
Malay	Malaysia, Indonesia
Maltese	Malta
Maori*	New Zealand
Marathi	Maharashtra (India)
Mongolian	Mongolia
Nepali	Nepal
Norwegian	Norway
Polish	Poland
Portuguese	Portugal, Brazil, Angola, Mozambique,
Punjabi	India, Pakistan

Romanian	Romania
Russian	Russia, Ukraine
Samoan	Samoa
Scots Gaelic*	Scotland
Serbian	Bosnia-Herzegovina
Slovak	Slovakia
Slovenian	Slovenia
Somali	Somalia
Spanish	Latin America, South America, Spain
Sundanese	Sudan
Swahili	Tanzania, Kenya, Uganda, the Democratic Republic of Congo
Swedish	Sweden, Finland
Tajik	Tajikistan
Tamil	Tamil Nadu (India)
Telugu	Southeast India
Thai	Thailand
Turkish	Turkey, Cyprus
Turkmen	Turkmenistan
Ukrainian	Ukraine
Uzbek	Uzbekistan
Vietnamese	Vietnam
Welsh*	Wales
Yiddish*	Israel, Russia
Zulu	Zululand (South Africa)

Language status source: https://www.theguardian.com/news/datablog/2011/apr/15/language-extinct-endangered

CONTENTS

18 Piece of cake.

19 Houston, we have a problem.

20 Inconceivable!

21 Who let the tiger in?

22 No thank you. I already ate monkey today.

23 I've rescued forty-eight cats.

24 What's for dinner?

25 One does not simply walk into Mordor.

26 Is that peg leg a rental?

27 Simon says, "Pick your nose."

28 It was an accident!

29 We need a bigger boat.

30 Stop!

31 The plunger broke.

32 Say hello to my little friend.

33 What big teeth you have!

34 Elementary, Watson.

35 My brain died.

36 Epic!

37 Join the club.

38 Is that a tornado?

39 Made you look.

40 Are we lost?

41 The sky is falling!

42 Who clogged the toilet?

43 Not it!

44 Be my guest.

45 I do not like green eggs and ham.

46 You cheated.

47 Nice pumpkin head.

48 Step on it!

49 I'm getting nothing for Christmas.

50 Four score and seven years ago . . .

51 The vampires are here again.

52 I'm sure these screws aren't important.

53 Fly, you fools!

54 This tastes like sewage.

55 Can I borrow a cup of sugar?

56 Old soldiers never die.

57 Do not pass "Go." Do not collect $200.

58 Who wrote this book?!?

1 I have to poop!

AFRIKAANS

Ek moet poep!

ALBANIAN

Duhet te bej kaken!

AMHARIC

መፀዳዳት አለብኝ!

Mewasheti ālebinyi!

ARABIC

لا بد لي من أنبوب!

Yajib 'an 'ataghuta!

ARMENIAN

Ես պետք է թրցնեմ:

Yes petk' e t'rrts'nem!

AZERBAIJANI

Qusmalıyam!

BASQUE

Kaka egin behar dut!

BELARUSIAN

Я павінен какаць!

Ja pavinien kakać!

BOSNIAN

Moram kakiti!

BULGARIAN

Трябва да какам!

Tryabva da akam!

BURMESE

ငါစုပ်ရမယ်။

Ngar hcote ramaal!

CATALAN

He de fer caca!

CEBUANO

Kinahanglan nako magbulsa!

MANDARIN CHINESE

我要拉屎！

Wǒ yào lā shǐ!

CORSICAN

Aghju da cacà!

CROATIAN

Moram kakati!

CZECH

Musím kakat!

DANISH

Jeg skal lave pølser!

DUTCH

Ik moet poepen!

ESPERANTO

Mi devas feki!

ESTONIAN

Ma pean kakama!

FILIPINO

Kailangan kong mag-tae!

FINNISH

Täytyy kakkailla!

FRENCH

Je dois faire caca!

GALICIAN

Teño que facer caca!

GEORGIAN

უნდა ვიხურო!

Unda vikhumro!

GERMAN

Ich muss kacken!

GREEK

Πρέπει να σκάσω!

Prépei na kakáro!

HAITIAN CREOLE

Mwen gen poupou!

HAUSA

Dole ne in yi kumbura!

HAWAIIAN

Pono wau e poop!

HINDI

मुझे शौच करना है!

Mujhe bevaqoof banana hoga!

HMONG

Kuv yuav tsum quav!

HUNGARIAN

Kakilnom kell!

ICELANDIC

Ég verð að kúka!

IGBO

Ekwesịrị m ịkụ azụ!

INDONESIAN

Aku harus buang air besar!

IRISH

Caithfidh mé poop!

ITALIAN

Devo fare la cacca!

JAPANESE

うんちしなきゃ！

Unchi shinakya!

JAVANESE

Aku kudu poop!

KANNADA

ನಾನು ಮಲಗಬೇಕು!

Nānu malagabēku!

KAZAKH

Мен нәжіс шығаруым керек!

Men näjis şığarwım kerek!

KINYARWANDA

Ngomba kwikubita hasi!

KOREAN

똥을 싸야해!

Ttong-eul ssayahae!

KURDISH

Divê ez pûç bikim!

KYRGYZ

Мен сыгышым керек!

Men sıgışım kerek!

LATVIAN

Man jākakā!

LITHUANIAN

Aš turiu kakuoti!

LUXEMBOURGISH

Ech muss drénken!

MACEDONIAN

Морам да какам!

Moram da kakam!

MALAGASY

Tsy maintsy mikorisa aho!

MALAY

Saya mesti buang!

MALTESE

Għandi nagħmel ħmieġ!

MAORI

Me poopati au!

MARATHI

मला पळवावा लागेल!

Malā paḷavāvā lāgēla!

MONGOLIAN

Би хахах хэрэгтэй!

Bi khündrekh kheregtei baina!

NEPALI

मैले पिट्नु पर्छ!

Mailē piṭnu parcha!

NORWEGIAN

Jeg må bæsje!

NYANJA

Ndiyenera kutulutsa!

POLISH

Muszę zrobić kupę!

PORTUGUESE

Eu tenho que fazer cocô!

PUNJABI

ਮੈਨੂੰ ਹਿਲਾਉਣਾ ਪਏਗਾ!

Mainū hilā'uṇā pa'ēgā!

ROMANIAN

Trebuie să fac caca!

RUSSIAN

Мне надо какать!

Mne nuzhno pokakat'!

SAMOAN

E tatau ona ou alu!

SCOTS GAELIC

Feumaidh mi poop!

SERBIAN

Морам какати!

Moram da kakim!

SLOVAK

Musím kakať!

SLOVENIAN

Moram pokakati!

SOMALI

Waa inaan salaaxaa!

SPANISH

¡Tengo que hacer caca!

SUNDANESE

Abdi kedah kotoran!

SWAHILI

Lazima ninywe!

SWEDISH

Jag måste bajsa!

TAJIK

Ман мачбурам!

Man maçвuram!

TAMIL

நான் மலம் கழிக்க வேண்டும்!

Nāṉ malam kaḻikka vēṇṭum!

TELUGU

నేను విసర్జించాలి!

Nēnu visarjiñcāli!

THAI

ฉันต้องเซ่อ!

Chạn t̂xng sèu!

TURKISH

Kaka yapmalıyım!

TURKMEN

Men açmaly!

UKRAINIAN

Я мушу какати!

Ya mushu kakaty!

UZBEK

Men qichishishim kerak!

VIETNAMESE

Tôi phải đi ị!

VIETNAMESE

Mae'n rhaid i mi poop!

YIDDISH

איך האָבן צו פּופּ!

Ikh hobn tsu pup!

ZULU

Kumele ngichithe!

2 Dracula is your cousin? How nice.

AFRIKAANS

Is Dracula jou neef? Hoe lekker.

ALBANIAN

Drakula është kushëriri juaj? Sa mirë.

AMHARIC

ድራኩላ የአጎት ልጅህ ነው? እንዴት ደስ ይላል።

Dirakula ye'āgoti lijihi newi? Inidēti desi yilali.

ARABIC

دراكولا هو ابن عمك؟ كم هو جميل.

Darakula hu abn eumka? Kam hu jamil.

ARMENIAN

Դրակուլան քո զարմիկն է: Ինչքան գեղեցիկ.

Drakulan k'vo zarmikn e: Inch'k'an geghets'ik.

AZERBAIJANI

Dracula əminiz oğludur? Necə də gözəl.

BASQUE

Drakula zure lehengusua da? Zein ona.

BELARUSIAN

Дракула - твой стрыечны брат? Як прыемна.

Drakula - tvoj stryječny brat? Jak pryjemna.

BOSNIAN

Drakula je tvoj rođak? Kako lijepo.

BULGARIAN

Дракула твой братовчед ли е? Колко хубаво.

Drakula tvoĭ bratovched li e? Kolko khubavo.

BURMESE

Dracula မင်းရဲ့ဝမ်းကွဲလား။ ဘယ်လောက်ကောင်းလိုက်လဲ။

Dracula mainnrae wamkwal larr? Bhaallout kaungg lite lell.

CATALAN

Dràcula és el teu cosí? Que bé.

CEBUANO

Si Dracula imong ig-agaw? Unsa ka nindot.

MANDARIN CHINESE

德古拉是你表妹？多好。

Dé gŭ lā shì nĭ biăomèi? Duō hăo.

CORSICAN

Dracula hè u to cuginu? Chì bellu.

CROATIAN

Drakula je vaš rođak? Kako lijepo.

CZECH

Dracula je tvůj bratranec? Jak milé.

DANISH

Dracula er din fætter? Hvor fint.

DUTCH

Dracula is je neef? Wat leuk.

ESPERANTO

Drakulo estas via kuzo? Kiel bela.

ESTONIAN

Dracula on su nõbu? Kui kena.

FILIPINO

Si Dracula ay pinsan mo? Magaling.

FINNISH

Dracula on serkkusi? Kuinka mukavaa.

FRENCH

Dracula est ton cousin? Comme c'est gentil.

GALICIAN

Drácula é a túa curmá? Qué ben.

GEORGIAN

დრაკულა შენი ბიძაშვილია? რა კარგია.

Drak'ula sheni bidzashvilia? A k'argia.

GERMAN

Dracula ist dein Cousin? Wie schön.

GREEK

Ο Δράκουλας είναι ξάδερφος σου; Τι ωραία.

O Drákoulas einai xáderfos sou? Ti oraía.

HAITIAN CREOLE

Dracula se kouzen ou? Ala bèl.

HAUSA

Dracula dan uwanku ne? Yaya kyau.

HAWAIIAN

ʻO Dracula kou hoahānau? Pehea ka maikaʻi.

HINDI

ड्रैकुला आपका चचेरा भाई है? कितना अच्छा।

draikula aapaka chachera bhaee hai? kitana achchha.

HMONG

Dracula puas yog koj tus npawg? Zoo nkauj npaum cas.

HUNGARIAN

Drakula az unokatestvéred? De kedves.

ICELANDIC

Dracula er frændi þinn? En fínt.

IGBO

Dracula bụ nwa nwanne nna gị? Ọ dị mma.

INDONESIAN

Drakula adalah sepupumu? Bagusnya.

IRISH

Is é Dracula do chol ceathrar? Nach deas é.

ITALIAN

Dracula è tuo cugino? Che carino.

JAPANESE

ドラキュラはあなたのいとこですか？なんて素敵だ。

Dorakyura wa anata no itokodesu ka? Nante sutekida.

JAVANESE

Dracula iku sedulurmu? Apik tenan.

KANNADA

ಡ್ರಾಕುಲಾ ನಿಮ್ಮ ಸೋದರಸಂಬಂಧಿ? ಎಷ್ಟು ಚೆಂದ.

Ḍrākulā nim'ma sōdarasambandhi? Eṣṭu cenda.

KAZAKH

Дракула сенің туысың ба? Қандай керемет.

Drakwla seniñ twısıñ ba? Qanday keremet.

KINYARWANDA

Dracula ni mubyara wawe? Nibyiza.

KOREAN

드라큘라가 당신의 사촌입니까? 얼마나 좋은지.

Deulakyullaga dangsin-ui sachon-ibnikka? Eolmana joh-eunji.

KURDISH

Dracula pismamê te ye? Çiqas xweş e.

KYRGYZ

Дракула сенин жеңби? Кандай сонун.

Drakula senin ejeŋbi? Kanday sonun.

LATVIAN

Drakula ir tava māsīca? Cik jauki.

LITHUANIAN

Drakula yra tavo pusbrolis? Kaip miela.

LUXEMBOURGISH

Den Dracula as äre koseng? Wéi schéin.

MACEDONIAN

Дракула ти е братучед? Колку убаво.

Drakula ti e bratučed? Kolku ubavo.

MALAGASY

Dracula no zanak'olo-mpiray tam-po aminao? Tsara be.

MALAY

Dracula adalah sepupu anda? Bagusnya.

MALTESE

Dracula huwa l-kuġin tiegħek? Xi hlew.

MAORI

Ko Dracula to whanaunga? Ano te pai.

MARATHI

ड्रॅकुला तुमचा चुलत भाऊ आहे का? किती छान.

Ḍrĕkulā tumacā culata bhā'ū āhē kā? Kitī chāna.

MONGOLIAN

Дракула бол таны үеэл үү? Ямар сайхан юм бэ.

Drakula bol tany üyeel üü? Yamar saikhan yum be.

NEPALI

ड्रेकुला तिम्रो चचेरो भाई हो? कति राम्रो।

Ḍrēkulā timrō cacērō bhā'ī hō? Kati rāmrō.

NORWEGIAN

Dracula er fetteren din? Så fint.

NYANJA

Dracula ndi msuweni wako? Ndizabwino bwanji.

POLISH

Dracula jest twoim kuzynem? Jak miło.

PORTUGUESE

Drácula é seu primo? Que legal.

PUNJABI

ਡ੍ਰੈਕੁਲਾ ਤੁਹਾਡਾ ਚਚੇਰੇ ਭਰਾ ਹੈ? ਕਿੰਨਾ ਚੰਗਾ.

Ḍraikulā tuhāḍā cacērē bharā hai? Kinā cagā.

ROMANIAN

Dracula este vărul tău? Ce drăguț.

RUSSIAN

Дракула - твой двоюродный брат? Как мило.

Drakula - tvoy dvoyurodnyy brat? Kak milo.

SAMOAN

Dracula o lou tausoga? Manaia tele.

SCOTS GAELIC

Is e Dracula do cho-ogha? Cho snog.

SERBIAN

Дракула је твој рођак? Баш лепо.

Drakula je tvoj rođak? Baš lepo.

SLOVAK

Dracula je tvoj bratranec? Aké milé.

SLOVENIAN

Drakula je vaš bratranec? Kako lepo.

SOMALI

Dracula waa ina -adeerkaa? Sidee fiican.

SPANISH

¿Drácula es tu primo? Que agradable.

SUNDANESE

Dracula téh misan anjeun? Kumaha saé.

SWAHILI

Dracula ni binamu yako? Jinsi nzuri.

SWEDISH

Dracula är din kusin? Vad trevligt.

TAJIK

Дракула ҷияни шумо аст? Чӣ хуб.

Drakula çijani şumo ast? Cī хив.

TAMIL

டிராகுலா உங்கள் உறவினர்? எவ்வளவு அருமை.

Ṭirākulā uṅkaḷ uṟaviṉar? Evvaḷavu arumai.

TELUGU

డ్రాక్యులా మీ కజిన్? చాలా మంచి.

Ḍrākyulā mī kajin? Cālā man̄ci.

THAI

แดร็กคิวล่าเป็นลูกพี่ลูกน้องคุณเหรอ? ดีแค่ไหน.

Dæ r̆k khiw l̀ā pĕn lūkphī̀lūkn̂xng khuṇ h̄e rx? Dī khæ̀ h̄ịn.

TURKISH

Drakula senin kuzenin mi? Ne güzel.

TURKMEN

Drakula doganoglanymy? Nähili gowy.

UKRAINIAN

Дракула, твій двоюрідний брат? Як гарно.

Drakula, tviy dvoyuridnyy brat? Yak harno.

UZBEK

Drakula sizning qarindoshingizmi? Qanday yaxshi.

VIETNAMESE

Dracula là anh họ của bạn? Thật tuyệt.

VIETNAMESE

Dracula ydy'ch cefnder? Mor braf.

YIDDISH

דראַקולאַ איז דיין קוזינע? ווי שיין.

Drakula iz deyn kuzine? Vi sheyn.

ZULU

U Dracula umzala wakho? Kwakuhle.

3 I should have stayed home today.

AFRIKAANS

Ek moes vandag tuis gebly het.

ALBANIAN

Duhet të kisha qëndruar sot në shtëpi.

AMHARIC

ዛሬ ቤት መቆየት ነበረብኝ።

Zarē bēti mek'oyeti neberebinyi.

ARABIC

كان يجب أن أبقى في المنزل اليوم.

Kan yajib 'an 'abqaa fi almanzil alyawma.

ARMENIAN

Ես այսօր պետք է տանը մնայի:

Yes aysor petk' e tany mnayi:

AZERBAIJANI

Bu gün evdə qalmalıydım.

BASQUE

Gaur etxean egon beharko nuke.

BELARUSIAN

Я павінен быў застацца дома сёння.

Ja pavinien byŭ zastacca doma sionnia.

BOSNIAN

Trebao sam danas ostati kod kuće.

BULGARIAN

Трябваше да остана вкъщи днес.

Tryabvashe da ostana vkŭshti dnes.

BURMESE

ငါဒီနေ့အိမ်မှာနေခဲ့သင့်တယ်။

Ngar denae aainmhar nay hkae sang taal.

CATALAN

Avui m'hauria d'haver quedat a casa.

CEBUANO

Kinahanglan unta ako magpabilin sa balay karon.

MANDARIN CHINESE

我今天應該待在家裡。

Wǒ jīntiān yìng gāi dài zài jiālǐ.

CORSICAN

Avissi duvutu stà in casa oghje.

CROATIAN

Danas sam trebao ostati kod kuće.

CZECH

Měl jsem dnes zůstat doma.

DANISH

Jeg skulle have været hjemme i dag.

DUTCH

Ik had vandaag thuis moeten blijven.

ESPERANTO

Mi devintus resti hejme hodiaŭ.

ESTONIAN

Oleksin pidanud täna koju jääma.

FILIPINO

Dapat ay nanatili ako sa bahay ngayon.

FINNISH

Minun olisi pitänyt jäädä kotiin tänään.

FRENCH

J'aurais dû rester à la maison aujourd'hui.

GALICIAN

Debería quedar hoxe na casa.

GEORGIAN

დღეს სახლში უნდა დავრჩენილიყავი.

Dghes sakhlshi unda davrcheniliq'avi.

GERMAN

Ich hätte heute zu hause bleiben sollen.

GREEK

Έπρεπε να μείνω σπίτι σήμερα.

Éprepe na meíno spíti símera.

HAITIAN CREOLE

Mwen ta dwe rete lakay mwen jodi a.

HAUSA

Yakamata in zauna gida yau.

HAWAIIAN

Ua noho wau i ka home i kēia lā.

HINDI

मुझे आज घर पर ही रहना चाहिए था।

Mujhe aaj ghar par hee rahana chaahie tha.

HMONG

Kuv yuav tsum tau nyob hauv tsev hnub no.

HUNGARIAN

Ma otthon kellett volna maradnom.

ICELANDIC

Ég hefði átt að vera heima í dag.

IGBO

M gaara anọ n'ụlọ taa.

INDONESIAN

Seharusnya aku tinggal di rumah hari ini.

IRISH

Ba chóir dom a bheith tar éis fanacht sa bhaile inniu.

ITALIAN

Sarei dovuto restare a casa oggi.

JAPANESE

今日は家にいるべきだった。

Kyō wa ie ni irubekidatta.

JAVANESE

Aku kudune wis nginep dina iki.

KANNADA

ನಾನು ಇಂದು ಮನೆಯಲ್ಲೇ ಇರಬೇಕಿತ್ತು.

Nānu indu maneyallē irabēkittu.

KAZAKH

Мен бүгін үйде қалуым керек еді.

Men bügin üyde qalwım kerek edi.

KINYARWANDA

Nari nkwiye kuguma mu rugo uyu munsi.

KOREAN

오늘은 집에 있었어야 했다.

Oneul-eun jib-e iss-eoss-eoya haessda.

KURDISH

Divê ez îro li malê bimama.

KYRGYZ

Мен бүгүн үйдө калышым керек болчу.

Men bügün üydö kalışım kerek bolçu.

LATVIAN

Man šodien vajadzēja palikt mājās.

LITHUANIAN

Šiandien turėjau likti namuose.

LUXEMBOURGISH

Ech sollt haut doheem bleiwen.

MACEDONIAN

Денес требаше да останам дома.

Denes trebaše da ostanam doma.

MALAGASY

Tokony nijanona tao an-trano aho androany.

MALAY

Saya sepatutnya tinggal di rumah hari ini.

MALTESE

Kelli nibqa d-dar illum.

MAORI

Ahau i noho ki te kainga i tenei ra.

MARATHI

मी आज घरीच थांबायला हवे होते.

Mī āja gharīca thāmbāyalā havē hōtē.

MONGOLIAN

Би өнөөдөр гэртээ үлдэх ёстой байсан.

Bi önöödör gertee üldekh yostoi baisan.

NEPALI

म आज घरमै बस्नु पर्ने थियो।

Ma āja gharamai basnu parnē thiyō.

NORWEGIAN

Jeg burde vært hjemme i dag.

NYANJA

Ndikanayenera kukhala kunyumba lero.

POLISH

Powinienem był zostać dzisiaj w domu.

PORTUGUESE

Eu deveria ter ficado em casa hoje.

PUNJABI

ਮੈਨੂੰ ਅੱਜ ਘਰ ਰਹਿਣਾ ਚਾਹੀਦਾ ਸੀ.

Mainū aja ghara rahiṇā cāhīdā sī.

ROMANIAN

Ar fi trebuit să rămân acasă astăzi.

RUSSIAN

Мне следовало сегодня остаться дома.

Mne sledovalo segodnya ostat'sya doma.

SAMOAN

Sa tatau ona ou nofo i le fale i le aso.

SCOTS GAELIC

Bu chòir dhomh a bhith air fuireach dhachaigh an-diugh.

SERBIAN

Данас сам требао остати код куће.

Danas sam trebao ostati kod kuće.

SLOVAK

Dnes som mal zostať doma.

SLOVENIAN

Danes bi moral ostati doma.

SOMALI

Waxay ahayd inaan maanta guriga joogo.

SPANISH

Debería haberme quedado en casa hoy.

SUNDANESE

Abdi kedah cicing di bumi dinten ayeuna.

SWAHILI

Nilipaswa kukaa nyumbani leo.

SWEDISH

Jag borde ha stannat hemma idag.

TAJIK

Ман бояд имрӯз дар хона мебудам.

Man вojad imrūz dar xona меvudam.

TAMIL

நான் இன்று வீட்டில் தங்கியிருக்க வேண்டும்.

Nāṉ iṉṟu vīṭṭil taṅkiyirukka vēṇṭum.

TELUGU

నేను ఈ రోజు ఇంట్లో ఉండి ఉండాలి.

Nēnu ī rōju iṇṭlō uṇḍi uṇḍāli.

THAI

วันนี้ฉันควรจะอยู่บ้าน

Wạn nî c̄hạn khwr ca xyū̀ b̂ān

TURKISH

Bugün evde kalmalıydım.

TURKMEN

Men şu gün öýde galmalydym.

UKRAINIAN

Мені сьогодні мало залишитися вдома.

Meni s'ohodni malo zalyshytysya vdoma.

UZBEK

Men bugun uyda qolishim kerak edi.

VIETNAMESE

Đáng lẽ hôm nay tôi nên ở nhà.

VIETNAMESE

Dylwn i fod wedi aros adref heddiw.

YIDDISH

איך זאָל האָבן סטייד היים הײַנט.

ikh zol hobn steyd heym haynt.

ZULU

Bekufanele ngihlale ekhaya namuhla.

❹ The book was better.

AFRIKAANS

Die boek was beter.

ALBANIAN

Libri ishte më i mirë.

AMHARIC

መጽሐፉ የተሻለ ነበር።

Mets'iḥāfu yeteshale neberi.

ARABIC

كان الكتاب أفضل.

Kan alkitab 'afdala.

ARMENIAN

Գիրքն ավելի լավն էր։

Girk'n aveli lavn er:

AZERBAIJANI

Kitab daha yaxşı idi.

BASQUE

Liburua hobea zen.

BELARUSIAN

Кніга была лепшай.

Kniha byla liepšaj.

BOSNIAN

Knjiga je bila bolja.

BULGARIAN

Книгата беше по -добра.

Knigata beshe po -dobra.

BURMESE

င်းစာအုပ်သည်ပိုမိုကောင်းမွန်သည်။

Inn hcaraote sai pomo kaunggmwan sai.

CATALAN

El llibre era millor.

CEBUANO

Mas maayo ang libro.

MANDARIN CHINESE

這本書更好。

Zhè běnshū gèng hǎo.

CORSICAN

U libru era megliu.

CROATIAN

Knjiga je bila bolja.

CZECH

Kniha byla lepší.

DANISH

Bogen var bedre.

DUTCH

Het boek was beter.

ESPERANTO

La libro estis pli bona.

ESTONIAN

Raamat oli parem.

FILIPINO

Ang libro ay mas mahusay.

FINNISH

Kirja oli parempi.

FRENCH

Le livre était mieux.

GALICIAN

O libro era mellor.

GEORGIAN

წიგნი უკეთესი იყო.

Ts'igni uk'etesi iq'o.

GERMAN

Das buch war besser.

GREEK

Το βιβλίο ήταν καλύτερο.

To vivlío ítan kalýtero.

HAITIAN CREOLE

Liv la te pi bon.

HAUSA

Littafin ya fi kyau.

HAWAIIAN

ʻOi aku ka maikaʻi o ka puke.

HINDI

किताब बेहतर थी।

Kitaab behatar thee.

HMONG

Phau ntawv tau zoo dua.

HUNGARIAN

A könyv jobb volt.

ICELANDIC

Bókin var betri.

IGBO

Akwụkwọ ahụ ka mma.

INDONESIAN

Buku itu lebih baik.

IRISH

Bhí an leabhar níos fearr.

ITALIAN

Il libro era migliore.

JAPANESE

本の方が良かった。

Sono moto wa motto yokatta.

JAVANESE

Bukune luwih apik.

KANNADA

ಪುಸ್ತಕವು ಉತ್ತಮವಾಗಿತ್ತು.

Pustakavu uttamavāgittu.

KAZAKH

Кітап жақсы болды.

Kitap jaqsı boldı.

KINYARWANDA

Igitabo cyari cyiza.

KOREAN

책이 더 좋았다.

Chaeg-i deo joh-assseubnida.

KURDISH

Pirtûk çêtir bû.

KYRGYZ

Китеп жакшы болчу.

Kitep jakşı bolçu.

LATVIAN

Grāmata bija labāka.

LITHUANIAN

Knyga buvo geresnė.

LUXEMBOURGISH

D'buch war besser.

MACEDONIAN

Книгата беше подобра.

Knigata beše podobra.

MALAGASY

Tsara kokoa ilay boky.

MALAY

Buku itu lebih baik.

MALTESE

Il-ktieb kien aħjar.

MAORI

He pai ake te pukapuka.

MARATHI

पुस्तक चांगले होते.

Pustaka cāṅgalē hōtē.

MONGOLIAN

Ном илүү дээр байсан.

Nom ilüü deer baisan.

NEPALI

पुस्तक अझ राम्रो थियो।

Pustaka ajha rāmrō thiyō.

NORWEGIAN

Boken var bedre.

NYANJA

Bukulo linali labwino.

POLISH

Książka była lepsza.

PORTUGUESE

O livro era melhor.

PUNJABI

ਕਿਤਾਬ ਬਿਹਤਰ ਸੀ.

Kitāba bihatara sī.

ROMANIAN

Cartea a fost mai bună.

RUSSIAN

Книга получше была.

Kniga byla luchshe.

SAMOAN

Sa sili atu le tusi.

SCOTS GAELIC

Bha an leabhar na b ’fheàrr.

SERBIAN

Књига је била боља.

Knjiga je bila bolja.

SLOVAK

Kniha bola lepšia.

SLOVENIAN

Knjiga je bila boljša.

SOMALI

Buuggu wuu fiicnaa.

SPANISH

El libro fue mejor.

SUNDANESE

Buku na langkung saé.

SWAHILI

Kitabu kilikuwa bora.

SWEDISH

Boken var bättre.

TAJIK

Китоб беҳтар буд.

Kitoв behtar вud.

TAMIL

புத்தகம் சிறப்பாக இருந்தது.

Puttakam ciṟappāka iruntatu.

TELUGU

పుస్తకం మెరుగ్గా ఉంది.

Pustakaṁ meruggā undi.

THAI

หนังสือเล่มนี้ดีกว่า

Nạngs̄ụ̄x lèm nî dī kẁā.

TURKISH

Kitap daha güzeldi.

TURKMEN

Kitap has gowudy.

UKRAINIAN

Книга була кращою.

Knyha bula krashchoyu.

UZBEK

Kitob yaxshiroq edi.

VIETNAMESE

Cuốn sách đã tốt hơn.

VIETNAMESE

Roedd y llyfr yn well.

YIDDISH

דער בוך איז געווען בעסער.

Der bukh iz geven beser.

ZULU

Incwadi yayingcono.

5 Why didn't I wear a parachute?

AFRIKAANS

Waarom het ek nie 'n valskerm gedra nie?

ALBANIAN

Pse nuk kam veshur një parashutë?

AMHARIC

ለምን ፓራሹት አልለበስኩም?

Lemini parashuti ālilebesikumi?

ARABIC

لماذا لم ألبس المظلة؟

Limadha lam 'artadi mizalatan?

ARMENIAN

Ինչու ես պարաշյուտ չկրեցի:

Inch'u yes parashyut ch'em hagel.

AZERBAIJANI

Niyə paraşüt taxmadım?

BASQUE

Zergatik ez nuen paraxutik jantzi?

BELARUSIAN

Чаму я не насіў парашут?

Čamu ja nie nasiŭ parašut?

BOSNIAN

Zašto nisam nosio padobran?

BULGARIAN

Защо не носех парашут?

Zashto ne nosekh parashut?

BURMESE

ငါဘာလို့လေထီးမဝတ်ခဲ့တာလဲ။

Ngar bharlhoet layhtee m waat hkae tarlell.

CATALAN

Per què no portava un paracaigudes?

CEBUANO

Ngano nga wala ako magsul-ob og parachute?

MANDARIN CHINESE

為什麼我沒有帶降落傘？

Wèishéme wǒ méiyǒu dài jiàngluòsǎn?

CORSICAN

Perchè ùn aghju micca purtatu un parachute?

CROATIAN

Zašto nisam nosio padobran?

CZECH

Proč jsem nenosil padák?

DANISH

Hvorfor havde jeg ikke en faldskærm på?

DUTCH

Waarom droeg ik geen parachute?

ESPERANTO

Kial mi ne portis paraŝuton?

ESTONIAN

Miks ma ei kandnud langevarju?

FILIPINO

Bakit hindi ako nagsuot ng parachute?

FINNISH

Miksi en käyttänyt laskuvarjoa?

FRENCH

Pourquoi n'ai-je pas mis de parachute?

GALICIAN

Por que non levei un paracaídas?

GEORGIAN

რატომ არ ჩავიცვი პარაშუტი?

Rat'om ar chavitsvi p'arashut'i?

GERMAN

Warum habe ich keinen fallschirm getragen?

GREEK

Γιατί δεν φόρεσα αλεξίπτωτο

Giatí den fóresa alexíptoto?

HAITIAN CREOLE

Poukisa mwen pa t 'mete yon parachit?

HAUSA

Me yasa ban sa parachute ba?

HAWAIIAN

No ke aha i komo ʻole ai au i kahi parachute?

HINDI

मैंने पैराशूट क्यों नहीं पहना?

Mainne pairaashoot kyon nahin pahana?

HMONG

Vim li cas kuv thiaj tsis hnav lub kaus mom hlau?

HUNGARIAN

Miért nem hordtam ejtőernyőt?

ICELANDIC

Hvers vegna var ég ekki með fallhlíf?

IGBO

Kedu ihe kpatara na anaghị m eyi parashute?

INDONESIAN

Mengapa saya tidak memakai parasut?

IRISH

Cén fáth nár chaith mé paraisiúit?

ITALIAN

Perché non ho indossato un paracadute?

JAPANESE

なぜパラシュートを着なかったのですか？

Naze parashūto o kinakatta nodesu ka?

JAVANESE

Napa aku ora nganggo parasut?

KANNADA

ನಾನು ಯಾಕೆ ಧುಮುಕುಕೊಡೆ ಧರಿಸಲಿಲ್ಲ?

Nānu yāke dhumukukoḍe dharisalilla?

KAZAKH

Неге мен парашютпен жүрмедім?

Men nege paraşyutpen jürmedim?

KINYARWANDA

Kuki ntigeze nambara parasute?

KOREAN

나는 왜 낙하산을 착용하지 않았습니까?

Naneun wae naghasan-eul chag-yonghaji anh-assseubnikka?

KURDISH

Çima min paraşût li xwe nekir?

KYRGYZ

Эмнеге мен парашют кийбедим?

Emnege men paraşyut kiybedim?

LATVIAN

Kāpēc es nenēsāju izpletni?

LITHUANIAN

Kodėl aš nenešiojau parašiuto?

LUXEMBOURGISH

Firwat hunn ech kee fallschierm gedroen?

MACEDONIAN

Зошто не носев падобран?

Zošto ne nosev padobran?

MALAGASY

Fa maninona aho no tsy nanao parachute?

MALAY

Mengapa saya tidak memakai payung terjun?

MALTESE

Għaliex ma lbistix paraxut?

MAORI

He aha ahau i kore ai e mau i te parachute?

MARATHI

मी पॅराशूट का घातला नाही?

Mī pĕrāśūṭa kā ghātalā nāhī?

MONGOLIAN

Би яагаад шүхэр зүүгээгүй юм бэ?

Bi yaagaad shükher züügeegüi yum be?

NEPALI

मैले प्याराशूट किन लगाएको छैन?

Mailē pyārāśūṭa kina lagā'ēkō chaina?

NORWEGIAN

Hvorfor brukte jeg ikke fallskjerm?

NYANJA

Chifukwa chiyani sindinkavala parachuti?

POLISH

Dlaczego nie założyłem spadochronu?

PORTUGUESE

Por que não usei um pára-quedas?

PUNJABI

ਮੈਂ ਪੈਰਾਸ਼ੂਟ ਕਿਉਂ ਨਹੀਂ ਪਾਇਆ?

Maiṁ pairāśūṭa ki'uṁ nahīṁ pā'i'ā?

ROMANIAN

De ce nu am purtat o parașută?

RUSSIAN

Почему я не надел парашют?

Pochemu ya ne nadel parashyut?

SAMOAN

Aisea na ou le ofuina ai se parachute?

SCOTS GAELIC

Carson nach robh paraisiut orm?

SERBIAN

Зашто нисам носио падобран?

Zašto nisam nosio padobran?

SLOVAK

Prečo som nenosil padák?

SLOVENIAN

Zakaj nisem nosil padala?

SOMALI

Waa maxay sababta aan u xiran waayay baarashuud?

SPANISH

¿Por qué no usé un paracaídas?

SUNDANESE

Naha kuring henteu nganggo parasut?

SWAHILI

Kwa nini sikuvaa parachuti?

SWEDISH

Varför hade jag inte fallskärm?

TAJIK

Чаро ман парашют намепӯшам?

Caro man paraşjut namepūşam?

TAMIL

நான் ஏன் பாராசூட் அணியவில்லை?

Nāṉ ēṉ pārācūṭ aṇiyavillai?

TELUGU

నేను పారాచూట్ ఎందుకు ధరించలేదు?

Nēnu pārācūṭ enduku dhariñcalēdu?

THAI

ทำไมฉันไม่ใส่ร่มชูชีพ?

Thảmị c̄hạn mị̀ s̄ì r̀mchūchīph?

TURKISH

Neden paraşüt takmadım?

TURKMEN

Näme üçin paraşýut geýmedim?

UKRAINIAN

Чому я не одяг парашут?

Chomu ya ne odyahla parashut?

UZBEK

Nega men parashyut kiymadim?

VIETNAMESE

Tại sao tôi không mặc dù?

VIETNAMESE

Pam na wnes i wisgo parasiwt?

YIDDISH

פאַרוואָס האָב איך נישט טראָגן אַ פּאַראַשוט

Farvas hob ikh nisht trogn a parashut?

ZULU

Kungani ngingazange ngigqoke iparashute?

Are we there yet?

AFRIKAANS

Is ons al daar?

ALBANIAN

A jemi akoma atje?

AMHARIC

እኛ ገና አሉን?

Inya gena āluni?

ARABIC

هل وصلنا بعد؟

Hal wasalna?

ARMENIAN

Արդյո՞ք մենք դեռ այնտեղ ենք:

Menk' ayntegh ch'enk'?

AZERBAIJANI

Hələ oradayıq?

BASQUE

Han al gaude oraindik?

BELARUSIAN

Мы ўжо там?

My ŭžo tam?

BOSNIAN

Jesmo li stigli?

BULGARIAN

Още ли сме там?

Oshte li sme tam?

BURMESE

ငါတို့ရှိသေးလား။

Ngarthoet shisayylarr.

CATALAN

Ja hi som?

CEBUANO

Naa na ba kita?

MANDARIN CHINESE

我們到了嗎？

Wǒmen dàole ma?

CORSICAN

Ci simu dighjà?

CROATIAN

Jesmo li već stigli?

CZECH

Už jsme tam?

DANISH

Er vi der endnu?

DUTCH

Zijn we er al?

ESPERANTO

Ĉu ni jam estas tie?

ESTONIAN

Kas me oleme juba kohal?

FILIPINO

Nandyan na ba tayo?

FINNISH

Olemmeko vielä siellä?

FRENCH

Sommes-nous déjà là?

GALICIAN

¿Xa estamos alí?

GEORGIAN

ჯერ იქ ვართ?

Jer ik vart?

GERMAN

Sind wir schon da?

GREEK

Είμαστε ακόμα εκεί

Eímaste akómi ekeí?

HAITIAN CREOLE

Eske nou la deja?

HAUSA

Har yanzu muna can?

HAWAIIAN

Ma laila anei mākou?

HINDI

क्या हम अभी तक वहाँ हैं?

Kya ham ab bhee vahaan hain?

HMONG

Peb puas tseem muaj?

HUNGARIAN

Ott vagyunk már?

ICELANDIC

Erum við þar enn?

IGBO

Ànyị ka nọ ebe ahụ?

INDONESIAN

Apakah kita sudah sampai?

IRISH

An bhfuil muid ann fós?

ITALIAN

Siamo arrivati?

JAPANESE

私たちはもうそこにいますか？

Watashitachi wa mō soko ni imasu ka?

JAVANESE

Apa kita wis ana?

KANNADA

ನಾವು ಇನ್ನೂ ಅಲ್ಲಿದ್ದೇವೆಯೇ?

Nāvu innū alliddēveyē?

KAZAKH

Біз әлі бармыз ба?

Biz äli barmız ba?

KINYARWANDA

Turacyahari?

KOREAN

우리 아직 거기에 있습니까?

Ulineun ajig-issda?

KURDISH

Ma em hîn li wir in?

KYRGYZ

Биз дагы барбызбы?

Biz ali barbızbı?

LATVIAN

Vai mēs jau esam tur?

LITHUANIAN

Ar mes jau ten?

LUXEMBOURGISH

Sinn mir nach do?

MACEDONIAN

Дали сме таму уште?

Dali sme tamu ušte?

MALAGASY

Efa eo ve isika?

MALAY

Adakah kita masih ada?

MALTESE

Għadna hemm?

MAORI

Kei kona ano tatou?

MARATHI

आम्ही अजून तिथे आहोत का?

Āmhī ajūna tithē āhōta kā?

MONGOLIAN

Бид одоо хүртэл байна уу?

Bid odoo boltol baina uu?

NEPALI

के हामी अझै त्यहाँ छौं?

Kē hāmī ajhai tyahām̐ chaum̐?

NORWEGIAN

Er vi der ennå?

NYANJA

Kodi tili komweko?

POLISH

Czy już tam jesteśmy?

PORTUGUESE

Já estamos lá?

PUNJABI

ਕੀ ਅਸੀਂ ਅਜੇ ਉੱਥੇ ਹਾਂ?

Kī asīm ajē uthē hām?

ROMANIAN

Suntem deja acolo?

RUSSIAN

Мы уже там?

My uzhe na meste?

SAMOAN

O tatou i ai iina?

SCOTS GAELIC

A bheil sinn ann fhathast?

SERBIAN

Да ли смо већ стигли?

Da li smo već stigli?

SLOVAK

Už sme tam?

SLOVENIAN

Smo že tam?

SOMALI

Miyaan weli joognaa?

SPANISH

¿Ya llegamos?

SUNDANESE

Naha urang aya di dinya?

SWAHILI

Je! Tuko bado?

SWEDISH

Är vi där än?

TAJIK

Оё мо ҳанӯз дар он ҷоем?

Ojo mo hanūz dar on çoem?

TAMIL

நாம் இன்னும் அங்கு இருக்கிறோமா?

Nām iṉṉum aṅku irukkiṟōmā?

TELUGU

మనం ఇంకా అక్కడ ఉన్నామా?

Manaṁ iṅkā akkaḍa unnāmā?

THAI

เราอยู่ที่นั่นหรือยัง

Reā xyū̀ thī̀ nạ̀n h̄rụ̄x yạng

TURKISH

Henüz varmadık mı?

TURKMEN

Biz entek barmy?

UKRAINIAN

Ми вже там?

My vzhe tam?

UZBEK

Biz hali o'sha yerdamizmi?

VIETNAMESE

Chúng ta đã đến chưa?

VIETNAMESE

Ydyn ni yno eto?

YIDDISH

זענען מיר דאָרט נאָך?

Zenen mir shoyn dart?

ZULU

Ingabe sisekhona?

7 Brain freeze!

AFRIKAANS

Breinvasbrand!

ALBANIAN

Ngrij trurin!

AMHARIC

የአዕምሮ ቀዝቀዝ!

Ye'ā'imiro k'ezik'ezi!

ARABIC

تجميد الدماغ!

Tajmid aldimaghi!

ARMENIAN

Ուղեղի սառեցում:

Ugheghi sarrets'um!

AZERBAIJANI

Beyin donur!

BASQUE

Garuna izoztu!

BELARUSIAN

Замарожванне мазгоў!

Zamarožvannie mazhoŭ!

BOSNIAN

Zamrzavanje mozga!

BULGARIAN

Замразяване на мозъка!

Zamrŭzvane na mozŭka!

BURMESE

ဦး နှောက်အေးခဲခြင်

U nhaout aayy hkellhkyinn!

CATALAN

Congelació del cervell!

CEBUANO

Pag-freeze sa utok!

MANDARIN CHINESE

大腦凍結！

Dànǎo dòngjié!

CORSICAN

Congelà u cervellu!

CROATIAN

Zamrzavanje mozga!

CZECH

Zmrazení mozku!

DANISH

Hjernefrys!

DUTCH

Hersenen bevriezen!

ESPERANTO

Cerba frosto!

ESTONIAN

Aju külmub!

FILIPINO

Ang pag-freeze ng utak!

FINNISH

Jäätelöpäänsärky!

FRENCH

Gel de cerveau!

GALICIAN

Conxelación do cerebro!

GEORGIAN

ტვინის გაყინვა!

Tvinis gaq'inva!

GERMAN

Gehirn einfrieren!

GREEK

Πάγωμα μυαλού!

Págoma myaloú!

HAITIAN CREOLE

Friz nan sèvo!

HAUSA

Brain daskare!

HAWAIIAN

Hoʻoikaika ka lolo!

HINDI

दिमाग जाम!

Dimaag jaam!

HMONG

Lub hlwb khov!

HUNGARIAN

Az agy lefagy!

ICELANDIC

Heilastöðvun!

IGBO

Brain friza!

INDONESIAN

Pembekuan otak!

IRISH

Reo inchinn!

ITALIAN

Congelamento del cervello!

JAPANESE

思考力が低下する！

Shikō-ryoku ga teika suru!

JAVANESE

Otak beku!

KANNADA

ಮಿದುಳು ಫ್ರೀಜ್!

Miduḷu phrīj!

KAZAKH

Ми қатып қалды!

Mï qatıp qaldı!

KINYARWANDA

Guhagarika ubwonko!

KOREAN

아이스크림 두통!

Aiseukeulim dutong!

KURDISH

Brain freeze!

KYRGYZ

Мээ тоңуп калды!

Mee toŋup kaldı!

LATVIAN

Smadzenes sasalst!

LITHUANIAN

Smegenų sustingimas!

LUXEMBOURGISH

Gehir afréieren!

MACEDONIAN

Замрзнување на мозокот!

Zamrznuvanje na mozokot!

MALAGASY

Ny hatsiaka amin'ny ati-doha!

MALAY

Pembekuan otak!

MALTESE

Iffriżar tal-moħħ!

MAORI

Whakatio roro!

MARATHI

मेंदू काम न करणे!

Mēndū kāma na karaṇē!

MONGOLIAN

Тархи хөлдсөн!

Tarkhi khöldsön!

NEPALI

मस्तिष्क फ्रीज!

Mastiṣka phrīja!

NORWEGIAN

Hjernefrysing!

NYANJA

Ubongo umazizira!

POLISH

Zamrożenie mózgu!

PORTUGUESE

Congelamento do cérebro!

PUNJABI

ਦਿਮਾਗ ਫ੍ਰੀਜ਼!

Dimāga phrīza!

ROMANIAN

Înghețarea creierului!

RUSSIAN

Заморозка мозгов!

Zamorozka mozgov!

SAMOAN

Faʻamama le faiʻai!

SCOTS GAELIC

Reothadh eanchainn!

SERBIAN

Замрзнути мозак!

Zamrznuti mozak!

SLOVAK

Zmrazenie mozgu!

SLOVENIAN

Zamrznitev možganov!

SOMALI

Maskaxda qabooji!

SPANISH

¡Cerebro congelado!

SUNDANESE

Otak beku!

SWAHILI

Ubongo huganda!

SWEDISH

Hjärnfrys!

TAJIK

Майна яхкардааст!

Majna jaxkardaast!

TAMIL

மூளை முடக்கம்!

Mūḷai muṭakkam!

TELUGU

అయోమయంగా!

Ayōmayaṅgā!

THAI

สมองแข็ง!

S̄mxng k̄hæ̆ng!

TURKISH

Beyin durması!

TURKMEN

Beýni doňdur!

UKRAINIAN

Заморожування мозку!

Zamorozhuvannya mozku!

UZBEK

Miya muzlab qoldi!

VIETNAMESE

Buốt não!

VIETNAMESE

Rhewi'r ymennydd!

YIDDISH

מאַרך פרירן!

Markh frirn!

ZULU

Iqhwa lobuchopho!

8 Sorry, I'm allergic to unicorns.

AFRIKAANS

Jammer, ek is allergies vir eenhoorns.

ALBANIAN

Më falni, jam alergjik ndaj njëbrirësht.

AMHARIC

ይቅርታ ፣ ለዩኒኮዎች አለርጂ ነኝ።

Yik'irita - leyunīkowochi āleriјī nenyi.

ARABIC

آسف ، أعاني من حساسية تجاه وحيد القرن

Asf, 'ueani min hasasiat tijah wahid alqarani.

ARMENIAN

Կներեք, ես ալերգիա ունեմ միաեղջյուրների նկատմամբ:

Knerek', yes alergia unem miayeghjyurneri nkatmamb.

AZERBAIJANI

Bağışlayın, təkbaşlılara allergiyam var.

BASQUE

Sentitzen dut, alergia dut adarbakarrekiko.

BELARUSIAN

На жаль, у мяне алергія на аднарогаў.

Na žaĺ, u mianie alierhija na adnarohaŭ.

BOSNIAN

Izvinite, alergičan sam na jednoroge.

BULGARIAN

За съжаление съм алергичен към еднорози.

Za sŭzhalenie sŭm alergichen kŭm ednorozi.

BURMESE

◌ာင်းပန်ပါတယ်၊ ငါ unicorn တွေနဲ့ မတည့်ဘူး။

Taunggpaanpartaal, ngar unicorn twaynae m t ny bhuu.

CATALAN

Ho sento, sóc al·lèrgic als unicorns.

CEBUANO

Pasensya, alerdyik ako sa mga unicorn.

MANDARIN CHINESE

對不起，我對獨角獸過敏。

Duìbùqǐ, wǒ duì dú jiǎo shòu guòmǐn.

CORSICAN

Scusate, sò allergicu à l'unicorni.

CROATIAN

Nažalost, alergičan sam na jednoroge.

CZECH

Omlouvám se, jsem alergický na jednorožce.

DANISH

Beklager, jeg er allergisk over for enhjørninger.

DUTCH

Sorry, ik ben allergisch voor eenhoorns.

ESPERANTO

Pardonu, mi estas alergia kontraŭ unukornuloj.

ESTONIAN

Kahjuks olen ükssarvikute suhtes allergiline.

FILIPINO

Paumanhin, alerdyi ako sa mga unicorn.

FINNISH

Anteeksi, olen allerginen yksisarvisille.

FRENCH

Désolé, je suis allergique aux licornes.

GALICIAN

Sentímolo, son alérxico aos unicornios.

GEORGIAN

უკაცრავად, მე ალერგიული ვარ unicorns-ზე.

Uk'atsravad, me alergiuli var unicorns- ze.

GERMAN

Entschuldigung, ich bin allergisch gegen Einhörner.

GREEK

Συγγνώμη, είμαι αλλεργικός στους μονόκερους

Syngnómi, eímai allergikós stous monókerous.

HAITIAN CREOLE

Padon, mwen fè alèji ak likorn.

HAUSA

Yi haƙuri, Ina rashin lafiyan unicorns.

HAWAIIAN

E kala mai, ma'i wau i nā unicorn.

HINDI

क्षमा करें, मुझे गेंडा से एलर्जी है।

Kshama karen, mujhe genda se elarjee hai.

HMONG

Thov txim, kuv ua xua rau unicorns.

HUNGARIAN

Sajnos allergiás vagyok az unikornisokra.

ICELANDIC

Fyrirgefðu, ég er með ofnæmi fyrir einhyrningum.

IGBO

Ndo, enwere m ihe nfụkasị maka unicorns.

INDONESIAN

Maaf, saya alergi unicorn.

IRISH

Tá brón orm, tá mé ailléirgeach le haonbheannaigh.

ITALIAN

Scusa, sono allergico agli unicorni.

JAPANESE

すみません、ユニコーンにアレルギーがあります。

Sumimasen, yunikōn ni arerugī ga arimasu.

JAVANESE

Nuwun sewu, aku alergi marang unicorn.

KANNADA

ಕ್ಷಮಿಸಿ, ನನಗೆ ಯೂನಿಕಾರ್ನ್‌ಗಳಿಗೆ ಅಲರ್ಜಿ.

Kṣamisi, nanage yūnikārngaḷige alarji.

KAZAKH

Кешіріңіз, мен бірмүйізділерге аллергиям бар.

Keşiriñiz, men birmüyizdilerge allergïyam bar.

KINYARWANDA

Ihangane, ndi allergic kuri unicorn.

KOREAN

죄송합니다. 저는 유니콘에 알레르기가 있습니다.

Joesonghabnida jeoneun yunikon-e alleleugiga issseubnida.

KURDISH

Mixabin, ez alerjîk im ji yekdûzan.

KYRGYZ

Кечиресиз, мен жалгыз мүйүздүү малга аллергиямын.

Keçiresiz, men jalgız müyüzdüü malga allergiyamın.

LATVIAN

Diemžēl man ir alerģija pret vienradžiem.

LITHUANIAN

Atsiprašau, aš alergiškas vienaragiams.

LUXEMBOURGISH

Entschëllegt, ech sinn allergesch fir Eenhorn.

MACEDONIAN

Извинете, алергичен сум на еднорози.

Izvinete, alergičen sum na ednorozi.

MALAGASY

Miala tsiny, tsy mahazaka unicorn aho.

MALAY

Maaf, saya alah kepada unicorn.

MALTESE

Jiddispjacini, jien allerġiku għall-unicorns.

MAORI

Aroha mai, kei te mate au i nga unicorn.

MARATHI

क्षमस्व, मला युनिकॉर्नची ॲलर्जी आहे.

Kṣamasva, malā yunikŏrnacī ȧĕlarjī āhē.

MONGOLIAN

Уучлаарай, би ганц эвэрт харшилтай.

Uuchlaarai, bi gants evert kharshiltai.

NEPALI

माफ गर्नुहोस्, मलाई युनिकोर्न बाट एलर्जी छ।

Māpha garnuhōs, malā'ī yunikōrna bāṭa ēlarjī cha.

NORWEGIAN

Beklager, jeg er allergisk mot enhjørninger.

NYANJA

Pepani, sindigwirizana ndi zipembere.

POLISH

Przepraszam, mam alergię na jednorożce.

PORTUGUESE

Desculpe, sou alérgico a unicórnios.

PUNJABI

ਮੁਆਫ ਕਰਨਾ, ਮੈਨੂੰ ਯੂਨੀਕੋਰਨਸ ਤੋਂ ਐਲਰਜੀ ਹੈ.

Mu'āpha karanā, mainū yūnīkōranasa tōṁ ailarajī hai.

ROMANIAN

Îmi pare rău, sunt alergic la unicorni.

RUSSIAN

Извините, у меня аллергия на единорогов.

Izvinite, u menya allergiya na yedinorogov.

SAMOAN

Faamalie atu, ou te le fiafia i unicorn.

SCOTS GAELIC

Tha mi duilich, tha mi aileirgeach dha aon-chòrnach.

SERBIAN

Жао ми је, алергичан сам на једнороге.

Žao mi je, alergičan sam na jednoroge.

SLOVAK

Prepáčte, som alergický na jednorožce.

SLOVENIAN

Žal sem alergičen na samoroge.

SOMALI

Waan ka xumahay, waxaan xasaasiyad ka qabaa unicorns.

SPANISH

Lo siento, soy alérgico a los unicornios.

SUNDANESE

Hapunten, kuring alérgi kana unicorn.

SWAHILI

Samahani, mimi ni mzio wa nyati.

SWEDISH

Förlåt, jag är allergisk mot enhörningar.

TAJIK

Бубахшед, ман ба якрангҳо аллергия дорам.

Вubахşed, man ва jakrangho allergija doram.

TAMIL

மன்னிக்கவும், எனக்கு யூனிகார்ன் ஒவ்வாமை.

Maṉṉikkavum, eṉakku yūṉikārṉ ovvāmai.

TELUGU

క్షమించండి, నాకు యునికార్న్స్ అంటే అలర్జీ.

Kṣamiñcaṇḍi, nāku yunikārns aṇṭē alarjī.

THAI

ขอโทษ ฉันแพ้ยูนิคอร์น

Khxthoṣ̄' c̄hạn phæ̂ yū ni khxr̒n.

TURKISH

Üzgünüm, tek boynuzlu atlara alerjim var.

TURKMEN

Bagyşlaň, men ýekegözlere allergiýam ýok.

UKRAINIAN

Вибачте, у мене алергія на єдинорогів.

Vybachte, u mene alerhiya na yedynorohiv.

UZBEK

Kechirasiz, men yolg'iz hayvonlarga allergiyam bor.

VIETNAMESE

Xin lỗi, tôi bị dị ứng với kỳ lân.

VIETNAMESE

Mae'n ddrwg gennyf, mae gen i alergedd i unicornau.

YIDDISH

אנטשולדיגט, איך בין אַלערדזשיק צו וניקאָרנס

Antshuldigt, ikh bin alerjik tsu unikorns.

ZULU

Uxolo, angizwani nama-unicorn.

9 You smell like a monkey.

AFRIKAANS

Jy ruik soos 'n aap.

ALBANIAN

Keni erë majmuni.

AMHARIC

ዝንጀሮ ይሸታል።

Zinijero yishetali.

ARABIC

رائحتك مثل القرد.

Rayihatuk mithl alqirdu.

ARMENIAN

Կապիկի հոտ է գալիս:

Kapiki hot e galis.

AZERBAIJANI

Meymun kimi iy verirsən.

BASQUE

Tximino usaina duzu.

BELARUSIAN

Ты пахнеш малпай.

Ty pachnieš malpaj.

BOSNIAN

Mirišeš na majmuna.

BULGARIAN

Миришеш на маймуна.

Mirishesh na maĭmuna.

BURMESE

မင်းကမျောက်နံ့နံတယ်။

Mainn k myawwat nan nan taal.

CATALAN

Fa olor de mico.

CEBUANO

Humot ka sama sa usa ka unggoy.

MANDARIN CHINESE

你聞起來像一隻猴子。

Nǐ wén qǐlái xiàng yī zhī hóuzi.

CORSICAN

Sentite una scimmia.

CROATIAN

Mirišeš poput majmuna.

CZECH

Voníš jako opice.

DANISH

Du lugter som en abe.

DUTCH

Je ruikt als een aap.

ESPERANTO

Vi odoras kiel simio.

ESTONIAN

Sa lõhnad nagu ahv.

FILIPINO

Amoy unggoy ka.

FINNISH

Haistat apinalta.

FRENCH

Tu sens le singe.

GALICIAN

Cheiras a mono.

GEORGIAN

მაიმუნის სუნი გაქვს.

Maimunis suni gakvs.

GERMAN

Du riechst wie ein affe.

GREEK

Μυρίζεις σαν μαϊμού.

Myrízeis san maïmoú.

HAITIAN CREOLE

Ou pran sant tankou yon makak.

HAUSA

Kuna wari kamar biri.

HAWAIIAN

Honi ʻoe e like me ka moʻo.

HINDI

तुम बंदर की तरह महकते हो।

Aap bandar kee tarah gandh karate hain.

HMONG

Koj hnov tsw zoo li tus liab.

HUNGARIAN

Majomszagú vagy.

ICELANDIC

Þú lyktar eins og api.

IGBO

Ị na -esi ka enwe.

INDONESIAN

Anda berbau seperti monyet.

IRISH

Boladh tú cosúil le moncaí.

ITALIAN

Puzzi come una scimmia.

JAPANESE

あなたは猿のようなにおいがします。

Anata wa saru no yōna nioi ga shimasu.

JAVANESE

Sampeyan mambu kaya kethek.

KANNADA

ನೀವು ಕೋತಿಯಂತೆ ವಾಸನೆ ಮಾಡುತ್ತೀರಿ.

Nīvu kōtiyante vāsane māḍuttīri.

KAZAKH

Сіз маймылдың иісін сезесіз.

Siz maymıldıñ ïisin sezinesiz.

KINYARWANDA

Urumva nk'inguge.

KOREAN

원숭이 냄새가 난다.

Wonsung-i naemsaega naneyo.

KURDISH

Tu bêhna meymûnê dikî.

KYRGYZ

Сиз маймылдын жытын сезесиз.

Siz maymıldın jıtın sezesiz.

LATVIAN

Tu smaržo kā pērtiķis.

LITHUANIAN

Tu kvepi beždžionėle.

LUXEMBOURGISH

Dir richt wéi en Af.

MACEDONIAN

Мирисаш на мајмун.

Mirisaš na majmun.

MALAGASY

Maimbo ianao.

MALAY

Anda berbau seperti monyet.

MALTESE

Tħoss riħa ta 'xadina.

MAORI

He rite koe ki te makimaki.

MARATHI

तुला माकडासारखा वास येतो.

Tulā mākaḍāsārakhā vāsa yētō.

MONGOLIAN

Та сармагчин шиг үнэртэж байна.

Ta sarmagchin shig ünertej baina.

NEPALI

तिमीलाई बाँदर जस्तै गन्ध आउँछ।

Timīlā'ī bām̐dara jastai gandha ā'um̐cha.

NORWEGIAN

Du lukter som en ape.

NYANJA

Mukumva fungo la nyani.

POLISH

Pachniesz jak małpa.

PORTUGUESE

Você cheira a macaco.

PUNJABI

ਤੁਹਾਨੂੰ ਬਾਂਦਰ ਦੀ ਤਰ੍ਹਾਂ ਬਦਬੂ ਆਉਂਦੀ ਹੈ.

Tuhānū bāndara dī tar'hāṁ badabū ā'undī hai.

ROMANIAN

Miroși a maimuță.

RUSSIAN

Ты пахнешь обезьяной.

Ty pakhnesh' obez'yanoy.

SAMOAN

E manogi pei o se manuki.

SCOTS GAELIC

Bidh thu a 'fàileadh mar muncaidh.

SERBIAN

Миришеш на мајмуна.

Mirišeš na majmuna.

SLOVAK

Voníš ako opica.

SLOVENIAN

Dišiš kot opica.

SOMALI

Waxaad u uraysaa daanyeer.

SPANISH

Hueles a mono.

SUNDANESE

Anjeun bau kawas monyét.

SWAHILI

Unasikia harufu ya nyani.

SWEDISH

Du luktar som en apa.

TAJIK

Шумо бӯи маймунро ҳис мекунед.

Şumo būi majmunro his mekuned.

TAMIL

நீங்கள் ஒரு குரங்கின் வாசனை.

Nīṅkaḷ oru kuraṅkiṉ vācaṉai.

TELUGU

మీరు కోతిలా వాసన చూస్తున్నారు.

Mīru kōtilā vāsana cūstunnāru.

THAI

คุณมีกลิ่นเหมือนลิง

Khuṇ mī klìn h̄emụ̄xn ling.

TURKISH

Maymun gibi kokuyorsun.

TURKMEN

Maýmynyň ysy gelýär.

UKRAINIAN

Ти пахнеш мавпою.

Ty pakhnesh mavpoyu.

UZBEK

Siz maymunga o'xshaysiz.

VIETNAMESE

Bạn có mùi như một con khỉ.

VIETNAMESE

Rydych chi'n arogli fel mwnci.

YIDDISH

איר שמעקט ווי אַ מאַלפּע.

Ir shmekt vi a malpe.

ZULU

Unuka inkawu.

10 But Dad said . . .

AFRIKAANS

Maar pa het gesê . . .

ALBANIAN

Por babai tha . . .

AMHARIC

አባ ግን።

Aba gini . . .

ARABIC

فقال ابي

Lakina 'abi qal . . .

ARMENIAN

Բայց հայրիկն ասաց...

Bayts' hayrikn asats'. . .

AZERBAIJANI

Amma atam dedi . . .

BASQUE

Baina aitak esan zuen . . .

BELARUSIAN

Але тата сказаў . . .

Alie tata skazaŭ . . .

BOSNIAN

Ali tata je rekao . . .

BULGARIAN

Но татко каза . . .

No tatko kaza . . .

BURMESE

ဒါပေမယ့်အဖေကပြောတယ်။ . . .

Darpaymay a hpay k pyawwtaal . . .

CATALAN

Però va dir el pare . . .

CEBUANO

Apan giingon ni papa . . .

MANDARIN CHINESE

但是爸爸說。

Dànshì bàba shuō . . .

CORSICAN

Ma babbu hà dettu . . .

CROATIAN

Ali tata je rekao . . .

CZECH

Ale táta řekl . . .

DANISH

Men far sagde . . .

DUTCH

Maar papa zei . . .

ESPERANTO

Sed paĉjo diris . . .

ESTONIAN

Aga isa ütles . . .

FILIPINO

Pero sabi ni papa . . .

FINNISH

Mutta isä sanoi . . .

FRENCH

Mais papa a dit . . .

GALICIAN

Pero dixo papá. . .

GEORGIAN

მაგრამ მამამ თქვა

Magram mamam tkva . . .

GERMAN

Aber papa sagte . . .

GREEK

Αλλά ο μπαμπάς είπε

Allá eípe o bampás . . .

HAITIAN CREOLE

Men papa te di . . .

HAUSA

Sai baba yace . . .

HAWAIIAN

Akā ʻōlelo ʻo pāpā . . .

HINDI

परन्तु पिताजी ने कहा

Lekin paapa ne kaha . . .

HMONG

Tab sis txiv hais . . .

HUNGARIAN

De apa azt mondta . . .

ICELANDIC

En pabbi sagði . . .

IGBO

Ma papa m kwuru . . .

INDONESIAN

Tapi kata ayah . . .

IRISH

Ach dúirt daidí . . .

ITALIAN

Ma papà ha detto . . .

JAPANESE

でもお父さんは言った

Demo otōsan wa itta . . .

JAVANESE

Nanging bapak ngendika . . .

KANNADA

ಆದರೆ ತಂದೆ ಹೇಳಿದರು . . .

Ādare tande hēḷidaru . . .

KAZAKH

Бірақ әкем айтты . . .

Biraq äkem ayttı . . .

KINYARWANDA

Ariko papa yarabivuze . . .

KOREAN

하지만 아빠는 . . .

Geuleona appaneun malhaessda . . .

KURDISH

Lê bavo got . . .

KYRGYZ

Бирок атам айтты . . .

Birok atam ayttı . . .

LATVIAN

Bet tētis teica . . .

LITHUANIAN

Bet tėtis pasakė . . .

LUXEMBOURGISH

Awer de papp sot . . .

MACEDONIAN

Но тато рече . . .

No tato reče . . .

MALAGASY

Fa hoy i dada . . .

MALAY

Tetapi ayah berkata . . .

MALTESE

Imma missier qal . . .

MAORI

Engari i kii a papa . . .

MARATHI

पण बाबा म्हणाले . . .

Paṇa bābā mhaṇālē . . .

MONGOLIAN

Гэхдээ аав хэлэв . . .

Gekhdee aav khelev. . .

NEPALI

तर बुबाले भन्नुभयो

Tara bubālē bhannubhayō . . .

NORWEGIAN

Men pappa sa . . .

NYANJA

Koma bambo adati . . .

POLISH

Ale tata powiedział . . .

PORTUGUESE

Mas papai disse . . .

PUNJABI

ਪਰ ਪਿਤਾ ਜੀ ਨੇ ਕਿਹਾ . . .

Para pitā jī nē kihā . . .

ROMANIAN

Dar tata a spus . . .

RUSSIAN

Но папа сказал . . .

No papa skazal . . .

SAMOAN

Ae fai mai Tama . . .

SCOTS GAELIC

ACH THUIRT ATHAIR . . .

SERBIAN

Али тата је рекао . . .

Ali tata je rekao . . .

SLOVAK

Ale otec povedal . . .

SLOVENIAN

Toda oče je rekel . . .

SOMALI

Laakiin aabe ayaa yiri . . .

SPANISH

Pero papá dijo . . .

SUNDANESE

Tapi ceuk pa . . .

SWAHILI

Lakini baba alisema . . .

SWEDISH

Men pappa sa . . .

TAJIK

Аммо падарам гуфт . . .

Ammo padar guft . . .

TAMIL

ஆனால் அப்பா
சொன்னார் . . .

Āṉāl appā coṉṉār . . .

TELUGU

కానీ నాన్న చెప్పారు . . .

Kānī nānna ceppāru . . .

THAI

แต่พ่อบอกว่า . . .

Tæ ph̀x bxk ẁā . . .

TURKISH

Ama baba dedi . . .

TURKMEN

Emma kakam aýtdy . . .

UKRAINIAN

Але тато сказав . . .

Ale tato skazav . . .

UZBEK

Lekin dadam aytdi . . .

VIETNAMESE

Nhưng bố nói . . .

VIETNAMESE

Ond meddai tad . . .

YIDDISH

אבער טאטע האט געזאגט

Aber tate hat gezagt . . .

ZULU

Kodwa ubaba wathi . . .

11 We're not in Kansas anymore.

AFRIKAANS

Ons is nie meer in Kansas nie.

ALBANIAN

Ne nuk jemi më në Kansas.

AMHARIC

እኛ ካንሳስ ውስጥ አይደለንም።

Inya Kanisasi wisit'i āyidelenimi.

ARABIC

لم نعد في كانساس بعد الآن.

Lam naeud fi Kansas baed alan.

ARMENIAN

Մենք այլևս Կանզասում չենք:

Menk' aylevs Kanzasum ch'enk'.

AZERBAIJANI

Artıq Kanzasda deyilik.

BASQUE

Kansasen ez gaude jada.

BELARUSIAN

Мы больш не ў Канзасе.

My boĺš nie ŭ Kanzasie.

BOSNIAN

Nismo više u Kanzasu.

BULGARIAN

Вече не сме в Канзас.

Veche ne sme v Kanzas.

BURMESE

ငါတို့ Kansas မှာမရှိတော့ဘူး။

Ngarthoet Kansas mhar mashitotbhuu.

CATALAN

Ja no som a Kansas.

CEBUANO

Wala na kita sa Kansas.

MANDARIN CHINESE

我們不在堪薩斯了。

Wǒmen bùzài Kānsàsīle.

CORSICAN

Ùn simu più in Kansas.

CROATIAN

Nismo više u Kansasu.

CZECH

Už nejsme v Kansasu.

DANISH

Vi er ikke i Kansas længere.

DUTCH

We zijn niet meer in Kansas.

ESPERANTO

Ni ne plu estas en Kansaso.

ESTONIAN

Me ei ole enam Kansases.

FILIPINO

Wala na kami sa Kansas.

FINNISH

Emme ole enää Kansasissa.

FRENCH

Nous ne sommes plus au Kansas.

GALICIAN

Xa non estamos en Kansas.

GEORGIAN

ჩვენ აღარ ვართ კანზასში

Chven aghar vart K'anzasshi.

GERMAN

Wir sind nicht mehr in Kansas.

GREEK

Δεν είμαστε πλέον στο Κάνσας

Den eímaste pia sto Kánsas.

HAITIAN CREOLE

Nou pa nan Kansas ankò.

HAUSA

Ba mu cikin Kansas kuma.

HAWAIIAN

ʻAʻole mākou ma Kansas hou.

HINDI

हम अब कंसास में नहीं हैं।

Ham ab Kaansaas mein nahin hain.

HMONG

Peb tsis nyob hauv Kansas lawm.

HUNGARIAN

Már nem Kansasban vagyunk.

ICELANDIC

Við erum ekki lengur í Kansas.

IGBO

Anyị anọghị na Kansas ọzọ.

INDONESIAN

Kami tidak di Kansas lagi.

IRISH

Níl muid i Kansas níos mó.

ITALIAN

Non siamo più in Kansas.

JAPANESE

私たちはもうカンザスにいません。

Watashitachi wa mō Kanzasu ni imasen.

JAVANESE

Kita ora ana ing Kansas maneh.

KANNADA

ನಾವು ಇನ್ನು ಕಾನ್ಸಾಸ್‌ನಲ್ಲಿಲ್ಲ.

Nāvu innu Kānsāsnallilla.

KAZAKH

Біз енді Канзаста емеспіз.

Biz endi Kanzasta emespiz.

KINYARWANDA

Ntitukiri muri Kansas.

KOREAN

우리는 더 이상 캔자스에 있지 않습니다.

Ulineun deo isang Kaenjaseue issji anhseubnida.

KURDISH

Em êdî ne li Kansas in.

KYRGYZ

Биз эми Канзаста эмеспиз.

Biz emi Kanzasta emespiz.

LATVIAN

Mēs vairs neesam Kanzasā.

LITHUANIAN

Mes jau ne Kanzase.

LUXEMBOURGISH

Mir sinn net méi zu Kansas.

MACEDONIAN

Не сме повеќе во Канзас.

Ne sme poveḱe vo Kanzas.

MALAGASY

Tsy any Kansas intsony izahay.

MALAY

Kami tidak lagi berada di Kansas.

MALTESE

M'għadniex Kansas.

MAORI

Kaore matou i Kansas.

MARATHI

आम्ही आता कॅन्ससमध्ये नाही.

Amhī ātā Kĕnsasamadhyē nāhī.

MONGOLIAN

Бид Канзаст байхгүй болсон.

Bid Kanzast baikhgüi bolson.

NEPALI

हामी अब कान्सास मा छैनौं।

Hāmī aba Kānsāsa mā chainaum̐.

NORWEGIAN

Vi er ikke i Kansas lenger.

NYANJA

Sitilinso ku Kansas.

POLISH

Nie jesteśmy już w Kansas.

PORTUGUESE

Não estamos mais no Kansas.

PUNJABI

ਅਸੀਂ ਹੁਣ ਕੰਸਾਸ ਵਿੱਚ ਨਹੀਂ ਹਾਂ.

Asīṁ huṇa Kasāsa vica nahīṁ hāṁ.

ROMANIAN

Nu mai suntem în Kansas.

RUSSIAN

Мы больше не в Канзасе.

My bol'she ne v Kanzase.

SAMOAN

Matou te le o toe i Kansas.

SCOTS GAELIC

Chan eil sinn ann an Kansas tuilleadh.

SERBIAN

Више нисмо у Канзасу.

Više nismo u Kanzasu.

SLOVAK

Už nie sme v Kansase.

SLOVENIAN

Nismo več v Kansasu.

SOMALI

Ma joogno Kansas hadda.

SPANISH

Ya no estamos en Kansas.

SUNDANESE

Kami henteu di Kansas deui.

SWAHILI

Hatuko Kansas tena.

SWEDISH

Vi är inte i Kansas längre.

TAJIK

Мо дигар дар Канзас нестем.

Mo digar dar Kanzas nestem.

TAMIL

நாங்கள் இனி கன்சாஸில் இல்லை.

Nāṅkaḷ iṉi Kaṉcāsil illai.

TELUGU

మేము ఇప్పుడు కాన్సాస్‌లో లేము.

Mēmu ippuḍu Kānsāslō lēmu.

THAI

เราไม่ได้อยู่ในแคนซัสอีกต่อไป

Reā mị̀ dị̂ xyū̀ nı Khænsạs̄ xīk t̀x pị.

TURKISH

Artık Kansas'ta değiliz.

TURKMEN

Indi Kanzasda däl.

UKRAINIAN

Ми більше не в Канзасі.

My bil'she ne v Kanzasi.

UZBEK

Biz endi Kanzasda emasmiz.

VIETNAMESE

Chúng tôi không còn ở Kansas nữa.

VIETNAMESE

Nid ydym yn Kansas bellach.

YIDDISH

מיר זענען ניט מער אין קאַנסאַס.

Mir zenen nit mer in Kansas.

ZULU

Asisekho eKansas.

12 This is my pet dinosaur.

AFRIKAANS

Dit is my troeteldier dinosourus.

ALBANIAN

Ky është dinozauri im i përkëdhelur.

AMHARIC

ይህ የእኔ የቤት እንስሳት ዳይኖሰር ነው።

Yihi ye'inē yebēti inisisati dayinoseri newi.

ARABIC

هذا هو ديناصور المفضل لدي.

Hadha hu aldiynasur almufadal liday.

ARMENIAN

Սա իմ ընտանի դինոզավրն է:

Sa im yntani dinozavrn e.

AZERBAIJANI

Bu mənim ev heyvanı dinozavrımdır.

BASQUE

Hau da nire maskota dinosauroa.

BELARUSIAN

Гэта мой дыназаўр.

Heta moj chatni dynazaŭr.

BOSNIAN

Ovo je moj dinosaurus.

BULGARIAN

Това е моят домашен любимец динозавър.

Tova e moyat domashen lyubimets dinozavŭr.

BURMESE

ဒါကငါ့ရဲ့အိမ်မွေးတိရစ္ဆာန်ဒိုင်နိုဆော ပါ။

Dark ngarrae aain mway tirahcsaran dinenosaw par.

CATALAN

Aquest és el meu dinosaure mascota.

CEBUANO

Kini ang akong binuhi nga dinosaur.

MANDARIN CHINESE

這是我的寵物恐龍。

Zhè shì wǒ de chǒngwù kǒnglóng.

CORSICAN

Questu hè u mo dinosauru animale.

CROATIAN

Ovo je moj dinosaurus za kućne ljubimce.

CZECH

Toto je můj mazlíček dinosaurus.

DANISH

Dette er min kæledyrsdinosaur.

DUTCH

Dit is mijn huisdierendinosaurus.

ESPERANTO

Jen mia dorlotbesto.

ESTONIAN

See on minu lemmikloomade dinosaurus.

FILIPINO

Ito ang aking alagang dinosauro.

FINNISH

Tämä on lemmikkini dinosaurus.

FRENCH

C'est mon dinosaure de compagnie.

GALICIAN

Este é o meu dinosauro mascota.

GEORGIAN

ეს არის ჩემი შინაური დინოზავრი

Es aris chemi shinauri dinozavri.

GERMAN

Das ist mein haustier-Dinosaurier.

GREEK

Αυτός είναι ο κατοικίδιος δεινόσαυρος μου.

Aftós eínai o katoikídios deinósavros mou.

HAITIAN CREOLE

Sa a se dinozò bèt kay mwen an.

HAUSA

Wannan shine dinosaur dabbona.

HAWAIIAN

ʻO kaʻu dinosaur holoholona kēia.

HINDI

यह मेरा पालतू डायनासोर है।

Yah mera paalatoo daayanaasor hai.

HMONG

Nov yog kuv tus tsiaj dinosaur.

HUNGARIAN

Ez a kedvenc dinoszauruszom.

ICELANDIC

Þetta er risaeðla mín fyrir gæludýr.

IGBO

Nke a bụ dinosaur anụ ụlọ m.

INDONESIAN

Ini dinosaurus peliharaan saya.

IRISH

Seo mo dhineasáir peataí.

ITALIAN

Questo è il mio dinosauro domestico.

JAPANESE

これは私のペットの恐竜です。

Kore wa watashi no petto no kyōryūdesu.

JAVANESE

Iki dinosaurus pet.

KANNADA

ಇದು ನನ್ನ ಮುದ್ದಿನ ಡೈನೋಸಾರ್.

Idu nanna muddina ḍainōsār.

KAZAKH

Бұл менің үй жануарларының динозавры.

Bul meniñ üy janwarlarınıñ dïnozavrı.

KINYARWANDA

Iyi ni inyamanswa yanjye dinosaur.

KOREAN

이것은 내 애완용 공룡입니다.

Igeos-eun nae aewan-yong gonglyong-ibnida.

KURDISH

Ev dînazora heywanê min e.

KYRGYZ

Бул менин үй жаныбарым динозавр.

Bul menin üy janıbarım dinozavr.

LATVIAN

Šis ir mans mīlulis dinozaurs.

LITHUANIAN

Tai mano augintinis dinozauras.

LUXEMBOURGISH

Dëst as mäi Hausdéier Dinosaurier.

MACEDONIAN

Ова е мојот миленик диносаурус.

Ova e mojot milenik dinosaurus.

MALAGASY

Ity no dinôzôro biby fiompiko.

MALAY

Ini adalah dinosaur haiwan kesayangan saya.

MALTESE

Dan huwa d-dinosawru domestiku tiegħi.

MAORI

Koinei taku mokoweri mokoweri.

MARATHI

हा माझा पाळीव प्राणी डायनासोर आहे.

Hā mājhā pāḷīva prāṇī ḍāyanāsōra āhē.

MONGOLIAN

Энэ бол миний гэрийн тэжээмэл үлэг гүрвэл юм.

Ene bol minii geriin tejeemel üleg gürvel yum.

NEPALI

यो मेरो पाल्तु जनावर डायनासोर हो।

Yō mērō pāltu janāvara ḍāyanāsōra hō.

NORWEGIAN

Dette er min kjæledyrdinosaur.

NYANJA

Ichi ndi dinosaur wanga wang'ombe.

POLISH

To mój zwierzęcy dinozaur.

PORTUGUESE

Este é meu dinossauro de estimação.

PUNJABI

ਇਹ ਮੇਰਾ ਪਾਲਤੂ ਜਾਨਵਰ ਡਾਇਨਾਸੌਰ ਹੈ.

Iha mērā pālatū jānavara ḍā'ināsaura hai.

ROMANIAN

Acesta este dinozaurul meu animal de companie.

RUSSIAN

Это мой домашний динозавр.

Eto moy domashniy dinozavr.

SAMOAN

O la'u dinosauro fagafao lea.

SCOTS GAELIC

Is e seo an dineosaur peata agam.

SERBIAN

Ово је мој диносаурус.

Ovo je moj dinosaurus.

SLOVAK

Toto je môj domáci dinosaurus.

SLOVENIAN

To je moj hišni dinozaver.

SOMALI

Kani waa dinosaurkayga xayawaanka ah.

SPANISH

Este es mi dinosaurio mascota.

SUNDANESE

Ieu dinosaurus piaraan kuring.

SWAHILI

Huyu ndiye dinosaur yangu kipenzi.

SWEDISH

Detta är min sällskapsdinosaur.

TAJIK

Ин динозаври хонагии ман аст.

In dinozavri xonagii man ast.

TAMIL

இது என் செல்ல டைனோசர்.

Itu eṉ cella ṭaiṉōcar.

TELUGU

ఇది నా పెంపుడు జంతువు డైనోసార్.

Idi nā pempuḍu jantuvu ḍainōsār.

THAI

นี่คือไดโนเสาร์สัตว์เลี้ยงของฉัน

Nì khụ̄x dịnos̄eār̒ s̄ạtw̒ leī̂yng k̄hxng c̄hạn.

TURKISH

Bu benim evcil dinozorum.

TURKMEN

Bu meniň haýwan dinozawrym.

UKRAINIAN

Це мій домашній динозавр.

Tse miy domashniy dynozavr.

UZBEK

Bu mening uy hayvonim dinozavr.

VIETNAMESE

Đây là con khủng long cưng của tôi.

VIETNAMESE

Dyma fy deinosor anifail anwes.

YIDDISH

דאָס איז מיין ליבלינג דיינאַסאָר.

Dos iz meyn libling deynasor.

ZULU

Lesi yisibankwakazi sami esifuywayo.

13 The bread is moldy.

AFRIKAANS

Die brood is muf.

ALBANIAN

Buka është e mykur.

AMHARIC

ዳቦው ሻጋታ ነው።

Dabowi shagata newi.

ARABIC

الخبز عفن.

Alkhubz muteafini.

ARMENIAN

Հացը բորբոսնած է:

Hats'y borbosnats e:

AZERBAIJANI

Çörək küflüdür.

BASQUE

Ogia lizuna da.

BELARUSIAN

Хлеб запляснеў.

Chlieb zapliasnie.

BOSNIAN

Hleb je pljesniv.

BULGARIAN

Хлябът е мухъл.

Khlyabŭt e mukhŭl.

BURMESE

ပေါင်မုန့်သည်မှိုတက်သည်။

Paung mu n sai mhao taat sai.

CATALAN

El pa és florid.

CEBUANO

Amag ang tinapay.

MANDARIN CHINESE

麵包發霉了。

Miànbāo fāméile.

CORSICAN

U pane hè muffa.

CROATIAN

Kruh je pljesniv.

CZECH

Chléb je plíseň.

DANISH

Brødet er mugent.

DUTCH

Het brood is beschimmeld.

ESPERANTO

La pano estas muldita.

ESTONIAN

Leib on hallitanud.

FILIPINO

Ang tinapay ay amag.

FINNISH

Leipä on homeista.

FRENCH

Le pain est moisi.

GALICIAN

O pan está mofo.

GEORGIAN

პური გახურებულია

P'uri gakhurebulia.

GERMAN

Das brot ist schimmelig.

GREEK

Το ψωμί μουχλιάζει

To psomí mouchliázei.

HAITIAN CREOLE

Pen an mwazi.

HAUSA

Gurasar tana da m.

HAWAIIAN

Mouldy ka palaoa.

HINDI

रोटी फफूंदी लगी है।

Rotee dheelee hai.

HMONG

Lub khob cij yog pwm.

HUNGARIAN

A kenyér penészes.

ICELANDIC

Brauðið er mygla.

IGBO

Achịcha ahụ bụ ebu.

INDONESIAN

Rotinya berjamur.

IRISH

Tá an t-arán múnlaithe.

ITALIAN

Il pane è ammuffito.

JAPANESE

パンはカビが生えています。

Pan wa kabi ga haete imasu.

JAVANESE

Roti cetakan.

KANNADA

ಬ್ರೆಡ್ ಅಚ್ಚಾಗಿದೆ.

Breḍ accāgide.

KAZAKH

Нан көгерген.

Nan kögergen.

KINYARWANDA

Umugati uroroshye.

KOREAN

빵에 곰팡이가 핀다.

Ppang-eun gompang-iga pinda.

KURDISH

Nan qalib e.

KYRGYZ

Нан көгөрүп кетти.

Nan kögörüp ketken.

LATVIAN

Maize ir sapelējusi.

LITHUANIAN

Duona supelijusi.

LUXEMBOURGISH

D'brout as mëll.

MACEDONIAN

Лебот е мувлосан.

Lebot e muvlosan.

MALAGASY

Mamy ny mofo.

MALAY

Roti berkulat.

MALTESE

Il-ħobż huwa moffa.

MAORI

Ko te paraoa he pokepokea ai.

MARATHI

भाकरी बुरशीयुक्त आहे.

Bhākarī buraśīyukta āhē.

MONGOLIAN

Талх хөгцөрсөн байна.

Talkh khögtsörsön baina.

NEPALI

रोटी मोल्डी छ।

Rōṭī mōlḍī cha.

NORWEGIAN

Brødet er muggent.

NYANJA

Mkate ndi wa nkhungu.

POLISH

Chleb to pleśń.

PORTUGUESE

O pão está mofado.

PUNJABI

ਰੋਟੀ ਉੱਲੀ ਹੈ.

Rōṭī ulī hai.

ROMANIAN

Pâinea este mucegai.

RUSSIAN

Хлеб плесень.

Khleb zaplesnevelyy.

SAMOAN

E magumagu le falaoa.

SCOTS GAELIC

Tha an t-aran air a chumadh.

SERBIAN

Хлеб је буђ.

Hleb je buđ.

SLOVAK

Chlieb je pleseň.

SLOVENIAN

Kruh je plesniv.

SOMALI

Roodigu waa caaryaar.

SPANISH

El pan está mohoso.

SUNDANESE

Roti na kapang.

SWAHILI

Mkate ni ukungu.

SWEDISH

Brödet är mögligt.

TAJIK

Нон қолаби аст.

Non qolaвi ast.

TAMIL

ரொட்டி அச்சு.

Roṭṭi accu.

TELUGU

రొట్టె అచ్చు.

Roṭṭe accu.

THAI

ขนมปังเป็นแบบรา

Khnmpạng pĕn bæb rā.

TURKISH

Ekmek küflü.

TURKMEN

Çörek galyndy.

UKRAINIAN

Хліб - цвіль.

Khlib plisnyaviye.

UZBEK

Non mog'orlangan.

VIETNAMESE

Bánh mì bị mốc.

VIETNAMESE

Mae'r bara yn fowldig.

YIDDISH

די ברויט איז פורעם.

Di broyt iz farshimlt.

ZULU

Isinkwa sikhuntile.

14 Science: it's like magic.

AFRIKAANS

Wetenskap: dit is soos towerkuns.

ALBANIAN

Shkenca: është si magji.

AMHARIC

ሳይንስ - እንደ ምትሃት ነው።

Sayinisi - inide mitihati newi.

ARABIC

العلم: إنه مثل السحر.

Aleilmu: 'iinah mithl alsahri.

ARMENIAN

Գիտություն. Դա կախարդության է նման:

Gitut'yun. Da nman e kakhardut'yan.

AZERBAIJANI

Elm: sehr kimidir.

BASQUE

Zientzia: magia bezalakoa da.

BELARUSIAN

Навука: гэта як магія.

Navuka: heta jak mahija.

BOSNIAN

Nauka: to je poput magije.

BULGARIAN

Наука: това е като магия.

Nauka: tova e kato magiya.

BURMESE

သိပ္ပံ၊ ၎င်းသည်မှော်ပညာနှင့်တူသည်။

Sippan: darhar mhaaw nae tuutaal.

CATALAN

Ciència: és com màgia.

CEBUANO

Siyensya: kini sama sa mahika.

MANDARIN CHINESE

科學：就像魔術一樣。

Kēxué: Jiù xiàng móshù yīyàng.

CORSICAN

Scienza: hè cum'è magia.

CROATIAN

Znanost: to je poput magije.

CZECH

Věda: je to jako kouzlo.

DANISH

Videnskab: det er som magi.

DUTCH

Wetenschap: het is als magie.

ESPERANTO

Scienco: ĝi estas kiel magio.

ESTONIAN

Teadus: see on nagu maagia.

FILIPINO

Agham: parang mahika.

FINNISH

Tiede: se on kuin taikuutta.

FRENCH

Science : c'est comme par magie.

GALICIAN

Ciencia: é como maxia.

GEORGIAN

მეცნიერება: ის ჯადოს ჰგავს

Metsniereba: is jados hgavs.

GERMAN

Wissenschaft: es ist wie magie.

GREEK

Επιστήμη: είναι σαν μαγεία

Epistími: eínai san mageía.

HAITIAN CREOLE

Syans: se tankou maji.

HAUSA

Kimiyya: kamar sihiri ne.

HAWAIIAN

ʻEpekema: like ia me ka hoʻokalakupua.

HINDI

विज्ञान: यह जादू की तरह है।

Vigyaan: yah jaadoo kee tarah hai.

HMONG

Kev tshawb fawb: nws zoo li khawv koob.

HUNGARIAN

Tudomány: olyan, mint a varázslat.

ICELANDIC

Vísindi: það er eins og galdur.

IGBO

Sayensị: ọ dị ka anwansi.

INDONESIAN

Sains: itu seperti sihir.

IRISH

Eolaíocht: tá sé cosúil le draíocht.

ITALIAN

Scienza: è come per magia.

JAPANESE

科学：それは魔法のようなものです。

Kagaku: sore wa mahō no yōna monodesu.

JAVANESE

Ilmu: kaya sihir.

KANNADA

ವಿಜ್ಞಾನ: ಇದು ಮ್ಯಾಜಿಕ್ ಹಾಗೆ.

Vijñāna: Idu myājik hāge.

KAZAKH

Ғылым: бұл сиқырға ұқсайды.

Ğılım: bul sïqırğa uqsaydı.

KINYARWANDA

Ubumenyi: ni nkuburozi.

KOREAN

과학: 마법과 같습니다.

Gwahag: mabeobgwa gatseubnida.

KURDISH

Zanist: ew mîna sêrbaziyê ye.

KYRGYZ

Илим: бул сыйкыр сыяктуу.

İlim: bul sıykır sıyaktuu.

LATVIAN

Zinātne: tas ir kā maģija.

LITHUANIAN

Mokslas: tai tarsi magija.

LUXEMBOURGISH

Wëssenschaft: et as wéi magie.

MACEDONIAN

Наука: тоа е како магија.

Nauka: toa e kako magija.

MALAGASY

Siansa: toy ny majia io.

MALAY

Ilmu: ia seperti sihir.

MALTESE

Xjenza: hija bħall-maġija.

MAORI

Pūtaiao: he rite ki te makutu.

MARATHI

विज्ञान: हे जादूसारखे आहे.

Vijñāna: hē jādūsārakhē āhē.

MONGOLIAN

Шинжлэх ухаан: Энэ бол ид шид шиг.

Shinjlekh ukhaan: ene bol id shid shig.

NEPALI

विज्ञान: यो जादू जस्तै हो।

Vijñāna: yō jādū jastai hō.

NORWEGIAN

Vitenskap: det er som magi.

NYANJA

Sayansi: zili ngati matsenga.

POLISH

Nauka: to jak magia.

PORTUGUESE

Ciência: é como mágica.

PUNJABI

ਵਿਗਿਆਨ: ਇਹ ਜਾਦੂ ਵਰਗਾ ਹੈ.

Vigi'āna: iha jādū varagā hai.

ROMANIAN

Știință: este ca magia.

RUSSIAN

Наука: это как волшебство.

Nauka: eto kak volshebstvo.

SAMOAN

Saienisi: e pei o faataulaitu.

SCOTS GAELIC

Saidheans: tha e coltach ri draoidheachd.

SERBIAN

Наука: то је попут магије.

Nauka: to je poput magije.

SLOVAK

Veda: je to ako mágia.

SLOVENIAN

Znanost: to je kot čarovnija.

SOMALI

Sayniska: waa sida sixirka oo kale.

SPANISH

Ciencia: es como magia.

SUNDANESE

Élmu: siga sihir.

SWAHILI

Sayansi: ni kama uchawi.

SWEDISH

Vetenskap: det är som magi.

TAJIK

Илм: он мисли ҷодугарӣ аст.

Ilm: on misli çodugarī ast.

TAMIL

அறிவியல்: இது மந்திரம் போன்றது.

Ar̲iviyal: itu mantiram pōn̲r̲atu.

TELUGU

సైన్స్: ఇది మేజిక్ లాంటిది.

Sains: idi mējik lāṇṭidi.

THAI

วิทยาศาสตร์: มันเหมือนกับเวทมนตร์

Withyāṣ̄āstr̒: mạn h̄emụ̄xnkạb wethmntr̒

TURKISH

Bilim: sihir gibi.

TURKMEN

Ylym: bu jady ýaly.

UKRAINIAN

Наука: це як магія.

Nauka: tse yak mahiya.

UZBEK

Ilm: bu sehrga o'xshaydi.

VIETNAMESE

Khoa học: nó giống như phép thuật.

VIETNAMESE

Gwyddoniaeth: mae fel hud.

YIDDISH

וויסנשאַפֿט: דאָס איז ווי מאַגיש.

Visnshaft: dos iz vi magish.

ZULU

Isayensi: kufana nomlingo.

15 Got milk?

AFRIKAANS

Het melk?

ALBANIAN

Mori qumështin?

AMHARIC

ወተት አለዎት?

Weteti ālewoti?

ARABIC

هل لديك حليب؟

Ladaa halibi?

ARMENIAN

Կար ունե՞ք:

Kat' unek'?

AZERBAIJANI

Süd var?

BASQUE

Esnea al duzu?

BELARUSIAN

У вас ёсць малако?

Josć malako?

BOSNIAN

Imam mlijeka?

BULGARIAN

Имате ли мляко?

Imam mlyako?

BURMESE

နို့ရပြီလား။

Nhoet r pyelarr.

CATALAN

Tinc llet?

CEBUANO

Adunay gatas?

MANDARIN CHINESE

有牛奶嗎？

Yǒu niúnǎi ma?

CORSICAN

Avete u latte?

CROATIAN

Imaš mlijeka?

CZECH

Dostal mléko?

DANISH

Fik mælk?

DUTCH

Heb melk?

ESPERANTO

Ĉu lakton vi havas?

ESTONIAN

Kas sa said piima?

FILIPINO

May gatas ba?

FINNISH

Sai maitoa?

FRENCH

Avoir du lait?

GALICIAN

Ten leite?

GEORGIAN

მიიღეთ რძე?

Miighet rdze?

GERMAN

Hast du milch?

GREEK

Έχετε γάλα

Píra gála?

HAITIAN CREOLE

Gen lèt?

HAUSA

Samun madara?

HAWAIIAN

Loa‘a ka waiū?

HINDI

दूध मिला?

Doodh mil gaya?

HMONG

Tau mis?

HUNGARIAN

Tejet kapott?

ICELANDIC

Áttu mjólk?

IGBO

Enwere mmiri ara?

INDONESIAN

Mendapat susu?

IRISH

Fuair tú bainne?

ITALIAN

Hai il latte?

JAPANESE

牛乳ある？

Miruku o eta?

JAVANESE

Entuk susu?

KANNADA

ಹಾಲು ಸಿಕ್ಕಿದೆಯೇ?

Hālu sikkideyē?

KAZAKH

Сүт алдың ба?

Süt aldıñ ba?

KINYARWANDA

Kubona amata?

KOREAN

우유 있어요?

Uyuleul eod-eossda?

KURDISH

Şîr heye?

KYRGYZ

Сүт алдыңбы?

Süt aldıŋbı?

LATVIAN

Vai jums piens?

LITHUANIAN

Turiu pieno?

LUXEMBOURGISH

Huet mëllech?

MACEDONIAN

Доби млеко?

Dobi mleko?

MALAGASY

Nahazo ronono?

MALAY

Ada susu?

MALTESE

Għandek ħalib?

MAORI

He miraka kau?

MARATHI

दूध मिळाले?

Dūdha miḷālē?

MONGOLIAN

Сүү авсан уу?

Süü avsan?

NEPALI

दूध पाउनुभयो?

Dūdha pā'unubhayō?

NORWEGIAN

Fikk melk?

NYANJA

Muli ndi mkaka?

POLISH

Masz mleko?

PORTUGUESE

Tenho leite?

PUNJABI

ਦੁੱਧ ਮਿਲਿਆ?

Dudha mili'ā?

ROMANIAN

Am lapte?

RUSSIAN

Есть молоко?

Yest' moloko?

SAMOAN

Maua susu?

SCOTS GAELIC

A bheil bainne agad?

SERBIAN

Имаш млека?

Imaš mleka?

SLOVAK

Dostal mlieko?

SLOVENIAN

Imaš mleko?

SOMALI

Caano ma heshay?

SPANISH

¿Tienes leche?

SUNDANESE

Ngagaduhan susu?

SWAHILI

Una maziwa?

SWEDISH

Har mjölk?

TAJIK

Шир гирифтед?

Şir girifted?

TAMIL

பால் கிடைத்தது?

Pāl kiṭaittatu?

TELUGU

పాలు దొరికాయి?

Pālu dorikāyi?

THAI

มีนมไหม?

Mī nm h̄ịm?

TURKISH

Süt var mı?

TURKMEN

Süyt bar?

UKRAINIAN

Є молоко?

Ye moloko?

UZBEK

Sut oldingizmi?

VIETNAMESE

Có sữa?

VIETNAMESE

Oes gennych chi laeth?

YIDDISH

גאַט מילך?

Gat milkh?

ZULU

Unobisi?

16 Who took the toilet paper?

AFRIKAANS

Wie het die toiletpapier geneem?

ALBANIAN

Kush e mori letrën e tualetit?

AMHARIC

የሽንት ቤት ወረቀቱን ማን ወሰደ?

Yeshiniti bēti werek'etuni mani wesede?

ARABIC

من أخذ ورق التواليت؟

Man 'akhadh waraq altawalitu?

ARMENIAN

Ո՞վ վերցրեց զուգարանի թուղթը։

Vo v e verts'rel zugarani t'ught'y?

AZERBAIJANI

Tualet kağızı kim aldı?

BASQUE

Nork hartu du komuneko papera?

BELARUSIAN

Хто ўзяў туалетную паперу?

Chto ŭziaŭ tualietnuju papieru?

BOSNIAN

Ko je uzeo toaletni papir?

BULGARIAN

Кой взе тоалетната хартия?

Koĭ vze toaletnata khartiya?

BURMESE

အိမ်သာသုံးစက္ကူကိုဘယ်သူယူတာလဲ။

Aainsar sone hcakkuu ko bhaalsuu yuu tarlell.

CATALAN

Qui es va emportar el paper higiènic?

CEBUANO

Kinsa ang nagkuha sa papel sa kasilyas?

MANDARIN CHINESE

誰拿走了衛生紙？

Shuí ná zǒule wèishēngzhǐ?

CORSICAN

Quale hè chì hà pigliatu a carta igienica?

CROATIAN

Tko je uzeo toaletni papir?

CZECH

Kdo vzal toaletní papír?

DANISH

Hvem tog toiletpapiret?

DUTCH

Wie heeft het toiletpapier meegenomen?

ESPERANTO

Kiu prenis la necesejan paperon?

ESTONIAN

Kes võttis tualettpaberi?

FILIPINO

Sino ang kumuha ng toilet paper?

FINNISH

Kuka otti vessapaperin?

FRENCH

Qui a pris le papier toilette?

GALICIAN

Quen levou o papel hixiénico?

GEORGIAN

ვინ აიღო ტუალეტის ქაღალდი?

Vin aigho t'ualet'is kaghaldi?

GERMAN

Wer hat das klopapier genommen?

GREEK

Ποιος πήρε το χαρτί τουαλέτας

Poios píre to chartí toualétas?

HAITIAN CREOLE

Ki moun ki te pran papye twalèt la?

HAUSA

Wanene ya ɗauki takardar bayan gida?

HAWAIIAN

Na wai i lawe ka pepa lua?

HINDI

टॉयलेट पेपर किसने लिया?

Toyalet pepar kisane liya?

HMONG

Leej twg nqa daim ntawv tso quav?

HUNGARIAN

Ki vette a vécépapírt?

ICELANDIC

Hver tók klósettpappírinn?

IGBO

Kedu onye were akwụkwọ mposi?

INDONESIAN

Siapa yang mengambil kertas toilet?

IRISH

Cé a thóg an páipéar leithris?

ITALIAN

Chi ha preso la carta igienica?

JAPANESE

トイレットペーパーは誰が取ったのですか？

Toirettopēpā wa dare ga totta no?

JAVANESE

Sapa sing njupuk kertas toilet?

KANNADA

ಟಾಯ್ಲೆಟ್ ಪೇಪರ್ ತೆಗೆದುಕೊಂಡವರು ಯಾರು?

Ṭāyleṭ pēpar tegedukoṇḍavaru yāru?

KAZAKH

Дəретхана қағазын кім алды?

Däretxana qağazın kim aldı?

KINYARWANDA

Ninde wafashe impapuro z'umusarani?

KOREAN

누가 화장지를 가져갔나요?

Nuga hwajangjileul gajyeogassnayo?

KURDISH

Kê kaxeza tuwaletê bir?

KYRGYZ

Даарат кагазын ким алган?

Daarat kagazın kim aldı?

LATVIAN

Kas paņēma tualetes papīru?

LITHUANIAN

Kas paėmė tualetinį popierių?

LUXEMBOURGISH

Wien huet d'Toilettepabeier geholl?

MACEDONIAN

Кој ја зеде тоалетната хартија?

Koj zede toaletna hartija?

MALAGASY

Iza no naka ny taratasy fidiovana?

MALAY

Siapa yang mengambil kertas tandas?

MALTESE

Min ħa t-toilet paper?

MAORI

Na wai i tango te pepa wharepaku?

MARATHI

टॉयलेट पेपर कोणी घेतला?

Ṭŏyalēṭa pēpara kōṇī ghētalā?

MONGOLIAN

Ариун цэврийн цаасыг хэн авсан бэ?

Ariun tsevriin tsaasyg khen avsan be?

NEPALI

ट्वाइलेट पेपर कसले लिएको हो?

Ṭvā'ilēṭa pēpara kasalē li'ēkō hō?

NORWEGIAN

Hvem tok toalettpapiret?

NYANJA

Ndani adatenga pepala lakachimbudzi?

POLISH

Kto zabrał papier toaletowy?

PORTUGUESE

Quem pegou o papel higiênico?

PUNJABI

ਟਾਇਲਟ ਪੇਪਰ ਕੌਣ ਲੈ ਗਿਆ?

Ṭā'ilaṭa pēpara kauṇa lai gi'ā?

ROMANIAN

Cine a luat hârtia igienică?

RUSSIAN

Кто взял туалетную бумагу?

Kto vzyal tualetnuyu bumagu?

SAMOAN

O ai na aveina le pepa faletaele?

SCOTS GAELIC

Cò ghlac am pàipear toileat?

SERBIAN

Ко је узео тоалетни папир?

Ko je uzeo toaletni papir?

SLOVAK

Kto vzal toaletný papier?

SLOVENIAN

Kdo je vzel toaletni papir?

SOMALI

Yaa qaatay warqadda musqusha?

SPANISH

¿Quién se llevó el papel higiénico?

SUNDANESE

Saha anu nyandak tisu wc?

SWAHILI

Nani alichukua karatasi ya choo?

SWEDISH

Vem tog toalettpapper?

TAJIK

Кӣ коғази ҳоҷатхонаро гирифтааст?

Kī koƣazi hoçatxonaro giriftaast?

TAMIL

கழிப்பறை காகிதத்தை எடுத்தது யார்?

Kaḻippaṟai kākitattai eṭuttatu yār?

TELUGU

టాయిలెట్ పేపర్ ఎవరు తీసుకున్నారు?

Ṭāyileṭ pēpar evaru tīsukunnāru?

THAI

ใครเอากระดาษชำระไป?

Khır xeā kradāš' chảra pị?

TURKISH

Tuvalet kağıdını kim aldı?

TURKMEN

Hajathana kagyzyny kim aldy?

UKRAINIAN

Хто взяв туалетний папір?

Khto vzyav tualetnyy papir?

UZBEK

Tualet qog'ozini kim oldi?

VIETNAMESE

Ai đã lấy giấy vệ sinh?

VIETNAMESE

Pwy gymerodd y papur toiled?

YIDDISH

ווער האָט גענומען די קלאָזעט פּאַפיר?

Ver hot genumen di klozet papir?

ZULU

Ngubani othathe iphepha langasese?

17 That's a big cockroach.

AFRIKAANS

Dit is 'n groot kakkerlak.

ALBANIAN

Kjo është një kacabu i madh.

AMHARIC

ያ ትልቅ በረሮ ነው።

Ya tilik'i berero newi.

ARABIC

هذا صرصور كبير

Hadha sarsur kabirun.

ARMENIAN

Դա մեծ ուտիճ է:

Da mets utich e.

AZERBAIJANI

Bu, böyük bir tarakan.

BASQUE

Labezomorro handia da hori.

BELARUSIAN

Гэта вялікі прусак.

Heta vialiki prusak.

BOSNIAN

To je veliki žohar.

BULGARIAN

Това е голяма хлебарка.

Tova e golyama khlebarka.

BURMESE

အဲဒါပိုးဟပ်ကြီး။

Aelldar poehaut kyee.

CATALAN

Això és una gran panerola.

CEBUANO

Kana usa ka dako nga ipis.

MANDARIN CHINESE

那是一隻大蟑螂。

Nà shì yī zhī dà zhāngláng.

CORSICAN

Eccu un grande scarafaghju.

CROATIAN

To je veliki žohar.

CZECH

To je velký šváb.

DANISH

Det er en stor kakerlak.

DUTCH

Dat is een grote kakkerlak.

ESPERANTO

Tio estas granda blato.

ESTONIAN

See on suur prussakas.

FILIPINO

Malaking ipis iyon.

FINNISH

Se on iso torakka.

FRENCH

C'est un gros cafard.

GALICIAN

Iso é unha gran cascuda.

GEORGIAN

ეს დიდი ტარაკანია

Es didi t'arak'ania.

GERMAN

Das ist eine große kakerlake.

GREEK

Αυτό είναι μια μεγάλη κατσαρίδα.

Aftó eínai mia megáli katsarída.

HAITIAN CREOLE

Sa se yon gwo ravèt.

HAUSA

Wannan babban kyankyasai ne.

HAWAIIAN

He ipukukui nui kēlā.

HINDI

यह एक बड़ा कॉकरोच है।

Yah ek bada kokaroch hai.

HMONG

Qhov ntawd yog kab laum loj.

HUNGARIAN

Ez egy nagy csótány.

ICELANDIC

Þetta er stór kakkalakki.

IGBO

Nke ahụ bụ nnukwu ọchịcha.

INDONESIAN

Itu kecoa besar.

IRISH

Sin cockroach mór.

ITALIAN

Questo è un grosso scarafaggio.

JAPANESE

それは大きなゴキブリです。

Sore wa ōkina gokiburidesu.

JAVANESE

Iki kecoak gedhe.

KANNADA

ಅದು ದೊಡ್ಡ ಜಿರಲೆ.

Adu doḍḍa jirale.

KAZAKH

Бұл үлкен тарақан.

Bul ülken taraqan.

KINYARWANDA

Iyo ni isake nini.

KOREAN

그것은 큰 바퀴벌레입니다.

Geugeos-eun keun bakwibeolleibnida.

KURDISH

Ew kêzikek mezin e.

KYRGYZ

Бул чоң таракан.

Bul çoŋ tarakan.

LATVIAN

Tas ir liels tarakāns.

LITHUANIAN

Tai didelis tarakonas.

LUXEMBOURGISH

Dat as e grousse kakerlak.

MACEDONIAN

Тоа е голема тавтабита.

Toa e golema tavtabita.

MALAGASY

Kalalao lehibe izany.

MALAY

Itu lipas besar.

MALTESE

Dak hu wirdien kbir.

MAORI

He tiiwhana nui tera.

MARATHI

हा एक मोठा झुरळ आहे.

Hā ēka mōṭhā jhuraḷa āhē.

MONGOLIAN

Энэ бол том жоом.

Ene bol tom joom.

NEPALI

त्यो एउटा ठूलो काक्रोच हो।

Tyō ē'uṭā ṭhūlō kākrōca hō.

NORWEGIAN

Det er en stor kakerlakk.

NYANJA

Ameneyo ndi tambala wamkulu.

POLISH

To wielki karaluch.

PORTUGUESE

Essa é uma grande barata.

PUNJABI

ਇਹ ਇੱਕ ਵੱਡਾ ਕਾਕਰੋਚ ਹੈ.

Iha ika vaḍā kākarōca hai.

ROMANIAN

Este un gândac mare.

RUSSIAN

Это большой таракан.

Eto bol'shoy tarakan.

SAMOAN

O se lapisi tele.

SCOTS GAELIC

Is e cockroach mòr a tha sin.

SERBIAN

То је велики жохар.

To je veliki žohar.

SLOVAK

To je veľký šváb.

SLOVENIAN

To je velik ščur.

SOMALI

Taasi waa baranbaro weyn.

SPANISH

Esa es una gran cucaracha.

SUNDANESE

Éta kecoak ageung.

SWAHILI

Hiyo ni mende mkubwa.

SWEDISH

Det är en stor kackerlacka.

TAJIK

Ин як тараканы калон аст.

In jak tarakani kalon ast.

TAMIL

அது பெரிய கரப்பான் பூச்சி.

Atu periya karappāṉ pūcci.

TELUGU

అది పెద్ద బొద్దింక.

Adi pedda boddiṅka.

THAI

นั่นเป็นแมลงสาบตัวใหญ่

Nạ̀n pĕn mælngs̄āb tạw h̄ıỵ̀

TURKISH

Bu büyük bir hamamböceği.

TURKMEN

Bu ullakan tarakan.

UKRAINIAN

Це великий тарган.

Tse velykyy tarhan.

UZBEK

Bu katta tarakan.

VIETNAMESE

Đó là một con gián lớn.

VIETNAMESE

Mae hynny'n chwilod duon mawr.

YIDDISH

דאָס איז אַ גרויס קאַקער.

Dos iz a groys kaker.

ZULU

Lokho kukhulu kakhulu.

18 Piece of cake.

AFRIKAANS

N stukkie koek.

ALBANIAN

Copë torte.

AMHARIC

ቁራጭ ኬክ።

K'urach'i kēki.

ARABIC

قطعة كيك.

Qiteat min alkaeki.

ARMENIAN

կտոր տորթ:

Tort'i ktor.

AZERBAIJANI

ədəd tort.

BASQUE

Tarta zati.

BELARUSIAN

кавалачкаў торта.

Kavalak piraha.

BOSNIAN

Komad torte.

BULGARIAN

парчета торта.

Parche torta.

BURMESE

ကိတ်မုန့်အပိုင်းအစ။

Kate mu n aapineaahc.

CATALAN

Tros de pastís.

CEBUANO

Tipik nga cake.

MANDARIN CHINESE

小菜一碟。

Xiǎocài yī dié.

CORSICAN

Pezzu di torta.

CROATIAN

Mačji kašalj.

CZECH

Kus dortu.

DANISH

Stykke kage.

DUTCH

Fluitje van een cent.

ESPERANTO

Peco de kuko.

ESTONIAN

Käkitegu.

FILIPINO

Madali lang.

FINNISH

Pala kakkua.

FRENCH

Part de gâteau.

GALICIAN

Anaco de torta.

GEORGIAN

ნამცხვრის ნაჭერი

Namtskhvris nach'eri.

GERMAN

Stück kuchen.

GREEK

Πανεύκολο.

Panéfkolo.

HAITIAN CREOLE

Mòso gato.

HAUSA

Abun kek.

HAWAIIAN

ʻĀpana keke.

HINDI

तुच्छ बात।

Tuchchh baat.

HMONG

Daim ncuav mog qab zib.

HUNGARIAN

Szelet torta.

ICELANDIC

Ekkert mál.

IGBO

Iberibe achicha.

INDONESIAN

Sepotong kue.

IRISH

Píosa cáca.

ITALIAN

Pezzo di torta.

JAPANESE

ケーキ。

Kēki.

JAVANESE

Jajan jajan.

KANNADA

ಕೇಕಿನ ತುಂಡು.

Kēkina tuṇḍu.

KAZAKH

Бәліш тілімі.

Bäliş tilimi.

KINYARWANDA

Igice cya keke.

KOREAN

케이크 조각.

Keikeu jogag.

KURDISH

Parçeyek kek.

KYRGYZ

Торт кесеги.

Tort kesegi.

LATVIAN

Kūkas gabals.

LITHUANIAN

Gabalėlis pyrago.

LUXEMBOURGISH

Stéck vum kuch.

MACEDONIAN

Парче торта.

Parče torta.

MALAGASY

Mofomamy.

MALAY

Sangat mudah.

MALTESE

Biċċa kejk.

MAORI

Kihi keke.

MARATHI

केक तुकडा.

Kēka tukaḍā.

MONGOLIAN

Зүсэм бялуу.

Züsem byaluu.

NEPALI

केकको टुक्रा।

Kēkakō ṭukrā.

NORWEGIAN

Lett som bare det.

NYANJA

Chidutswa cha mkate.

POLISH

Bułka z masłem.

PORTUGUESE

Pedaco de bolo.

PUNJABI

ਕੇਕ ਦਾ ਟੁਕੜਾ.

Kēka dā ṭukaṛā.

ROMANIAN

Bucată de tort.

RUSSIAN

Кусок пирога.

Kusok piroga.

SAMOAN

Fasi keke.

SCOTS GAELIC

Pìos cèic.

SERBIAN

Просто као пасуљ.

Prosto kao pasulj.

SLOVAK

Kúsok koláča.

SLOVENIAN

Malenkost.

SOMALI

Cad cad.

SPANISH

Pedazo de pastel.

SUNDANESE

Sapotong jajan.

SWAHILI

Kipande cha keki.

SWEDISH

Lätt som en plätt.

TAJIK

Як пораи торт.

Jak porai tort.

TAMIL

கேக் துண்டு.

Kēk tuṇṭu.

TELUGU

కేకు ముక్క.

Kēku mukka.

THAI

เค้กชิ้น.

Khêk chîn.

TURKISH

Kekin parçası.

TURKMEN

Bir bölek tort.

UKRAINIAN

Шматок торту.

Shmatok tortu.

UZBEK

Kek bo'lagi.

VIETNAMESE

Miếng bánh.

VIETNAMESE

Darn o gacen.

YIDDISH

שטיקל קוכן.

Shtikl kukhn.

ZULU

Ucezu lwekhekhe.

19 Houston, we have a problem.

AFRIKAANS

Houston, ons het n probleem.

ALBANIAN

Houston, ne kemi një problem.

AMHARIC

ሂውስተን ፤ ችግር አለብን።

Hīwisiteni - chigiri ālebini.

ARABIC

هيوستن ، لدينا مشكلة.

Hiustun ladayna mushkilatun.

ARMENIAN

Հյուստոն, մենք խնդիր ունենք:

Hyust'von, menk' khndir unenk'.

AZERBAIJANI

Hyuston, bir problemimiz var.

BASQUE

Houston, arazo bat dugu.

BELARUSIAN

Х'юстан, у нас праблема.

CHjustan, u nas prabliema.

BOSNIAN

Houston, imamo problem.

BULGARIAN

Хюстън, имаме проблем.

Khyustŭn imame problem.

BURMESE

ဟူစတန်၊ ငါတို့မှာပြဿနာတစ်ခုရှိတယ်။

Huuhcataan, ngarthoetmhar pyanar taithkushitaal.

CATALAN

Houston, tenim un problema.

CEBUANO

Houston, naa tay problema.

MANDARIN CHINESE

休斯頓，我們有一個問題。

Xiūsīdùn, wǒmen yǒu yīgè wèntí.

CORSICAN

Houston, avemu un prublema.

CROATIAN

Houston, imamo problem.

CZECH

Houstone máme problém.

DANISH

Houston vi har et problem.

DUTCH

Houston we hebben een probleem.

ESPERANTO

Houston, ni havas problemon.

ESTONIAN

Houston, meil on probleem.

FILIPINO

Houston, may problema tayo.

FINNISH

Houston, meillä on ongelma.

FRENCH

Houston nous avons un problème.

GALICIAN

Houston, temos un problema.

GEORGIAN

ჰიუსტონ პრობლემა გვაქვს.

Hiust'on p'roblema gvakvs.

GERMAN

Houston, wir haben ein problem.

GREEK

Χιούστον, έχουμε πρόβλημα

Chioúston, échoume próvlima.

HAITIAN CREOLE

Houston, nou gen yon pwoblèm.

HAUSA

Houston, muna da matsala.

HAWAIIAN

ʻO Houston, he pilikia kā mākou.

HINDI

हॉस्टन हमारे पास समस्या है।

Hostan hamaare paas samasya he.

HMONG

Houston, peb muaj teeb meem.

HUNGARIAN

Houston van egy kis problémánk.

ICELANDIC

Houston, við eigum í vandræðum.

IGBO

Houston, anyị nwere nsogbu.

INDONESIAN

Houston kita punya masalah.

IRISH

Houston, tá fadhb againn.

ITALIAN

Houston abbiamo un problema.

JAPANESE

ヒューストン、問題があります。

Hyūsuton, mondai ga arimasu.

JAVANESE

Houston, kita duwe masalah.

KANNADA

ಹೂಸ್ಟನ್, ನಮಗೆ ಸಮಸ್ಯೆ ಇದೆ.

Hūsṭan, namage samasye ide.

KAZAKH

Хьюстон, бізде мәселе бар.

Xyuston, bizde mäsele bar.

KINYARWANDA

Houston, dufite ikibazo.

KOREAN

휴스턴, 우리에게 문제가 생겼다.

Hyuseuteon, uliege munjega saeng-gyeossda.

KURDISH

Houston, pirsgirêkek me heye.

KYRGYZ

Houston, бизде көйгөй бар.

Houston, bizde köygöy bar.

LATVIAN

Hjūston, mums ir problēma.

LITHUANIAN

Hiustonai, turime problemą.

LUXEMBOURGISH

Houston, mir hunn e problem.

MACEDONIAN

Хјустон, имаме проблем.

Hjuston, imame problem.

MALAGASY

Houston, manana olana isika.

MALAY

Houston, kita mempunyai masalah.

MALTESE

Houston, għandna problema.

MAORI

Houston, he raru kei a tatou.

MARATHI

ह्यूस्टन, आम्हाला एक समस्या आहे.

Hyūsṭana, āmhālā ēka samasyā āhē.

MONGOLIAN

Хьюстон, бидэнд асуудал байна.

Khiyuston, bidend asuudal baina.

NEPALI

ह्युस्टन, हामी एक समस्या छ।

Hyusṭana, hāmī ēka samasyā cha.

NORWEGIAN

Houston vi har et problem.

NYANJA

Houston, tili ndi vuto.

POLISH

Houston, mamy problem.

PORTUGUESE

Houston, nós temos um problema.

PUNJABI

Houston, ਸਾਨੂੰ ਇੱਕ ਸਮੱਸਿਆ ਹੈ.

Houston, sānū ika samasi'ā hai.

ROMANIAN

Houston avem o problema.

RUSSIAN

Хьюстон, у нас проблема.

Kh'yuston, u nas problema.

SAMOAN

Houston, o lo'o iai lo matou fa'afitauli.

SCOTS GAELIC

Houston, tha duilgheadas againn.

SERBIAN

Хјустон имамо проблем.

Hjuston imamo problem.

SLOVAK

Houston, máme problém.

SLOVENIAN

Houston, imamo problem.

SOMALI

Houston, waxaan qabnaa dhibaato.

SPANISH

Houston, tenemos un problema.

SUNDANESE

Houston, urang ngagaduhan masalah.

SWAHILI

Houston, tuna shida.

SWEDISH

Houston vi har ett problem.

TAJIK

Хьюстон, мо мушкилот дорем.

X'juston, mo muşkilot dorem.

TAMIL

ஹூஸ்டன், எங்களுக்கு ஒரு பிரச்சனை இருக்கிறது.

Hūsṭaṉ, eṅkaḷukku oru piraccaṉai irukkiṟatu.

TELUGU

హౌస్టన్, మాకు ఒక సమస్య ఉంది.

Hausṭan, māku oka samasya undi.

THAI

ฮูสตันพวกเรามีปัญหา.

Ḥūs̄ tạn phwk reā mī pạỵh̄ā.

TURKISH

Bir problemimiz var Houston.

TURKMEN

Hýuston, bizde bir mesele bar.

UKRAINIAN

Х'юстон, у нас проблема.

KH'yuston, u nas problema.

UZBEK

Xyuston, bizda muammo bor.

VIETNAMESE

Houston chúng ta có một vấn đề.

VIETNAMESE

Houston, mae gennym broblem.

YIDDISH

האָוסטאָן, מיר האָבן אַ פּראָבלעם.

Houston, mir hobn a problem.

ZULU

Houston, sinenkinga.

20 Inconceivable!

AFRIKAANS

Ondenkbaar!

ALBANIAN

E paimagjinueshme!

AMHARIC

የማይታሰብ!

Yemayitasebi!

ARABIC

لا يمكن تصوره!

La yumkin tasawuruhu!

ARMENIAN

Անհնար է:

Anhavanakan!

AZERBAIJANI

Ağlasığmaz!

BASQUE

Pentsaezina!

BELARUSIAN

Неймаверна!

Niejmavierna!

BOSNIAN

Nezamislivo!

BULGARIAN

Немислимо!

Nemislimo!

BURMESE

မယုံကြည်နိုင်စရာ!

M yonekyininehcarar!

CATALAN

Inconcebible!

CEBUANO

Dili masabtan!

MANDARIN CHINESE

不可思議！

Bùkěsīyì!

CORSICAN

Impussibule!

CROATIAN

Nezamislivo!

CZECH

Nepředstavitelné!

DANISH

Ufatteligt!

DUTCH

Onvoorstelbaar!

ESPERANTO

Neimagebla!

ESTONIAN

Mõeldamatu!

FILIPINO

Hindi mawari!

FINNISH

Käsittämätöntä!

FRENCH

Inconcevable!

GALICIAN

¡Inconcibible!

GEORGIAN

წარმოუდგენელია!

Ts'armoudgenelia!

GERMAN

Undenkbar!

GREEK

Αδιανόητος!

Adianóitos!

HAITIAN CREOLE

Enposib!

HAUSA

Wanda ba a iya tunaninsa!

HAWAIIAN

Hoʻohuli ʻole!

HINDI

अकल्पनीय!

Awkalpaneey!

HMONG

Inconceivable!

HUNGARIAN

Elképzelhetetlen!

ICELANDIC

Óskiljanlegt!

IGBO

Enweghị atụmanya!

INDONESIAN

Tak terbayangkan!

IRISH

Dochreidte!

ITALIAN

Inconcepibile!

JAPANESE

想像を絶する！

Sōzō o zessuru!

JAVANESE

Ora bisa dingerteni!

KANNADA

ಅಚಿಂತ್ಯ!

Acintya!

KAZAKH

Ақылға сыймайтын!

Aqılğa sıymaytın!

KINYARWANDA

Ntibishoboka!

KOREAN

말도 안돼!

Maldo andwae!

KURDISH

Inconceivable!

KYRGYZ

Акылга сыйбаган!

Akılga sıybagan!

LATVIAN

Neiedomājami!

LITHUANIAN

Neįsivaizduojama!

LUXEMBOURGISH

Ondenkbar!

MACEDONIAN

Незамисливо!

Nezamislivo!

MALAGASY

Tsy takatry ny saina!

MALAY

Tidak dapat difahami!

MALTESE

Inkonċepibbli!

MAORI

Kaore e taea te whakaaro!

MARATHI

अकल्पनीय!

Akalpanīya!

MONGOLIAN

Санаанд багтамгүй!

Sanaand bagtamgüi!

NEPALI

अकल्पनीय!

Akalpanīya!

NORWEGIAN

Utenkelig!

NYANJA

Zosatheka!

POLISH

Niepojęty!

PORTUGUESE

Inconcebível!

PUNJABI

ਸਮਝ ਤੋਂ ਬਾਹਰ!

Samajha tōṁ bāhara!

ROMANIAN

Neconceput!

RUSSIAN

Немыслимо!

Nemyslimo!

SAMOAN

Le talitonuina!

SCOTS GAELIC

Do-chreidsinneach!

SERBIAN

Незамисливо!

Nezamislivo!

SLOVAK

Nepredstaviteľné!

SLOVENIAN

Nepredstavljivo!

SOMALI

Lama malayn karo!

SPANISH

¡Inconcebible!

SUNDANESE

Teu kapendak!

SWAHILI

Haiwezekani!

SWEDISH

Otänkbart!

TAJIK

Акл бовар қилмайди!

Aql вovar qilmajdi!

TAMIL

நினைத்துப் பார்க்க முடியாதது!

Niṉaittup pārkka muṭiyātatu!

TELUGU

ఊహించలేనిది!

Ūhiñcalēnidi!

THAI

นึกไม่ถึง!

Nụk mị̀ t̄hụng!

TURKISH

Akıl almaz!

TURKMEN

Düşünip bolmaýar!

UKRAINIAN

Немислимо!

Nemyslymo!

UZBEK

Mantiqsiz!

VIETNAMESE

Không thể tưởng tượng được!

VIETNAMESE

Yn annirnadwy!

YIDDISH

!אוממעגלעך

Aummeglekh!

ZULU

Akucabangeki!

21 Who let the tiger in?

AFRIKAANS

Wie het die tier ingelaat?

ALBANIAN

Kush e la tigrin të hyjë?

AMHARIC

ነብርን ማን አስገባው?

Nebirini mani āsigebawi?

ARABIC

من سمح للنمر بالدخول؟

Man samah lilnamir bialdukhuli?

ARMENIAN

Ո՞վ ներս թողեց վագրին:

Vo v e vagrin ners t'voghel?

AZERBAIJANI

Pələngi kim içəri buraxdı?

BASQUE

Nork utzi zion tigreari?

BELARUSIAN

Хто ўпусціў тыгра?

Chto ŭpusciŭ tyhra?

BOSNIAN

Ko je pustio tigra unutra?

BULGARIAN

Кой пусна тигъра?

Koĭ pusna tigŭra?

BURMESE

ကျားကိုဘယ်သူခွင့်ပြုတာလဲ။

Kyarr ko bhaalsuu lwhaat tarlell.

CATALAN

Qui va deixar entrar el tigre?

CEBUANO

Kinsa ang gipasulod sa tigre?

MANDARIN CHINESE

誰讓老虎進來的？

Shuí ràng lǎohǔ jìnlái de?

CORSICAN

Quale hè chì hà intrutu u tigru?

CROATIAN

Tko je pustio tigra?

CZECH

Kdo pustil tygra dovnitř?

DANISH

Hvem slap tigeren ind?

DUTCH

Wie heeft de tijger binnengelaten?

ESPERANTO

Kiu enlasis la tigron?

ESTONIAN

Kes lasi tiigri sisse?

FILIPINO

Sino ang nagpasok ng tigre?

FINNISH

Kuka päästi tiikerin sisään?

FRENCH

Qui a laissé entrer le tigre?

GALICIAN

Quen deixou entrar o tigre?

GEORGIAN

ვინ შეუშვა ვეფხვი?

Vin sheushva vepkhvi?

GERMAN

Wer hat den Tiger reingelassen?

GREEK

Ποιος άφησε την τίγρη να μπει

Poios áfise tin tígri na bei?

HAITIAN CREOLE

Ki moun ki kite tig la antre?

HAUSA

Wanene ya bari damisa ta shiga?

HAWAIIAN

Na wai e hoʻokuʻu i ka tiger i loko?

HINDI

बाघ को किसने अंदर जाने दिया?

Baagh ko kisane andar jaane diya?

HMONG

Leej twg cia tus tsov nyob hauv?

HUNGARIAN

Ki engedte be a tigrist?

ICELANDIC

Hver hleypti tígrisdýrinu inn?

IGBO

Kedu onye kwere ka agụ banye?

INDONESIAN

Siapa yang membiarkan harimau masuk?

IRISH

Cé a lig an tíogair isteach?

ITALIAN

Chi ha fatto entrare la tigre?

JAPANESE

誰が虎を入れましたか？

Dare ga tora o iremashita ka?

JAVANESE

Sapa sing nglilani macan?

KANNADA

ಹುಲಿಯನ್ನು ಒಳಗೆ ಬಿಟ್ಟವರು ಯಾರು?

Huliyannu oḷage biṭṭavaru yāru?

KAZAKH

Жолбарысты кім кіргізді?

Jolbarıstı kim kirgizdi?

KINYARWANDA

Ninde warekuye ingwe?

KOREAN

누가 호랑이를 들여보냈습니까?

Nuga holang-ileul deul-yeobonaessseubnikka?

KURDISH

Kê piling berda hundir?

KYRGYZ

Жолборсту ким киргизди?

Jolborstu kim kirgizdi?

LATVIAN

Kas ielaida tīģeri?

LITHUANIAN

Kas įleido tigrą?

LUXEMBOURGISH

Wie loosst den Tiger eran?

MACEDONIAN

Кој го пушти тигарот?

Koj go pušti tigarot?

MALAGASY

Iza no namela ny tigra?

MALAY

Siapa yang membiarkan harimau masuk?

MALTESE

Min ħalla t-tigra tidħol?

MAORI

Na wai i tuku te tiger ki roto?

MARATHI

वाघाला कोणी आत येऊ दिले?

Vāghālā kōṇī āta yē'ū dilē?

MONGOLIAN

Барыг хэн оруулсан бэ?

Baryg khen oruulsan be?

NEPALI

कसले बाघलाई भित्र पस्न दियो?

Kasalē bāghalā'ī bhitra pasna diyō?

NORWEGIAN

Hvem slapp tigeren inn?

NYANJA

Ndani analola kambukuyu?

POLISH

Kto wpuścił tygrysa?

PORTUGUESE

Quem deixou o tigre entrar?

PUNJABI

ਕਿਸਨੇ ਟਾਈਗਰ ਨੂੰ ਅੰਦਰ ਜਾਣ ਦਿੱਤਾ?

Kisanē ṭā'īgara nū adara jāṇa ditā?

ROMANIAN

Cine a lăsat tigrul să intre?

RUSSIAN

Кто впустил тигра?

Kto vpustil tigra?

SAMOAN

O ai na fa'atagaina le taika i totonu?

SCOTS GAELIC

Cò leig an tìgear a-steach?

SERBIAN

Ко је пустио тигра?

Ko je pustio tigra?

SLOVAK

Kto pustil tigra dnu?

SLOVENIAN

Kdo je spustil tigra?

SOMALI

Yaa shabeelka soo geliyey?

SPANISH

¿Quién dejó entrar al tigre?

SUNDANESE

Saha anu ngantepkeun macan?

SWAHILI

Nani alimwacha tiger aingie?

SWEDISH

Vem släppte in tigern?

TAJIK

Кӣ палангро иҷозат дод?

Kī palangro içozat dod?

TAMIL

புலியை உள்ளே அனுமதித்தது யார்?

Puliyai uḷḷē aṉumatittatu yār?

TELUGU

పులిని ఎవరు లోపలికి అనుమతించారు?

Pulini evaru lōpaliki anumatiñcāru?

THAI

ใครให้เสือเข้ามา?

Khır h̄ı̂ s̄eụ̄x k̄hêā mā?

TURKISH

Kaplanı kim içeri aldı?

TURKMEN

Igerolbars kim girdi?

UKRAINIAN

Хто впустив тигра?

Khto vpustyv tyhra?

UZBEK

Yo'lbarsni kim kiritdi?

VIETNAMESE

Ai cho hổ vào?

VIETNAMESE

Pwy adawodd y teigr i mewn?

YIDDISH

ווער האט אריינגעלאזט דעם טיגער?

Ver hat areyngelazt dem tiger?

ZULU

Ngubani ovumele ihlosi lingene?

22 No thank you. I already ate monkey today.

AFRIKAANS

Nee dankie. Ek het vandag al aap geëet.

ALBANIAN

Jo faleminderit. Unë tashmë kam ngrënë majmun sot.

AMHARIC

አይ አመሰግናለሁ። ዛሬ ጦጣ በልቼ ነበር።

Ayi āmeseginalehu - zarē t'ot'a belichē neberi.

ARABIC

لا، شكرا. لقد أكلت القرد بالفعل اليوم.

La, shukra. laqad 'ukilt alqird bialfiel alyawma.

ARMENIAN

Ոչ, շնորհակալ եմ. Այսօր արդեն կապիկ եմ կերել:

Voch', shnorhakal yem. Aysor arden kapik yem kerel.

AZERBAIJANI

Xeyr, sağ olun. Bu gün artıq meymun yedim.

BASQUE

Ez eskerrik asko. Gaur dagoeneko tximua jan dut.

BELARUSIAN

Не, дзякуй. Я ўжо еў малпу сёння.

Nie, dziakuj. Ja ŭžo jeŭ malpu sionnia.

BOSNIAN

Ne hvala. Danas sam već jeo majmuna.

BULGARIAN

Не благодаря. Днес вече ядох маймуна.

Ne blagodarya. Dnes veche yadokh maĭmuna.

BURMESE

မဟုတ်ဘူးကျေးဇူးတင်ပါတယ်။ ငါဒီနေ့မျောက်စားပြီးပြီ။

Mahotebhuu kyaayyjuutainpartaal. Ngar denae myawwat hcarr pyeepye.

CATALAN

No gràcies. Avui ja he menjat mico.

CEBUANO

Dili salamat. Nikaon na ako unggoy karon.

MANDARIN CHINESE

不，謝謝。我今天已經吃了猴子。

Bù, xièxiè. Wǒ jīntiān yǐjīng chīle hóuzi.

CORSICAN

Innò vi ringraziu. Aghju digià manghjatu scimmia oghje.

CROATIAN

Ne hvala. Danas sam već jeo majmuna.

CZECH

Ne, děkuji. Dnes jsem už jedl opici.

DANISH

Nej tak. Jeg har allerede spist abe i dag.

DUTCH

Nee, dank u. Ik heb vandaag al aap gegeten.

ESPERANTO

Ne dankon. Mi jam manĝis simion hodiaŭ.

ESTONIAN

Ei aitäh. Täna sõin juba ahvi.

FILIPINO

Hindi, salamat. Kumain na ako ng unggoy ngayon.

FINNISH

Ei kiitos. Tänään söin jo apinan.

FRENCH

Non, merci. J'ai déjà mangé du singe aujourd'hui.

GALICIAN

Non grazas. Hoxe xa comín mono.

GEORGIAN

არა გმადლობთ. დღეს უკვე მაიმუნი ვჭამე

Ara gmadlobt. Dghes uk've maimuni vch'ame.

GERMAN

Nein danke. Ich habe heute schon affen gegessen.

GREEK

Οχι ευχαριστώ. Έφαγα ήδη μαϊμού σήμερα.

Ochi efcharistó. Éfaga ídi maïmoú símera.

HAITIAN CREOLE

Non mèsi. Mwen deja manje makak jodi a.

HAUSA

A'a na gode. Na riga na ci biri a yau.

HAWAIIAN

'A'ole mahalo. Ua 'ai mua wau i ka mōneka i kēia lā.

HINDI

नहीं धन्यवाद। मैंने आज ही बंदर खा लिया।

Nahin dhanyavaad. Mainne aaj hee bandar kha liya.

HMONG

Tsis ua tsaug. Kuv twb tau noj liab hnub no lawm.

HUNGARIAN

Nem, köszönöm. Ma már majmot ettem.

ICELANDIC

Nei takk. Ég borðaði nú þegar api í dag.

IGBO

Mba daalụ. Eriela m enwe taa.

INDONESIAN

Tidak terima kasih. Saya sudah makan monyet hari ini.

IRISH

Níl maith agat. D'ith mé moncaí inniu.

ITALIAN

No grazie. Ho già mangiato la scimmia oggi.

JAPANESE

いいえ、結構です。今日はもう猿を食べました。

Īe, kekkōdesu. Kyō wa mō saru o tabemashita.

JAVANESE

Ora matur nuwun. Aku wis mangan kethek dina iki.

KANNADA

ಇಲ್ಲ ಧನ್ಯವಾದಗಳು. ನಾನು ಈಗಾಗಲೇ ಇಂದು ಕೋತಿಯನ್ನು ತಿಂದಿದ್ದೇನೆ.

Illa dhan'yavādagaḷu. Nānu īgāgalē indu kōtiyannu tindiddēne.

KAZAKH

Жоқ рахмет. Мен бүгін маймылды жеп қойдым.

Joq raxmet. Men bügin maymıldı jep qoydım.

KINYARWANDA

Oya urakoze. Uyu munsi nari maze kurya inkende.

KOREAN

아니요 괜찮습니다. 나는 오늘 이미 원숭이를 먹었다.

Aniyo gwaenchanhseubnida. Naneun oneul imi wonsung-ileul meog-eossda.

KURDISH

Na spas dikim. Min îro berê meymûn xwar.

KYRGYZ

Жок рахмат. Мен маймылды бүгүн эле жеп койгом.

Jok rahmat. Men maymıldı bügün ele jep koygom.

LATVIAN

Nē paldies. Šodien jau ēdu pērtiķi.

LITHUANIAN

Ne ačiū. Šiandien jau suvalgiau beždžionę.

LUXEMBOURGISH

Nee merci. Ech hunn haut schonn affen giess.

MACEDONIAN

Не благодарам. Денес веќе јадев мајмун.

Ne blagodaram. Denes veḱe jadev majmun.

MALAGASY

Tsia misaotra. Efa nihinana gidro aho androany.

MALAY

Tidak, terima kasih. Saya sudah makan monyet hari ini.

MALTESE

Le grazzi. Illum diġà kielt xadina.

MAORI

No mihi. Kua kai kētia ahau i tenei ra.

MARATHI

नको, धन्यवाद. मी आज आधीच माकड खाल्ले आहे.

Nakō, dhan'yavāda. Mī āja ādhīca mākaḍa khāllē āhē.

MONGOLIAN

Үгүй ээ баярлалаа. Би өнөөдөр аль хэдийн сармагчин идсэн.

Ügüi ee bayarlalaa. Bi önöödör ali khediin sarmagchin idsen.

NEPALI

हैन धन्यवाद। मैले आज नै बाँदर खाएको छु।

Haina dhan'yavāda. Mailē āja nai bām̐dara khā'ēkō chu.

NORWEGIAN

Nei takk. Jeg har allerede spist ape i dag.

NYANJA

Ayi zikomo. Ndadya kale nyani lero.

POLISH

Nie, dziękuję. Zjadłem już dziś małpę.

PORTUGUESE

Não, obrigado. Eu já comi macaco hoje.

PUNJABI

ਬੱਸ ਮਿਹਰਬਾਨੀ. ਮੈਂ ਅੱਜ ਹੀ ਬਾਂਦਰ ਖਾ ਲਿਆ ਹੈ.

Basa miharabānī. Maiṁ aja hī bāndara khā li'ā hai.

ROMANIAN

Nu, mulțumesc. Am mâncat deja maimuță azi.

RUSSIAN

Нет, спасибо. Я уже сегодня обезьяну съел.

Net, spasibo. Ya uzhe segodnya obez'yanu s"yel.

SAMOAN

Leai faafetai Ua uma ona ou 'ai manuki i le aso.

SCOTS GAELIC

Gun taing. Dh 'ith mi muncaidh an-diugh.

SERBIAN

Не хвала. Данас сам већ јео мајмуне.

Ne hvala. Danas sam već jeo majmune.

SLOVAK

Nie ďakujem. Dnes som už jedol opicu.

SLOVENIAN

Ne, hvala. Danes sem že jedel opice.

SOMALI

Maya mahadsanid. Hore ayaan u cunay maanta daanyeer.

SPANISH

No gracias. Ya comí mono hoy.

SUNDANESE

Henteu hatur nuhun. Abdi parantos tuang monyét dinten ayeuna.

SWAHILI

Hapana asante. Nimekula nyani leo.

SWEDISH

Nej tack. Jag har redan ätit apa idag.

TAJIK

Не рахмат. Ман аллакай маймун хӯрдам.

Ne raxmat. Man allakaj majmun xūrdam.

TAMIL

பரவாயில்லை, நன்றி. நான் ஏற்கனவே இன்று குரங்கை சாப்பிட்டேன்.

Paravāyillai, naṉṟi. Nāṉ ēṟkaṉavē iṉṟu kuraṅkai cāppiṭṭēṉ.

TELUGU

అక్కర్లేదు. నేను ఈరోజు ఇప్పటికే కోతిని తిన్నాను.

Akkarlēdu. Nēnu īrōju ippaṭikē kōtini tinnānu.

THAI

ไม่เป็นไรขอบคุณ. วันนี้ฉันกินลิงไปแล้ว

Mị̀ pĕnrị k̄hxbkhuṇ. Wạn nī̂ c̄hạn kin ling pị læ̂w.

TURKISH

Hayır teşekkürler. Bugün zaten maymun yedim.

TURKMEN

Ýok, sagbol. Men bu gün maýmyny iýipdim.

UKRAINIAN

Ні, дякую. Я вже їв мавпу сьогодні.

Ni, dyakuyu. Ya vzhe yiv mavpu s'ohodni.

UZBEK

Rahmat kerak emas. Men bugun maymunni yeb qo'ydim.

VIETNAMESE

Không cám ơn. Tôi đã ăn thịt khỉ hôm nay.

VIETNAMESE

Dim diolch. Bwytais i fwnci heddiw.

YIDDISH

ניין א דאנק. איך האָב שוין געגעסן מאַלפּע הײַנט

Neyn a dank. Ikh hob shoyn gegesn malpe haynt.

ZULU

Cha ngiyabonga. Sengiyidlile inkawu namuhla.

23 I've rescued forty-eight cats.

AFRIKAANS

Ek het agt-en-veertig katte gered.

ALBANIAN

Kam shpëtuar dyzet e tetë mace.

AMHARIC

አርባ ስምንት ድመቶችን አዳንኩ።

Ariba siminiti dimetochini ādaniku

ARABIC

لقد أنقذت ثمانية وأربعين قطة.

Laqad 'unqidhat thamaniat wa'arbaein qitatan.

ARMENIAN

Ես փրկեցի քառասունութ կատու:

Yes p'rkets'i k'arrasunut' katu.

AZERBAIJANI

Qırx səkkiz pişiyi xilas etdim.

BASQUE

Berrogeita zortzi katu erreskatatu ditut.

BELARUSIAN

Я выратаваў сорак восем котак.

Ja vyratavaŭ sorak vosiem kotak.

BOSNIAN

Spasio sam četrdeset osam mačaka.

BULGARIAN

Спасих четиридесет и осем котки.

Spasikh chetirideset i osem kotki.

BURMESE

ကြောင်လေးဆယ့်ရှစ်ကောင်ကိုငါ ကယ်ခဲ့တယ်။

Kyaunglayy s y sht kaungko ngar kaal hkaetaal.

CATALAN

He rescatat quaranta-vuit gats.

CEBUANO

Naluwas nako ang kwarentay otso nga mga iring.

MANDARIN CHINESE

我救了四十八隻貓。

Wǒ jiùle sìshíbā zhī māo.

CORSICAN

Aghju salvatu quaranta ottu misgi.

CROATIAN

Spasio sam četrdeset osam mačaka.

CZECH

Zachránil jsem čtyřicet osm koček.

DANISH

Jeg har reddet otteogfyrre katte.

DUTCH

Ik heb achtenveertig katten gered.

ESPERANTO

Mi savis kvardek ok katojn.

ESTONIAN

Olen päästnud nelikümmend kaheksa kassi.

FILIPINO

Nailigtas ko ang apatnapu't walong mga pusa.

FINNISH

Olen pelastanut neljäkymmentäkahdeksan kissaa.

FRENCH

J'ai sauvé quarante-huit chats.

GALICIAN

Rescatei corenta e oito gatos.

GEORGIAN

მე გადავარჩინე ორმოცდარვა კატა

Me gadavarchine ormotsdarva k'at'a.

GERMAN

Ich habe 48 Katzen gerettet.

GREEK

Έχω σώσει σαράντα οκτώ γάτες.

Écho sósei saránta októ gátes.

HAITIAN CREOLE

Mwen te sove karant-uit chat.

HAUSA

Na ceto kuliyoyi arba'in da takwas.

HAWAIIAN

Ua hoʻopakele wau i nā pōpoki he kanahākūmāwalu.

HINDI

मैंने अड़तालीस बिल्लियों को बचाया है।

Mainne adataalees billiyon ko bachaaya hai.

HMONG

Kuv tau cawm plaub caug yim tus miv.

HUNGARIAN

Negyvennyolc macskát mentettem meg.

ICELANDIC

Ég hef bjargað fjörutíu og átta köttum.

IGBO

Azọpụtara m nwamba iri anọ na asatọ.

INDONESIAN

Saya telah menyelamatkan empat puluh delapan kucing.

IRISH

Tá daichead a hocht cait tarrtháilte agam.

ITALIAN

Ho salvato quarantotto gatti.

JAPANESE

私は48匹の猫を救出しました。

Watashi wa 48-biki no neko o kyūshutsu shimashita.

JAVANESE

Aku wis nylametake kucing patlikur wolu.

KANNADA

ನಾನು ನಲವತ್ತೆಂಟು ಬೆಕ್ಕುಗಳನ್ನು ರಕ್ಷಿಸಿದ್ದೇನೆ.

Nānu nalavatteṇṭu bekkugaḷannu rakṣisiddēne.

KAZAKH

Мен қырық сегіз мысықты құтқардым.

Men qırıq segiz mısıqtı qutqardım.

KINYARWANDA

Nakijije injangwe mirongo ine n'umunani.

KOREAN

나는 48마리의 고양이를 구출했습니다.

Naneun maheun-yeodeolb maliui goyang-ileul guhaessda.

KURDISH

Min çil û heşt pisîk rizgar kirin.

KYRGYZ

Мен кырк сегиз мышыкты куткардым.

Men kırk segiz mışıktı kutkardım.

LATVIAN

Esmu izglābis četrdesmit astoņus kaķus.

LITHUANIAN

Aš išgelbėjau keturiasdešimt aštuonias kates.

LUXEMBOURGISH

Ech hunn véierzeg aacht Kazen gerett.

MACEDONIAN

Спасив четириесет и осум мачки.

Spasiv četirieset i osum mački

.

MALAGASY

Nanavotra saka valo amby efapolo aho.

MALAY

Saya telah menyelamatkan empat puluh lapan kucing.

MALTESE

Jien salvajt tmienja u erbgħin qtates.

MAORI

Kua whakaorangia e ahau e wha tekau ma waru nga ngeru.

MARATHI

मी अठ्ठेचाळीस मांजरींची सुटका केली आहे.

Mī aṭhṭhēcāḷīsa mān̄jarīn̄cī suṭakā kēlī āhē.

MONGOLIAN

Би дөчин найман муурыг аварсан.

Bi döchin naiman muuryg avarsan.

NEPALI

मैले अट्ठालीस बिल्लियों लाई बचाएको छु।

Mailē aṭṭhālīsa billiyōṁ lā'ī bacā'ēkō chu.

NORWEGIAN

Jeg har reddet førtiåtte katter.

NYANJA

Ndapulumutsa amphaka makumi anayi mphambu zisanu ndi zitatu.

POLISH

Uratowałem czterdzieści osiem kotów.

PORTUGUESE

Eu resgatei quarenta e oito gatos.

PUNJABI

ਮੈਂ ਅੱਠ-ਅੱਠ ਬਿੱਲੀਆਂ ਨੂੰ ਬਚਾਇਆ ਹੈ.

Maiṁ aṭha-aṭha bilī'āṁ nū bacā'i'ā hai.

ROMANIAN

Am salvat patruzeci și opt de pisici.

RUSSIAN

Я спас сорок восемь кошек.

YA spas sorok vosem' koshek.

SAMOAN

Sa ou lavea'i pusi e fasefulu-valu.

SCOTS GAELIC

Tha mi air ceathrad 's a h-ochd cait a shàbhaladh.

SERBIAN

Спасио сам четрдесет осам мачака.

Spasio sam četrdeset osam mačaka.

SLOVAK

Zachránil som štyridsaťosem mačiek.

SLOVENIAN

Rešila sem oseminštirideset mačk.

SOMALI

Waxaan badbaadiyay siddeed iyo afartan bisadood.

SPANISH

He rescatado a cuarenta y ocho gatos.

SUNDANESE

Kuring parantos nyalametkeun opat puluh dalapan ucing.

SWAHILI

Nimeokoa paka arobaini na nane.

SWEDISH

Jag har räddat fyrtioåtta katter.

TAJIK

Ман чилу ҳашт гурба наҷот додам.

Man cilu haşt gurʙa naçot dodam.

TAMIL

நான் நாற்பத்தெட்டு பூனைகளை மீட்டுள்ளேன்.

Nāṉ nāṟpatteṭṭu pūṉaikaḷai mīṭṭuḷḷēṉ.

TELUGU

నేను నలభై ఎనిమిది పిల్లులను రక్షించాను.

Nēnu nalabhai enimidi pillulanu rakṣiñcānu.

THAI

ฉันช่วยชีวิตแมวสี่สิบแปดตัว

Chạn ch̀wy chīwit mæw s̄ī̀ s̄ib pæd tạw.

TURKISH

Kırk sekiz kediyi kurtardım.

TURKMEN

Men kyrk sekiz pişigi halas etdim.

UKRAINIAN

Я врятував сорок вісім котів.

Ya vryatuvav sorok visim kotiv.

UZBEK

Men qirq sakkizta mushukni qutqardim.

VIETNAMESE

Tôi đã giải cứu bốn mươi tám con mèo.

VIETNAMESE

Rydw i wedi achub pedwar deg wyth o gathod.

YIDDISH

איך'ווע רעסקיוד אַכט און פערציק.
קאַץ

Ikh've reskiud akht aun fertsik kats.

ZULU

Ngisindise amakati angamashumi amane nesishiyagalombili.

24 What's for dinner?

AFRIKAANS

Wat is vir aandete?

ALBANIAN

Cfare ka per darke?

AMHARIC

ለእራት ምንድነው?

Le'irati minidinewi?

ARABIC

ماذا للعشاء؟

Madha yujad lileasha'i?

ARMENIAN

Ի՞նչ է ընթրիքի համար։

Inch' e ynt'rik'i hamar.

AZERBAIJANI

Nahar üçün nə var?

BASQUE

Zer dago afaltzeko?

BELARUSIAN

Што на вячэру?

Što na viačeru?

BOSNIAN

Šta je za večeru?

BULGARIAN

Какво има за вечеря?

Kakvo ima za vecherya?

BURMESE

ညစာအတွက်ဘာစားမလဲ။

Nyahcar aatwat bhar hcarr malell.

CATALAN

Què hi ha per sopar?

CEBUANO

Unsa ang panihapon?

MANDARIN CHINESE

晚餐吃什麼？

Wǎncān chī shénme?

CORSICAN

Chì ci hè per cena?

CROATIAN

Što je za večeru?

CZECH

Co je k večeři?

DANISH

Hvad der er til middag?

DUTCH

Wat eten we?

ESPERANTO

Kio estas por vespermanĝo?

ESTONIAN

Mis õhtusöögiks on?

FILIPINO

Ano ang para sa hapunan?

FINNISH

Mitä on päivälliseksi?

FRENCH

Qu'y a-t-il pour le dîner?

GALICIAN

Que hai para cear?

GEORGIAN

რა არის სადილად?

ra aris sadilad?

GERMAN

Was gibt es zum Abendessen?

GREEK

Τι είναι για δείπνο?

Ti échei gia vradinó?

HAITIAN CREOLE

Sa ki nan pou dine?

HAUSA

Menene abincin dare?

HAWAIIAN

He aha ka mea no ka 'aina awakea?

HINDI

रात के खाने के लिए क्या है?

Raat ke khaane ke lie kya hai?

HMONG

Dab tsi rau noj hmo?

HUNGARIAN

Mi van vacsorára?

ICELANDIC

Hvað er í matinn?

IGBO

Kedu maka nri abalị?

INDONESIAN

Apa untuk makan malam?

IRISH

Cad atá ann don dinnéar?

ITALIAN

Cosa c'è per cena?

JAPANESE

夕食は何ですか？

Yūshoku wa nanidesu ka?

JAVANESE

Apa kanggo nedha bengi?

KANNADA

ಊಟಕ್ಕೆ ಏನು?

Ūṭakke ēnu?

KAZAKH

Кешкі асқа не?

Keşki asqa ne?

KINYARWANDA

Niki cyo kurya?

KOREAN

저녁은 뭐예요?

Jeonyeog sigsaneun mueos-ibnikka?

KURDISH

Ji bo xwarinê çi ye?

KYRGYZ

Кечки тамак эмне?

Keçki tamakka emne?

LATVIAN

Kas ir vakariņās?

LITHUANIAN

Kas vakarienei?

LUXEMBOURGISH

Wat as fir iessen?

MACEDONIAN

Што има за вечера?

Što ima za večera?

MALAGASY

Inona ny sakafo hariva?

MALAY

Apa untuk makan malam?

MALTESE

X'inhu għall-pranzu?

MAORI

He aha te kai tina?

MARATHI

डिनरसाठी काय आहे?

Ḍinarasāṭhī kāya āhē?

MONGOLIAN

Оройн хоолонд юу хэрэгтэй вэ?

Oroin khoolond yuu baina?

NEPALI

डिनर को लागी के हो?

Ḍinara kō lāgī kē hō?

NORWEGIAN

Hva er til middag?

NYANJA

Kodi chakudya chamadzulo ndi chiyani?

POLISH

Co jest na obiad?

PORTUGUESE

O que tem para o jantar?

PUNJABI

ਰਾਤ ਦੇ ਖਾਣੇ ਲਈ ਕੀ ਹੈ?

Rāta dē khāṇē la'ī kī hai?

ROMANIAN

Ce avem la cina?

RUSSIAN

Что на ужин?

Chto na obed?

SAMOAN

O le a le mea mo le ‘aiga o le afiafi?

SCOTS GAELIC

Dè a tha airson dinnear?

SERBIAN

Шта je за вечеру?

Šta je za večeru?

SLOVAK

Čo bude na večeru?

SLOVENIAN

Kaj je za večerjo?

SOMALI

Waa maxay casho?

SPANISH

¿Que hay para cenar?

SUNDANESE

Naon kanggo tuangeun?

SWAHILI

Ni nini kwa chakula cha jioni?

SWEDISH

Vad blir det till middag?

TAJIK

Барои хӯроки нисфирӯзӣ чӣ лозим аст?

Baroi xūroki nisfirūzī cī lozim ast?

TAMIL

இரவு உணவிற்கு என்ன இருக்கிறது?

Iravu uṇaviṟku eṉṉa irukkiṟatu?

TELUGU

విందు కోసం ఏమిటి?

Vindu kōsaṁ ēmiṭi?

THAI

มื้อเย็นกินอะไร?

Mụ̂x yĕn kin xarị?

TURKISH

Yemekte ne var?

TURKMEN

Agşamlyk näme?

UKRAINIAN

Що на вечерю?

Shcho na obid?

UZBEK

Kechki ovqat uchun nima?

VIETNAMESE

Ăn gì cho bữa tối?

VIETNAMESE

Beth sydd i ginio?

YIDDISH

וואָס ס פֿאַר מיטאָג?

Vos s far mitog?

ZULU

Yini ukudla kwakusihlwa?

25 One does not simply walk into Mordor.

AFRIKAANS

Mens loop nie sommer by Mordor in nie.

ALBANIAN

Dikush nuk hyn thjesht në Mordor.

AMHARIC

አንድ ሰው በቀላሉ ወደ ሞርዶር አይገባም።

Anidi sewi bek'elalu wede Moridori āyigebami.

ARABIC

لا يسير المرء ببساطة في موردور.

La yasir almar' bibasatat fi Murdur.

ARMENIAN

Մարդը պարզապես չի մտնում Մորդոր:

Mardy parzapes ch'i mtnum Mordor.

AZERBAIJANI

İnsan sadəcə Mordora getmir.

BASQUE

Ez da Mordorrera bakarrik ibiltzen.

BELARUSIAN

У Мардор нельга проста зайсці.

U Mardor nieĺha prosta zajsci.

BOSNIAN

Ne može se jednostavno ući u Mordor.

BULGARIAN

Човек не влиза просто в Мордор.

Chovek ne vliza prosto v Mordor.

BURMESE

တစ်ယောက်က Mordor ကို လမ်းလျှောက်တာမဟုတ်ဘူး။

Taityoutk Mordor ko lamshout tar mahotebhuu.

CATALAN

Un no només entra a Mordor.

CEBUANO

Ang usa dili yano nga maglakaw ngadto kang Moroor.

MANDARIN CHINESE

人們不會簡單地走進魔多。

Rénmen bù huì jiǎndān de zǒu jìn mó duō.

CORSICAN

Ùn si camina micca solu in Mordor.

CROATIAN

Ne može se jednostavno ući u Mordor.

CZECH

Člověk prostě nevejde do Mordoru.

DANISH

Man går ikke bare ind i Mordor.

DUTCH

Men loopt niet zomaar Mordor binnen.

ESPERANTO

Oni ne simple marŝas en Mordor.

ESTONIAN

Mordorisse lihtsalt ei kõnnita.

FILIPINO

Wlang taong simpleng makapunta sa Mordor.

FINNISH

Mordoriin ei yksinkertaisesti kävele.

FRENCH

On n'entre pas simplement dans le Mordor.

GALICIAN

Non se entra simplemente en Mordor.

GEORGIAN

ადამიანი უბრალოდ არ დადის მორდორში

Adamiani ubralod ar dadis Mordorshi.

GERMAN

Man betritt Mordor nicht einfach.

GREEK

Δεν μπαίνει κανείς στο Μόρντορ.

Den baínei kaneís sto Mórntor.

HAITIAN CREOLE

Youn pa tou senpleman mache nan Mordor.

HAUSA

Mutum baya shiga cikin Mordor kawai.

HAWAIIAN

ʻAʻole hele wale kekahi i loko o Moredor.

HINDI

कोई आसानी से मोरडोर में नहीं जाता है।

Koee aasaanee se Morador mein nahin jaata hai.

HMONG

Ib tus tsis yooj yim taug kev mus rau Mordor.

HUNGARIAN

Az ember nem egyszerűen besétál Mordorba.

ICELANDIC

Maður gengur ekki einfaldlega inn í Mordor.

IGBO

Otu anaghị abanye na Mordor.

INDONESIAN

Seseorang tidak begitu saja masuk ke Mordor.

IRISH

Ní shiúlann duine amháin isteach i Mordor.

ITALIAN

Non si entra semplicemente in Mordor.

JAPANESE

単にモルドールに足を踏み入れるだけではありません。

Tan'ni morudōru ni ashi o fumiireru dakede wa arimasen.

JAVANESE

Siji ora mung lumaku menyang Mordor.

KANNADA

ಒಬ್ಬರು ಕೇವಲ ಮೊರ್ಡೋರ್‌ಗೆ ಕಾಲಿಡುವುದಿಲ್ಲ.

Obbaru kēvala morḍōrge kāliḍuvudilla.

KAZAKH

Мордорға жай кіруге болмайды.

Mordorğa jay kirwge bolmaydı.

KINYARWANDA

Umuntu ntajya muri Mordor gusa.

KOREAN

단순히 모르도르에 들어가는 것이 아닙니다.

Dansunhi moleudoleue deul-eoganeun geos-i anibnida.

KURDISH

Meriv bi hêsanî naçe Mordor.

KYRGYZ

Бирөө жөн эле Мордорго кирбейт.

Biröö jön ele Mordorgo kirbeyt.

LATVIAN

Cilvēks neiet vienkārši Mordorā.

LITHUANIAN

Į Mordorą tiesiog neina.

LUXEMBOURGISH

Et geet net einfach an de Mordor.

MACEDONIAN

Не се оди едноставно во Мордор.

Ne se odi ednostavno vo Mordor.

MALAGASY

Ny olona iray dia tsy miditra ao amin'i Mordor fotsiny.

MALAY

Orang tidak hanya berjalan ke Mordor.

MALTESE

Wieħed ma jimxix sempliċement f'Mordor.

MAORI

Kaore tetahi e haere noa ki roto ki a Moror.

MARATHI

एक फक्त Mordor मध्ये चालत नाही.

Ēka phakta Mordor madhyē cālata nāhī.

MONGOLIAN

Хүн зүгээр л Мордор руу ордоггүй.

Khün zügeer l Mordor ruu ordoggüi.

NEPALI

एक मात्र Mordor मा हिंड्दैन।

Ēka mātra Mordor mā hiṇḍdaina.

NORWEGIAN

Man går bare ikke inn i Mordor.

NYANJA

Mmodzi samangolowa mu Mordor.

POLISH

Nie można po prostu wejść do Mordoru.

PORTUGUESE

Não se entra simplesmente em Mordor.

PUNJABI

ਕੋਈ ਸਿਰਫ ਮਾਰਡੋਰ ਵਿੱਚ ਨਹੀਂ ਜਾਂਦਾ.

Kō'ī sirapha Māraḍōra vica nahīṁ jāndā.

ROMANIAN

Nu mergi pur și simplu în Mordor.

RUSSIAN

В Мордор просто не попасть.

V Mordor prosto ne popast'.

SAMOAN

Tasi e le na o le savali i totonu o Moror.

SCOTS GAELIC

Chan eil aon a 'coiseachd a-steach do Mordor.

SERBIAN

Неко не може тек тако да ушета у Мордор.

Neko ne može tek tako da ušeta u Mordor.

SLOVAK

Do Mordoru sa jednoducho nevkročí.

SLOVENIAN

V Mordor se ne gre preprosto.

SOMALI

Midna si fudud uguma socdo Mordor.

SPANISH

Uno no simplemente camina hacia Mordor.

SUNDANESE

Salah henteu ngan saukur asup kana Mordor.

SWAHILI

Mtu haendi tu kwenda kwa Mordor.

SWEDISH

Man går inte bara in i Mordor.

TAJIK

Кас на танҳо ба Мордор медарояд.

Kas na tanho ва Mordor medarojad.

TAMIL

ஒருவர் வெறுமனே மொர்டோருக்குள் நுழைவதில்லை.

Oruvar ve̲rumaṉē morṭōrukkuḷ nu̲laivatillai.

TELUGU

ఒకరు కేవలం మోర్డోర్‌లోకి నడవరు.

Okaru kēvalaṁ Mōrḍōrlōki naḍavaru.

THAI

ไม่เพียงแค่เดินเข้าไปในมอร์ดอร์

Mị pheīyng khæ̀ dein k̄hêāpị nı Mxr̒dxr̒.

TURKISH

Kişi sadece Mordor'a girmez.

TURKMEN

Biri diňe Mordora girenok.

UKRAINIAN

До Мордору не просто зайти.

Do Mordoru ne prosto zayty.

UZBEK

Odam oddiygina Mordorga kirmaydi.

VIETNAMESE

Một người không chỉ đơn giản là đi bộ vào Mordor.

VIETNAMESE

Nid yw un yn syml yn cerdded i mewn i Mordor.

YIDDISH

מען גייט נישט פשוט אריין אין מרדור.

Men geyt nisht fshut areyn in Mrdur.

ZULU

Umuntu akavele angene ku Mordor.

26 Is that peg leg a rental?

AFRIKAANS

Is dit ‘n huurprothese?

ALBANIAN

A është kjo protezë me qira?

AMHARIC

ያ ሰው ሠራሽ ኪራይ ነው?

Ya sewi šerashi kīrayi newi?

ARABIC

هل هذه الأطراف الصناعية تأجير؟

Hal hadhih al'atraf alsinaeiat tajiru?

ARMENIAN

Այդ պրոթեզը վարձու՞մ է:

Ayd prot'ezy vardzu m e?

AZERBAIJANI

Bu protez kirayə verilirmi?

BASQUE

Protesi hori alokairua al da?

BELARUSIAN

Гэта пракат пратэза?

Heta prakat prateza?

BOSNIAN

Je li ta protetika iznajmljivanje?

BULGARIAN

Наемането на тази протеза ли е?

Naemaneto na tazi proteza li e?

BURMESE

၎င်းသည်ခြေတုလက်တုအငှားလား။

Innsai hkyay tu laat tu aanghar larr.

CATALAN

És una pròtesi un lloguer?

CEBUANO

Kana bang pagpamaligya usa ka abang?

MANDARIN CHINESE

那個假肢是出租的嗎？

Nàgè jiǎzhī shì chūzū de ma?

CORSICAN

Hè una prutesi in affitto?

CROATIAN

Je li ta protetika iznajmljivanje?

CZECH

Je to protetika půjčovna?

DANISH

Er det en udlejningsprotese?

DUTCH

Is die prothese te huur?

ESPERANTO

Ĉu tio protezas luon?

ESTONIAN

Kas see on proteesimine?

FILIPINO

Rentahan ba ang prosthetic na iyon?

FINNISH

Onko se proteesi vuokraus?

FRENCH

Est-ce que cette prothèse est une location?

GALICIAN

¿É unha prótese un aluguer?

GEORGIAN

ეს პროთეზი გაქირავებაა?

Es p'rotezi gakiravebaa?

GERMAN

Ist das eine leihprothese?

GREEK

Είναι αυτό προσθετικό για ενοικίαση?

Eínai aftó prosthetikó gia enoikíasi?

HAITIAN CREOLE

Èske sa pwotèz yon lokasyon?

HAUSA

Shin wannan sana'ar ta roba haya ce?

HAWAIIAN

He hoʻolimalima kēlā prosthetic?

HINDI

क्या वह प्रोस्थेटिक किराये पर है?

Kya vah prosthetik kiraaye par hai?

HMONG

Puas yog qhov khoom cua dag?

HUNGARIAN

Ez a protézis kölcsönzés?

ICELANDIC

Er það stoðtækaleiga?

IGBO

Nke ahụ prosthetic bụ mgbazinye?

INDONESIAN

Apakah itu prostetik sewaan?

IRISH

An cíos é an próistéitic sin?

ITALIAN

Quella protesi è a noleggio?

JAPANESE

その補綴物はレンタルですか？

Sono hoteibutsu wa rentarudesu ka?

JAVANESE

Apa prostitusi dadi sewa?

KANNADA

ಅದು ಪ್ರಾಸ್ಥೆಟಿಕ್ ಬಾಡಿಗೆಯೇ?

Adu prāstheṭik bāḍigeyē?

KAZAKH

Бұл протез жалдау ма?

Bul protez jaldaw ma?

KINYARWANDA

Iyo prostothique niyo ikodeshwa?

KOREAN

의수 대여인가요?

Uisu daeyeoingayo?

KURDISH

Ma ew protez kirê ye?

KYRGYZ

Бул протез ижарага берилгенби?

Bul protez ijaraga berilgenbi?

LATVIAN

Vai tā ir protēžu noma?

LITHUANIAN

Ar tai protezų nuoma?

LUXEMBOURGISH

As dat eng prothetesch locatioun?

MACEDONIAN

Дали е тоа протези за изнајмување?

Dali e toa protezi za iznajmuvanje?

MALAGASY

Fanofana ve izany?

MALAY

Adakah itu palsu?

MALTESE

Dik il-prostetika hija kiri?

MAORI

He riihi taua riiki?

MARATHI

ते कृत्रिम भाडे आहे का?

Tē kr̥trima bhāḍē āhē kā?

MONGOLIAN

Энэ хиймэл эрхтэн түрээслэх үү?

Ene khiimel erkhten türeeslekh üü?

NEPALI

के त्यो कृत्रिम भाडा हो?

Kē tyō kr̥trima bhāḍā hō?

NORWEGIAN

Er det en utleie av proteser?

NYANJA

Kodi kubwereketsa kuja ndi kubwereka?

POLISH

Czy ta proteza jest wypożyczona?

PORTUGUESE

Essa prótese é alugada?

PUNJABI

ਕੀ ਉਹ ਨਕਲੀ ਕਿਰਾਏ ਤੇ ਹੈ?

Kī uha nakalī kirā'ē tē hai?

ROMANIAN

Proteza este o închiriere?

RUSSIAN

Это протез аренда?

Eto protez arenda?

SAMOAN

O le pepelo lena o se lisi?

SCOTS GAELIC

A bheil am prosthetic sin na mhàl?

SERBIAN

Да ли се та протетика изнајмљује?

Da li se ta protetika iznajmljuje?

SLOVAK

Je to protetika požičovňa?

SLOVENIAN

Je ta protetika najem?

SOMALI

Ma jir -dhiskaasi ma kiro baa?

SPANISH

¿Esa prótesis es un alquiler?

SUNDANESE

Naha éta téh palsu?

SWAHILI

Je! Hiyo ni bandia ya kukodisha?

SWEDISH

Är det en protes att hyra?

TAJIK

Оё ин протез иҷора аст?

Ojo in protez içora ast?

TAMIL

அது செயற்கை வாடகையா?

Atu ceyaṟkai vāṭakaiyā?

TELUGU

ఆ ప్రొస్థెటిక్ అద్దెనా?

Ā prostheṭik addenā?

THAI

นั่นขาเทียมให้เช่าหรือเปล่า?

Nạn k̄hā theīym h̄ı̂ chèā h̄rụ̄x pel̀ā?

TURKISH

O protez kiralık mı?

TURKMEN

Bu protez kireýine berilýärmi?

UKRAINIAN

Це прокат протеза?

Tse prokat proteza?

UZBEK

Bu protez ijaraga olinadimi?

VIETNAMESE

Chân giả đó có phải là đồ cho thuê không?

VIETNAMESE

A yw'r prosthetig hwnnw'n rent?

YIDDISH

?איז דאָס אַ פּראָקאַט פּראָקאַט

Iz dos a prokat prokat?

ZULU

Ingabe lokho kwenziwa ngomzimba?

27 Simon says, “Pick your nose.”

AFRIKAANS

Simon sê: “Kies jou neus.”

ALBANIAN

Simon thotë: “Zgjidhe hundën”.

AMHARIC

ስምዖን - አፍንጫህን ምረጥ አለው።

Simi‘oni - āfinich’ahini miret’i ālewi.

ARABIC

قال سمعان: اختر أنفك.

Simun yaqul , “Akhtir ‘anfika.”

ARMENIAN

Սիմոնը ասում է. «Քիթդ վերցրու»:

Simony asum e. «K’it’d verts’ru».

AZERBAIJANI

Simon deyir: “Burnunu yığ”.

BASQUE

Simonek dio: “Aukeratu sudurra”.

BELARUSIAN

Сымон кажа: “Выберы нос”.

Symon kaža: “Vybiery nos”.

BOSNIAN

Simon kaže: “Izaberi nos.”

BULGARIAN

Саймън казва: „Избери си носа“.

Saĭmŭn kazva: „Izberi si nosa“.

BURMESE

Simon က “မင်းနှာခေါင်းကိုရွေး”

Simon k “ mainn nharhkaungg korway”.

CATALAN

Simon diu: “Tria el nas”.

CEBUANO

Miingon si Simon, “Pilia ang imong ilong.”

MANDARIN CHINESE

西蒙說：“挖你的鼻子。”

Xīméng shuō: “Wā nǐ de bízi.”

CORSICAN

Simon dice: “Sceglite u nasu”.

CROATIAN

Simon kaže: “Izaberi nos.”

CZECH

Simon říká: „Vezmi si nos.“

DANISH

Simon siger: “Vælg din næse.”

DUTCH

Simon zegt: “Knijp in je neus.”

ESPERANTO

Simon diras, “Elektu vian nazon.”

ESTONIAN

Simon ütleb: “Vali nina.”

FILIPINO

Sinabi ni Simon, “Piliin mo ang iyong ilong.”

FINNISH

Simon sanoo: “Nenäsi.”

FRENCH

Simon dit : “Cure-toi le nez.”

GALICIAN

Simon di: “Escolle o nariz”.

GEORGIAN

სიმონ ამბობს: “აიღე ცხვირი”.

Simon ambobs: “Aighe tskhviri”.

GERMAN

Simon sagt: “Nimm deine Nase.”

GREEK

Ο Σάιμον λέει: «Διάλεξε τη μύτη σου»

O Sáimon léei: «Diálexe ti mýti sou».

HAITIAN CREOLE

Simon di, “Chwazi nen ou.”

HAUSA

Simon ya ce, “Dauki hanci.”

HAWAIIAN

ʻLelo ʻo Simona, “E koho i kou ihu.”

HINDI

साइमन कहते हैं, "अपनी नाक उठाओ।"

Saiman kahate hain, "Apanee naak uthao."

HMONG

Simon hais tias, "Xaiv koj lub qhov ntswg."

HUNGARIAN

Simon azt mondja: "Vedd az orrodat!"

ICELANDIC

Simon segir: "Taktu nefið."

IGBO

Saịmọn na -ekwu, "Bulie imi gị."

INDONESIAN

Simon berkata, "Angkat hidungmu."

IRISH

Deir Simon, "Roghnaigh do shrón."

ITALIAN

Simon dice: "Scegli il naso".

JAPANESE

サイモンは「鼻をつまんで」と言います。

Saimon wa `hana o tsumande' to iimasu.

JAVANESE

Simon kandha, "Pilih irunge."

KANNADA

ಸೈಮನ್ ಹೇಳುತ್ತಾರೆ, "ನಿಮ್ಮ ಮೂಗು ಆರಿಸಿ."

Saiman hēḷuttāre, "Nim'ma mūgu ārisi."

KAZAKH

Саймон: «Мұрныңды ал» дейді.

Saymon: «Murnıñdı al» deydi.

KINYARWANDA

Simoni ati: "Tora izuru."

KOREAN

사이먼은 "코를 잡아라."라고 말합니다.

Saimeon-eun "koleul jab-ala." lago malhabnida.

KURDISH

Simonimûn dibêje, "Pozê xwe hilde."

KYRGYZ

Саймон: “Мурдуңду ал” дейт.

Saymon: “Murduŋdu al” deyt.

LATVIAN

Saimons saka: “Paņem degunu.”

LITHUANIAN

Simonas sako: „Nusikiš nosį“.

LUXEMBOURGISH

De Simon seet: “Wielt ar nues.”

MACEDONIAN

Симон вели: „Избери го носот“.

Simon veli: „Izberi go nosot“.

MALAGASY

Hoy i Simon: “Raiso ny oronao.”

MALAY

Simon berkata, “Pilihlah hidungmu.”

MALTESE

Simon jgħid, “Agħżel imnieħrek.”

MAORI

Ka kii a Haimona, “Tangohia to ihu.”

MARATHI

सायमन म्हणतो, “आपले नाक निवडा.”

Sāyamana mhaṇatō, “Apalē nāka nivaḍā.”

MONGOLIAN

Саймон “Хамараа сонгоорой” гэж хэлдэг.

Saimon “Khamaraa songooroi” gej kheldeg.

NEPALI

साइमन भन्छन्, “तपाइँको नाक छान्नुहोस्।”

Sā'imana bhanchan, “Tapā'im̐kō nāka chānnuhōs.”

NORWEGIAN

Simon sier: “Velg nesen din.”

NYANJA

Simon akuti, “Sankhani mphuno yako.”

POLISH

Simon mówi: „Dłubaj w nosie”.

PORTUGUESE

Simon diz: "Escolha seu nariz."

PUNJABI

ਸਾਈਮਨ ਕਹਿੰਦਾ ਹੈ, "ਆਪਣਾ ਨੱਕ ਚੁੱਕੋ."

Sā'īmana kahidā hai, "Apaṇā naka cukō."

ROMANIAN

Simon spune: „Alege-ți nasul".

RUSSIAN

Саймон говорит: «Ковыряйте в носу».

Saymon govorit: «Kovyryayte v nosu».

SAMOAN

Fai mai Simona, "Piki lou isu."

SCOTS GAELIC

Tha Sìm ag ràdh, "Tagh do shròn."

SERBIAN

Симон каже: "Изабери нос."

Simon kaže: "Izaberi nos."

SLOVAK

Simon hovorí: „Vyberte si nos."

SLOVENIAN

Simon pravi: "Poberi si nos."

SOMALI

Simon wuxuu leeyahay, sankaaga qaado.

SPANISH

Simón dice: "Métete la nariz".

SUNDANESE

Simon nyarios, "Candak irung anjeun."

SWAHILI

Simon anasema, "Chagua pua yako."

SWEDISH

Simon säger, "Välj din näsa."

TAJIK

Шимъӯн мегӯяд: "Бинии худро чин".

Şim'ūn megūjad: "Binii xudro cin".

TAMIL

சைமன் கூறுகிறார், "உங்கள் மூக்கை எடு."

Caiman̲ kūr̲ukir̲ār, "Uṅkaḷ mūkkai eṭu."

TELUGU

సైమన్, "మీ ముక్కును ఎంచుకోండి" అని చెప్పాడు.

Saiman, "mī mukkunu eñcukōṇḍi" ani ceppāḍu.

THAI

ไซม่อนพูดว่า "เลือกจมูกของคุณ"

Sị m̀xn phūd ẁā"leụ̄xk cmūk k̄hxng khuṇ"

TURKISH

Simon, "Burnunu seç" diyor.

TURKMEN

Simon: "Burnuňy al" diýýär.

UKRAINIAN

Саймон каже: "Вибери ніс".

Saymon kazhe: "Vybery nis".

UZBEK

Simon: "Burningni yig'", deydi.

VIETNAMESE

Simon nói, "Hãy ngoáy mũi."

VIETNAMESE

Dywed Simon, "Dewiswch eich trwyn."

YIDDISH

שמעון זאגט, "פּיק דיין נאָז."

Shmeun zagt, "Pik deyn noz."

ZULU

U Simon uthi, "Khetha ikhala lakho."

28 It was an accident!

AFRIKAANS

Dit was 'n ongeluk!

ALBANIAN

Ishte një aksident!

AMHARIC

አደጋ ነበር!

Adega neberi!

ARABIC

لقد كانت حادثة!

Laqad kanat hadithatan!

ARMENIAN

Դա դժբախտ պատահար էր:

Da dzhbakht patahar er!

AZERBAIJANI

Bu qəza idi!

BASQUE

Istripua izan zen!

BELARUSIAN

Гэта быў няшчасны выпадак!

Heta byŭ niaščasny vypadak!

BOSNIAN

To je bila nesreća!

BULGARIAN

Беше инцидент!

Stana sluchaĭno!

BURMESE

ဒါဟာမတော်တဆမှုတစ်ခုပဲ။

Darhar matawtasamhu hpyithkaesai!

CATALAN

Va ser un accident!

CEBUANO

Kini usa ka aksidente!

MANDARIN CHINESE

這是一場意外！

Zhè shì yīchǎng yìwài!

CORSICAN

Hè statu un accidente!

CROATIAN

To je bila nesreća!

CZECH

Byla to nehoda!

DANISH

Det var et uheld!

DUTCH

Het was een ongeluk!

ESPERANTO

Estis akcidento!

ESTONIAN

See oli õnnetus!

FILIPINO

Ito ay isang aksidente!

FINNISH

Se oli vahinko!

FRENCH

C'était un accident!

GALICIAN

Foi un accidente!

GEORGIAN

ეს უბედური შემთხვევა იყო!

Es ubeduri shemtkhveva iq'o!

GERMAN

Es war ein unfall!

GREEK

Ήταν ατύχημα!

Ítan atýchima!

HAITIAN CREOLE

Se te yon aksidan!

HAUSA

Hadari ne!

HAWAIIAN

He ulia ia!

HINDI

वह एक हादसा था!

Vah ek haadasa tha!

HMONG

Nws yog qhov xwm txheej!

HUNGARIAN

Baleset volt!

ICELANDIC

Þetta var slys!

IGBO

Ọ bụ ihe mberede!

INDONESIAN

Itu adalah sebuah kecelakaan!

IRISH

Timpiste a bhí ann!

ITALIAN

È stato un incidente!

JAPANESE

事故でした！

Jikodeshita!

JAVANESE

Iku kacilakan!

KANNADA

ಇದು ಅಪಘಾತ!

Idu apaghāta!

KAZAKH

Бұл апат болды!

Bul apat boldı!

KINYARWANDA

Byari impanuka!

KOREAN

사고였어!

Sagoyeoss-eo!

KURDISH

Ew qeza bû!

KYRGYZ

Бул кырсык болду!

Bul kırsık boldu!

LATVIAN

Tas bija nelaimes gadījums!

LITHUANIAN

Tai buvo nelaimingas atsitikimas!

LUXEMBOURGISH

Et war en accident!

MACEDONIAN

Тоа беше несреќа!

Toa beše nesreḱa!

MALAGASY

Loza izany!

MALAY

Ia adalah kemalangan!

MALTESE

Kien inċident!

MAORI

He aitua noa iho!

MARATHI

तो एक अपघात होता!

Tō ēka apaghāta hōtā!

MONGOLIAN

Энэ бол осол байсан!

Ene bol osol baisan!

NEPALI

यो एक दुर्घटना थियो!

Yō ēka durghaṭanā thiyō!

NORWEGIAN

Det var en ulykke!

NYANJA

Zinali ngozi!

POLISH

To był wypadek!

PORTUGUESE

Foi um acidente!

PUNJABI

ਇਹ ਇੱਕ ਦੁਰਘਟਨਾ ਸੀ!

Iha ika duraghaṭanā sī!

ROMANIAN

A fost un accident!

RUSSIAN

Это был несчастный случай!

Eto byl neschastnyy sluchay!

SAMOAN

O se mea na tupu faafuase'i!

SCOTS GAELIC

B 'e tubaist a bh' ann!

SERBIAN

То је била несрећа!

To je bila nesreća!

SLOVAK

Bola to nehoda!

SLOVENIAN

To je bila nesreča!

SOMALI

Waxay ahayd shil!

SPANISH

¡Fue un accidente!

SUNDANESE

Éta kacilakaan!

SWAHILI

Ilikuwa ajali!

SWEDISH

Det var en olycka!

TAJIK

Ин садама буд!

In sadama вud!

TAMIL

அது ஒரு விபத்து!

Atu oru vipattu!

TELUGU

ఇది ఒక ప్రమాదం!

Idi oka pramādaṁ!

THAI

มันเป็นอุบัติเหตุ!

Mạn pĕn xubạtihetu!

TURKISH

Bu bir kazaydı!

TURKMEN

Bu tötänlikdi!

UKRAINIAN

Це був нещасний випадок!

Tse buv neshchasnyy vypadok!

UZBEK

Bu tasodif edi!

VIETNAMESE

Nó là một tai nạn!

VIETNAMESE

Damwain oedd hi!

YIDDISH

!עס איז געווען אַ צופֿאַל

Es iz geven a tsufal!

ZULU

Kwakuyingozi!

29 We need a bigger boat.

AFRIKAANS

Ons het 'n groter boot nodig.

ALBANIAN

Kemi nevojë për një varkë më të madhe.

AMHARIC

ትልቅ ጀልባ እንፈልጋለን።

Tilik'i jeliba inifeligaleni.

ARABIC

نحن بحاجة إلى قارب أكبر.

Nahn bihajat 'iilaa qarib 'akbar.

ARMENIAN

Մեզ ավելի մեծ նավակ է պետք:

Mez aveli mets navak e petk'.

AZERBAIJANI

Daha böyük bir gəmiyə ehtiyacımız var.

BASQUE

Itsasontzi handiagoa behar dugu.

BELARUSIAN

Нам патрэбна большая лодка.

Nam patrebna boĺšaja lodka.

BOSNIAN

Treba nam veći brod.

BULGARIAN

Нуждаем се от по -голяма лодка.

Nuzhdaem se ot po -golyama lodka.

BURMESE

ငါတို့ပိုကြီးတဲ့လှေလိုတယ်။

Ngarthoet k pokyee tae lhaay lotaal.

CATALAN

Necessitem un vaixell més gran.

CEBUANO

Kinahanglan naton ang labi ka daghang bangka.

MANDARIN CHINESE

我們需要一艘更大的船。

Wǒmen xūyào yī sōu gèng dà de chuán.

CORSICAN

Avemu bisognu di una barca più grande.

CROATIAN

Treba nam veći brod.

CZECH

Potřebujeme větší loď.

DANISH

Vi har brug for en større båd.

DUTCH

We hebben een grotere boot nodig.

ESPERANTO

Ni bezonas pli grandan boaton.

ESTONIAN

Vajame suuremat paati.

FILIPINO

Kailangan natin ng mas malaking bangka.

FINNISH

Tarvitsemme isomman veneen.

FRENCH

Nous avons besoin d'un plus gros bateau.

GALICIAN

Necesitamos un barco máis grande.

GEORGIAN

ჩვენ გვჭირდება უფრო დიდი ნავი.

Chven gvch'irdeba upro didi navi.

GERMAN

Wir brauchen ein größeres boot.

GREEK

Χρειαζόμαστε ένα μεγαλύτερο σκάφος.

Chreiazómaste éna megalýtero skáfos.

HAITIAN CREOLE

Nou bezwen yon pi gwo bato.

HAUSA

Muna buƙatar babban jirgin ruwa.

HAWAIIAN

Pono mākou i kahi moku nui aʻe.

HINDI

हमें एक बड़ी नाव चाहिए।

Hamen ek badee naav chaahie.

HMONG

Peb xav tau lub nkoj loj dua.

HUNGARIAN

Nagyobb hajóra van szükségünk.

ICELANDIC

Við þurfum stærri bát.

IGBO

Anyị chọrọ nnukwu ụgbọ mmiri.

INDONESIAN

Kami membutuhkan kapal yang lebih besar.

IRISH

Tá bád níos mó ag teastáil uainn.

ITALIAN

Ci serve una barca più grande.

JAPANESE

もっと大きなボートが必要です。

Motto ōkina bōto ga hitsuyōdesu.

JAVANESE

Kita butuh kapal sing luwih gedhe.

KANNADA

ನಮಗೆ ದೊಡ್ಡ ದೋಣಿ ಬೇಕು.

Namage doḍḍa dōṇi bēku.

KAZAKH

Бізге үлкенірек қайық қажет.

Bizge ülkenirek qayıq qajet.

KINYARWANDA

Dukeneye ubwato bunini.

KOREAN

더 큰 배가 필요합니다.

deo keun baega pil-yohabnida.

KURDISH

Pêdiviya me bi keştiyek mezintir heye.

KYRGYZ

Бизге чоңураак кеме керек.

Bizge çoŋuraak keme kerek.

LATVIAN

Mums vajag lielāku laivu.

LITHUANIAN

Mums reikia didesnės valties.

LUXEMBOURGISH

Mir brauchen e gréissert boot.

MACEDONIAN

Ни треба поголем брод.

Ni treba pogolem brod.

MALAGASY

Mila sambo lehibe kokoa isika.

MALAY

Kita memerlukan kapal yang lebih besar.

MALTESE

Għandna bżonn dgħajsa akbar.

MAORI

Me nui ake te poti.

MARATHI

आम्हाला मोठ्या बोटीची गरज आहे.

Āmhālā mōṭhyā bōṭīcī garaja āhē.

MONGOLIAN

Бидэнд илүү том завь хэрэгтэй.

Bidend ilüü tom zavi kheregtei.

NEPALI

हामीलाई एउटा ठूलो डु डुगा चाहिन्छ।

Hāmīlā'ī ē'uṭā ṭhūlō ḍu dugā cāhincha.

NORWEGIAN

Vi trenger en større båt.

NYANJA

Tikufuna bwato lokulirapo.

POLISH

Potrzebujemy większej łodzi.

PORTUGUESE

Precisamos de um barco maior.

PUNJABI

ਸਾਨੂੰ ਇੱਕ ਵੱਡੀ ਕਿਸ਼ਤੀ ਦੀ ਲੋੜ ਹੈ.

Sānū ika vaḍī kiśatī dī lōṛa hai.

ROMANIAN

Avem nevoie de o barcă mai mare.

RUSSIAN

Нам нужна лодка побольше.

Nam nuzhna lodka pobol'she.

SAMOAN

Matou te mana'omia se va'a e sili atu.

SCOTS GAELIC

Feumaidh sinn bàta nas motha.

SERBIAN

Треба нам већи чамац.

Treba nam veći čamac.

SLOVAK

Potrebujeme väčšiu loď.

SLOVENIAN

Potrebujemo večji čoln.

SOMALI

Waxaan u baahannahay doon ka weyn.

SPANISH

Necesitamos un barco más grande.

SUNDANESE

Urang peryogi kapal anu langkung ageung.

SWAHILI

Tunahitaji mashua kubwa.

SWEDISH

Vi behöver en större båt.

TAJIK

Ба мо киштии калонтар лозим аст.

Ba mo kiştii kalontar lozim ast.

TAMIL

எங்களுக்கு ஒரு பெரிய படகு தேவை.

Eṅkaḷukku oru periya paṭaku tēvai.

TELUGU

మాకు పెద్ద పడవ కావాలి.

Māku pedda paḍava kāvāli.

THAI

เราต้องการเรือที่ใหญ่กว่า

Reā t̂xngkār reụ̄x thī̀ h̄ıỵ̀ kẁā.

TURKISH

Daha büyük bir tekneye ihtiyacımız var.

TURKMEN

Bize has uly gaýyk gerek.

UKRAINIAN

Нам потрібен більший човен.

Nam potriben bil'shyy choven.

UZBEK

Bizga kattaroq qayiq kerak.

VIETNAMESE

Chúng ta cần một chiếc thuyền lớn hơn.

VIETNAMESE

Mae angen cwch mwy arnom.

YIDDISH

מיר דאַרפֿן אַ גרעסערע שיפֿל.

Mir darfn a gresere shifl.

ZULU

Sidinga isikebhe esikhudlwana.

30 Stop!

AFRIKAANS

Stop!

ALBANIAN

Ndaloni!

AMHARIC

አቁም!

Ak'umi!

ARABIC

!توقف

Quf!

ARMENIAN

ԿԱՆԳՆԵ՛Ք:

Kangnets'row!

AZERBAIJANI

Dur!

BASQUE

Gelditu!

BELARUSIAN

Спыніся!

Spynisia!

BOSNIAN

Zaustavi!

BULGARIAN

Спри!

Sprise!

BURMESE

ရပ်!

Raut!

CATALAN

Atura!

CEBUANO

Hunong na!

MANDARIN CHINESE

停止！

Tíngzhǐ!

CORSICAN

Piantà!

CROATIAN

Prestani!

CZECH

Přestaň!

DANISH

Hold op!

DUTCH

Hou op!

ESPERANTO

Haltu!

ESTONIAN

Lõpeta!

FILIPINO

Tigilan mo na!

FINNISH

Lopettaa!

FRENCH

Arrêter!

GALICIAN

Pare!

GEORGIAN

გაჩერდი!

Gacherdi!

GERMAN

Halt!

GREEK

Να σταματήσει!

Na stamatísei!

HAITIAN CREOLE

Sispann!

HAUSA

Tsaya!

HAWAIIAN

Kū!

HINDI

विराम!

Viraam!

HMONG

Nres!

HUNGARIAN

Álljon meg!

ICELANDIC

Hættu!

IGBO

Kwụsị!

INDONESIAN

Berhenti!

IRISH

Stad!

ITALIAN

Fermare!

JAPANESE

やめる！

Yameru!

JAVANESE

Mandheg!

KANNADA

ನಿಲ್ಲಿಸು!

Nillisu!

KAZAKH

Тоқта!

Toqta!

KINYARWANDA

Hagarara!

KOREAN

중지!

Jungji!

KURDISH

Rawestan!

KYRGYZ

Токто!

Tokto!

LATVIAN

Beidz!

LITHUANIAN

Sustabdyti!

LUXEMBOURGISH

Stoppen!

MACEDONIAN

Застани!

Zastani!

MALAGASY

Mijanòna!

MALAY

Berhenti!

MALTESE

Waqfa!

MAORI

Kati!

MARATHI

थांबा!

Thāmbā!

MONGOLIAN

Зогс!

Zogs!

NEPALI

रोक!

Rōka!

NORWEGIAN

Stoppe!

NYANJA

Imani!

POLISH

Zatrzymać!

PORTUGUESE

Pare!

PUNJABI

ਰੁਕੋ!

Rūkō!

ROMANIAN

Încetează!

RUSSIAN

Прекрати!

Prekrati!

SAMOAN

Taofi!

SCOTS GAELIC

Stad!

SERBIAN

Зауставити!

Zaustaviti!

SLOVAK

Prestaň!

SLOVENIAN

Prenehaj!

SOMALI

Jooji!

SPANISH

¡Parada!

SUNDANESE

Eureun!

SWAHILI

Acha!

SWEDISH

Sluta!

TAJIK

Ист!

Ist!

TAMIL

நிறுத்து!

Niṟuttu!

TELUGU

ఆపు!

Āpu!

THAI

หยุด!

Hyud!

TURKISH

Durmak!

TURKMEN

Dur!

UKRAINIAN

стій!

Stiy!

UZBEK

To'xtating!

VIETNAMESE

Ngừng lại!

VIETNAMESE

Stopiwch!

YIDDISH

!אָפּשטעל

Opshtel!

ZULU

Ima!

31 The plunger broke.

AFRIKAANS

Die suier het gebreek.

ALBANIAN

Kumarxhiu u prish.

AMHARIC

አጥቂው ተሰበረ።

At'ik'īwi tesebere.

ARABIC

انكسر المكبس.

Ainkasar almikbasi.

ARMENIAN

Մխոցը կոտրվեց:

Mkhots'y kotrvets'.

AZERBAIJANI

Piston qırıldı.

BASQUE

Enborra hautsi zen.

BELARUSIAN

Поршань зламаўся.

Plunžer zlamaŭsia.

BOSNIAN

Klip se slomio.

BULGARIAN

Буталото се счупи.

Butaloto se schupi.

BURMESE

သံမဏိစက်ပျက်သွားသည်။

Sanmani hcaat pyetswarr sai.

CATALAN

L'èmbol es va trencar.

CEBUANO

Ang plunger nabali.

MANDARIN CHINESE

柱塞斷了。

Zhù sāi duànle.

CORSICAN

U stantu hè rottu.

CROATIAN

Klip se slomio.

CZECH

Píst se zlomil.

DANISH

Stemplet gik i stykker.

DUTCH

De zuiger brak.

ESPERANTO

La plonĝanto rompiĝis.

ESTONIAN

Kolb purunes.

FILIPINO

Nasira ang plunger.

FINNISH

Mäntä rikkoutui.

FRENCH

Le piston s'est cassé.

GALICIAN

O émbolo rompeu.

GEORGIAN

დგუში გატეხილია

Dgushi gat'ekhilia.

GERMAN

Der kolben brach.

GREEK

Το έμβολο έσπασε.

To émvolo éspase.

HAITIAN CREOLE

Plonje a kase.

HAUSA

Mai tsotsa ya karye.

HAWAIIAN

Haki ka mea palu.

HINDI

प्लंजर टूट गया।

Planjar toot gaya.

HMONG

Lub plunger tawg.

HUNGARIAN

A dugattyú eltört.

ICELANDIC

Stimpillinn brotnaði.

IGBO

Onye na -akwa akwa mebiri.

INDONESIAN

Plungernya pecah.

IRISH

Bhris an plunger.

ITALIAN

Lo stantuffo si è rotto.

JAPANESE

プランジャーが壊れた。

Puranjā ga kowareta.

JAVANESE

Plunger pecah.

KANNADA

ಪ್ಲಂಗರ್ ಮುರಿಯಿತು.

Plaṅgar muriyitu.

KAZAKH

Поршень сынды.

Porşen sındı.

KINYARWANDA

Umupanga yaravunitse.

KOREAN

플런저가 부러졌습니다.

Peulleonjeoga buleojyeossseubnida.

KURDISH

Plunger şikand.

KYRGYZ

Поршень сынып калды.

Plunjer sınıp kaldı.

LATVIAN

Virzulis salūza.

LITHUANIAN

Stūmoklis sulūžo.

LUXEMBOURGISH

De plunger as gebrach.

MACEDONIAN

Клипот се расипа.

Klipot se rasipa.

MALAGASY

Vaky ilay plunger.

MALAY

Pelocoknya pecah.

MALTESE

Il-planġer kissru.

MAORI

Ka pakaru te kaiuru.

MARATHI

प्लंगर तुटला.

Plaṅgara tuṭalā.

MONGOLIAN

Поршен тасарчээ.

Porshyen evderchee.

NEPALI

सवार भाँचियो।

Savāra bhām̐ciyō.

NORWEGIAN

Stempelet gikk i stykker.

NYANJA

Chombocho chinathyoka.

POLISH

Tłok pękł.

PORTUGUESE

O êmbolo quebrou.

PUNJABI

ਪਲੰਜਰ ਟੁੱਟ ਗਿਆ।

Palajara ṭuṭa gi'ā.

ROMANIAN

Pistonul s-a rupt.

RUSSIAN

Поршень сломался.

Porvalsya porshen'.

SAMOAN

Sa gagau le palau.

SCOTS GAELIC

Bhris an plunger.

SERBIAN

Клип се сломио.

Klip se slomio.

SLOVAK

Piest sa zlomil.

SLOVENIAN

Bat se je zlomil.

SOMALI

Tuugii ayaa jabay.

SPANISH

El émbolo se rompió.

SUNDANESE

Plunger peupeus.

SWAHILI

Kioevu kilivunjika.

SWEDISH

Kolven gick sönder.

TAJIK

Поршен шикаст.

Porşen şikast.

TAMIL

உலக்கை உடைந்தது.

Ulakkai uṭaintatu.

TELUGU

ప్లంగర్ విరిగింది.

Plaṅgar virigindi.

THAI

ลูกสูบแตก

Lūksūb tæk.

TURKISH

Piston kırıldı.

TURKMEN

Döküji döwüldi.

UKRAINIAN

Поршень порвався.

Porshen' porvavsya.

UZBEK

Piston buzildi.

VIETNAMESE

Pít tông bị gãy.

VIETNAMESE

Torrodd y plymiwr.

YIDDISH

דער פלאַנגער האָט זיך צעבראָכן.

Der flanger hat zikh tsebrakhn.

ZULU

I-plunger yaphuka.

32 Say hello to my little friend.

AFRIKAANS

Sê hallo vir my klein vriend.

ALBANIAN

Thuaj përshëndetje mikut tim të vogël.

AMHARIC

ለታናሽ ጓደኛዬ ሰላም በል።

Letanashi gwadenyayē selami beli.

ARABIC

قل مرحبا لصديقي الصغير.

Qul ahilan lisadiqi alsaghiri.

ARMENIAN

Բարևիր իմ փոքրիկ ընկերոջը:

Asa barev im p'vok'r ynkerojy.

AZERBAIJANI

Kiçik dostuma salam de.

BASQUE

Agurtu nire lagun txikiari.

BELARUSIAN

Павітайся з маім маленькім сябрам.

Pavitajsia z maim malieńkim siabram.

BOSNIAN

Reci zdravo mom malom prijatelju.

BULGARIAN

Поздрави моя малък приятел.

Kazhi zdraveĭ na malkiya mi priyatel.

BURMESE

ငါ့သူငယ်ချင်းကိုနှုတ်ဆက်ပါ။

Ngar suungaalhkyinnko nhuatsaat par.

CATALAN

Digues hola al meu amic petit.

CEBUANO

Kumusta sa akong gamay nga higala.

MANDARIN CHINESE

向我的小朋友問好。

Xiàng wǒ de xiǎopéngyǒu wènhǎo.

CORSICAN

Salute à u mo amicucciu.

CROATIAN

Pozdravi mog malog prijatelja.

CZECH

Pozdrav mého malého přítele.

DANISH

Sig hej til min lille ven.

DUTCH

Zeg hallo tegen mijn kleine vriend.

ESPERANTO

Diru saluton al mia malgranda amiko.

ESTONIAN

Ütle tere mu väikesele sõbrale.

FILIPINO

Kamustahin ang aking munting kaibigan.

FINNISH

Tervehdi pikku ystävääni.

FRENCH

Dis bonjour à mon petit ami.

GALICIAN

Saúda ao meu pequeno amigo.

GEORGIAN

მიესალმე ჩემს პატარა მეგობარს.

Miesalme chems p'at'ara megobars.

GERMAN

Sagen sie hallo zu meinem kleinen freund.

GREEK

Πες γεια στον μικρό μου φίλο.

Pes geia ston mikró mou filo.

HAITIAN CREOLE

Di ti zanmi mwen bonjou.

HAUSA

Ka gai da karamin abokina.

HAWAIIAN

Aloha i kuʻu hoa aloha.

HINDI

मेरे छोटे दोस्त को नमस्ते कहो।

Mere chhote dost ko namaste kaho.

HMONG

Hais nyob zoo rau kuv tus phooj ywg me.

HUNGARIAN

Köszönj a kis barátomnak.

ICELANDIC

Segðu hæ við litla vin minn.

IGBO

Kwuo obere enyi m.

INDONESIAN

Katakan halo untuk teman kecilku.

IRISH

Abair hello le mo chara beag.

ITALIAN

Saluta il mio piccolo amico.

JAPANESE

私の小さな友達に挨拶してください。

Watashi no chīsana tomodachi ni aisatsu.

JAVANESE

Salam karo kancaku cilik.

KANNADA

ನನ್ನ ಚಿಕ್ಕ ಸ್ನೇಹಿತನಿಗೆ ಹಲೋ ಹೇಳಿ.

Nanna cikka snēhitanige halō hēḷi.

KAZAKH

Менің кішкентай досыма сәлем айтыңыз.

Meniñ kişkentay dosıma sälem aytıñız.

KINYARWANDA

Mwaramutse inshuti yanjye nto.

KOREAN

내 작은 친구에게 인사하세요.

Nae jag-eun chinguege anbuleul jeonhaejuseyo.

KURDISH

Silav ji hevalê min ê piçûk re bêje.

KYRGYZ

Менин кичинекей досума салам айт.

Menin kiçinekey dosuma salam ayt.

LATVIAN

Sveiciniet manu mazo draugu.

LITHUANIAN

Pasisveikink su mano mažuoju draugu.

LUXEMBOURGISH

Soen hallo zu mengem klenge frënd.

MACEDONIAN

Поздрави го мојот мал пријател.

Pozdravi go mojot mal prijatel.

MALAGASY

Mampamangy any amin'ny namako keliko.

MALAY

Sampaikan salam kepada kawan kecil saya.

MALTESE

Isellem lill-ħabib żgħir tiegħi.

MAORI

Oha atu ki taku hoa iti.

MARATHI

माझ्या लहान मित्राला नमस्कार म्हणा.

Mājhyā lahāna mitrālā namaskāra mhaṇā.

MONGOLIAN

Миний бяцхан найзтай сайн уу гэж хэлээрэй.

Byatskhan naizdaa sain uu gej kheleerei.

NEPALI

मेरो सानो साथीलाई नमस्कार भन्नुहोस्।

Mērō sānō sāthīlā'ī namaskāra bhannuhōs.

NORWEGIAN

Si hallo til min lille venn.

NYANJA

Moni kwa mnzanga wamng'ono.

POLISH

Przywitaj się z moim małym przyjacielem.

PORTUGUESE

Diga olá para meu pequeno amigo.

PUNJABI

ਮੇਰੇ ਛੋਟੇ ਦੋਸਤ ਨੂੰ ਹੈਲੋ ਕਹੋ.

Mērē chōṭē dōsata nū hailō kahō.

ROMANIAN

Saluta-l pe micul meu prieten.

RUSSIAN

Передай привет моему маленькому другу.

Pereday privet moyemu malen'komu drugu.

SAMOAN

Talofa laʻu uo laititi.

SCOTS GAELIC

Abair hello ri mo charaid beag.

SERBIAN

Поздрави мог малог пријатеља.

Pozdravi mog malog prijatelja.

SLOVAK

Pozdrav môjho malého kamaráta.

SLOVENIAN

Pozdravi mojega malega prijatelja.

SOMALI

Salaan iga dheh saaxiibkayga yar.

SPANISH

Di hola a mi pequeño amigo.

SUNDANESE

Ngucap salam ka sobat alit kuring.

SWAHILI

Salamu kwa rafiki yangu mdogo.

SWEDISH

Säga hej till min lilla vän.

TAJIK

Ба дӯсти хурдиам салом гӯед.

Ba dūsti xurdiam salom gūed.

TAMIL

என் சிறிய நண்பருக்கு வணக்கம் சொல்லுங்கள்.

Eṉ ciṟiya naṇparukku vaṇakkam colluṅkaḷ.

TELUGU

నా చిన్న స్నేహితుడికి హలో చెప్పండి.

Nā cinna snēhituḍiki halō ceppaṇḍi.

THAI

ทักทายเพื่อนตัวน้อยของฉัน

Thạkthāy pheụ̄̀xn tạw n̂xy k̄hxng c̄hạn.

TURKISH

Küçük arkadaşıma merhaba de.

TURKMEN

Kiçijik dostuma salam aýdyň.

UKRAINIAN

Поздоровіться з моїм маленьким другом.

Pozdorovit'sya z moyim malen'kym druhom.

UZBEK

Mening kichkina do'stimga salom ayting.

VIETNAMESE

Nói xin chào với người bạn nhỏ của tôi.

VIETNAMESE

Dywedwch helo wrth fy ffrind bach.

YIDDISH

זאָגן העלא צו מיין קליין פֿרײַנד.

Zogn hela tsu meyn kleyn fraynd.

ZULU

Ngibingelele umngane wami omncane.

33 What big teeth you have!

AFRIKAANS

Jy het groot tande!

ALBANIAN

Keni dhëmbë të mëdhenj!

AMHARIC

ትላልቅ ጥርሶች አሉዎት!

Tilalik'i t'irisochi āluwoti!

ARABIC

لديك أسنان كبيرة!

Ladayk 'asnan kabiratun!

ARMENIAN

Դուք մեծ ատամներ ունեք:

Duk' unek' mets atamner!

AZERBAIJANI

Böyük dişləriniz var!

BASQUE

Hortz handiak dituzu!

BELARUSIAN

У цябе вялікія зубы!

U ciabie vialikija zuby!

BOSNIAN

Imate velike zube!

BULGARIAN

Имате големи зъби!

Imate golemi zŭbi!

BURMESE

မင်းမှာအံသွားကြီးရှိတယ်။

Mainnmhar aan swarr kyee shtaal!

CATALAN

Tens dents grosses!

CEBUANO

Daghang ngipon nimo!

MANDARIN CHINESE

你的牙齒好大啊！

Nǐ de yáchǐ hào dà a!

CORSICAN

Avete denti grossi!

CROATIAN

Imate velike zube!

CZECH

Máte velké zuby!

DANISH

Du har store tænder!

DUTCH

Je hebt grote tanden!

ESPERANTO

Vi havas grandajn dentojn!

ESTONIAN

Sul on suured hambad!

FILIPINO

Malaki ang ngipin mo!

FINNISH

Sinulla on isot hampaat!

FRENCH

Vous avez de grandes dents!

GALICIAN

Tes dentes grandes!

GEORGIAN

თქვენ გაქვთ დიდი კბილები!

Didi k'bilebi gakvs!

GERMAN

Du hast große zähne!

GREEK

Έχετε μεγάλα δόντια!

Écheis megála dóntia!

HAITIAN CREOLE

Ou gen gwo dan!

HAUSA

Kuna da manyan hakora!

HAWAIIAN

Nui kou mau niho!

HINDI

तुम्हारे बड़े दांत हैं!

Aapake bade daant hain!

HMONG

Koj muaj cov hniav loj!

HUNGARIAN

Nagy fogaid vannak!

ICELANDIC

Þú ert með stórar tennur!

IGBO

Ị nwere nnukwu ezé!

INDONESIAN

Anda memiliki gigi besar!

IRISH

Tá fiacla móra agat!

ITALIAN

Hai dei denti grandi!

JAPANESE

あなたは大きな歯を持っています！

Anata wa ōkina ha o motte imasu!

JAVANESE

Sampeyan duwe untu gedhe!

KANNADA

ನಿಮಗೆ ದೊಡ್ಡ ಹಲ್ಲುಗಳಿವೆ!

Nimage doḍḍa hallugaḷive!

KAZAKH

Сізде үлкен тістер бар!

Sizde ülken tister bar!

KINYARWANDA

Ufite amenyo manini!

KOREAN

당신은 큰 이빨을 가지고 있습니다!

Dangsin-eun keun ippal-eul gajigo issseubnida!

KURDISH

Diranên te yên mezin hene!

KYRGYZ

Сенин чоң тишиң бар!

Senin çoŋ tişiŋ bar!

LATVIAN

Tev ir lieli zobi!

LITHUANIAN

Jūs turite didelius dantis!

LUXEMBOURGISH

Dir hutt grouss zänn!

MACEDONIAN

Имаш големи заби!

Imate golemi zabi!

MALAGASY

Be nify ianao!

MALAY

Anda mempunyai gigi besar!

MALTESE

Għandek snien kbar!

MAORI

He niho nui tou!

MARATHI

तुमचे मोठे दात आहेत!

Tumacē mōṭhē dāta āhēta!

MONGOLIAN

Та том шүдтэй!

Ta tom shüdtei!

NEPALI

तपाइँसँग ठूलो दाँत छ!

Tapā'im̐samँga ṭhūlō dām̐ta cha!

NORWEGIAN

Du har store tenner!

NYANJA

Muli ndi mano akulu!

POLISH

Masz duże zęby!

PORTUGUESE

Você tem dentes grandes!

PUNJABI

ਤੁਹਾਡੇ ਵੱਡੇ ਦੰਦ ਹਨ!

Tuhāḍē vaḍē dada hana!

ROMANIAN

Ai dinți mari!

RUSSIAN

У тебя большие зубы!

U tebya bol'shiye zuby!

SAMOAN

E tele ou nifo!

SCOTS GAELIC

Tha fiaclan mòra agad!

SERBIAN

Имаш велике зубе!

Imaš velike zube!

SLOVAK

Máte veľké zuby!

SLOVENIAN

Imate velike zobe!

SOMALI

Waxaad leedahay ilko waaweyn!

SPANISH

¡Tienes dientes grandes!

SUNDANESE

Anjeun gaduh huntu ageung!

SWAHILI

Una meno makubwa!

SWEDISH

Du har stora tänder!

TAJIK

Шумо дандонҳои калон доред!

Şumo dandonhoi kalon dored!

TAMIL

உங்களுக்கு பெரிய பற்கள் உள்ளன!

Uṅkaḷukku periya paṟkaḷ uḷḷaṉa!

TELUGU

మీకు పెద్ద దంతాలు ఉన్నాయి!

Mīku pedda dantālu unnāyi!

THAI

คุณมีฟันที่ใหญ่!

Khuṇ mī fạn thī̀ h̄ıỵ̀!

TURKISH

Büyük dişlerin var!

TURKMEN

Uly dişleriňiz bar!

UKRAINIAN

У вас великі зуби!

U tebe velyki zuby!

UZBEK

Sizda katta tishlar bor!

VIETNAMESE

Bạn có hàm răng lớn!

VIETNAMESE

Mae gennych chi ddannedd mawr!

YIDDISH

איר האָט גרויס צייַן!

Ir hobn groys tseyn!

ZULU

Unamazinyo amakhulu!

34 Elementary, Watson.

AFRIKAANS

Elementêr, Watson.

ALBANIAN

Fillore, Watson.

AMHARIC

አንደኛ ደረጃ ፣ ዋትሰን።

Anidenya dereja Watiseni.

ARABIC

الابتدائية ، واتسون.

Alabtidayiyat, Watsun.

ARMENIAN

տարրական, Ուոթսոն:

Tarrakan, Uot'son.

AZERBAIJANI

Ibtidai, Watson.

BASQUE

Oinarrizkoa, Watson.

BELARUSIAN

Элементарнае, Уотсан.

Eliemientarna, Uotsan.

BOSNIAN

Osnovno, Watsone.

BULGARIAN

Елементарно, Уотсън.

Elementarno, Uot·sŭn.

BURMESE

မူလတန်း၊ Watson

Muulataann, Watson.

CATALAN

Elemental, Watson.

CEBUANO

Elementarya, Watson.

MANDARIN CHINESE

小學，沃森。

Xiǎoxué, Wò sēn.

CORSICAN

Elementariu, Watson.

CROATIAN

Osnovno, Watsone.

CZECH

Elementární, Watsone.

DANISH

Elementær, Watson.

DUTCH

Elementair, Watson.

ESPERANTO

Elementa, Vatsono.

ESTONIAN

Elementaarne, Watson.

FILIPINO

Elementarya, Watson.

FINNISH

Peruskoulu, Watson.

FRENCH

Élémentaire, Watson.

GALICIAN

Elemental, Watson.

GEORGIAN

დაწყებითი, უოტსონი

Dats'q'ebiti, Uot'soni.

GERMAN

Grundschule, Watson.

GREEK

στοιχειώδες, Γουότσον.

Stoicheiódes, Gouótson.

HAITIAN CREOLE

Elemantè, Watson.

HAUSA

Na farko, Watson.

HAWAIIAN

Kumumea, Watson.

HINDI

प्राथमिक, वाटसन।

Praathamik, Vaatasan.

HMONG

Theem pib, Watson.

HUNGARIAN

Elemi, Watson.

ICELANDIC

Grunnskóli, Watson.

IGBO

Elementrị, Watson.

INDONESIAN

Sd, Watson.

IRISH

Bunrang, Watson.

ITALIAN

Elementare, Watson.

JAPANESE

エレメンタリー、ワトソン。

Erementarī, Watoson.

JAVANESE

Sd, Watson.

KANNADA

ಪ್ರಾಥಮಿಕ, ವ್ಯಾಟ್ಸನ್

Prāthamika, Vyāṭsan.

KAZAKH

Бастауыш, Уотсон.

Bastawış, Wotson.

KINYARWANDA

Ibanze, Watson.

KOREAN

초등학교, 왓슨.

Chodeung, Was-seun.

KURDISH

Seretayî, Watson.

KYRGYZ

Башталгыч, Уотсон.

Baştalgıç, Uotson.

LATVIAN

Elementāri, Vatsons.

LITHUANIAN

Pradinis, Vatsonas.

LUXEMBOURGISH

Elementar, Watson.

MACEDONIAN

Основно, Вотсон.

Osnovno, Votson.

MALAGASY

Fototra, Watson.

MALAY

Dasar, Watson.

MALTESE

Elementari, Watson.

MAORI

Kura Tuatahi, Watson.

MARATHI

प्राथमिक, वॉटसन.

Prāthamika, Vŏṭasana.

MONGOLIAN

Анхан шатны, Ватсон.

Ankhan shatny, Vatson.

NEPALI

प्राथमिक, वाटसन।

Prāthamika, Vāṭasana.

NORWEGIAN

Elementær, Watson.

NYANJA

Zoyambira, Watson.

POLISH

Podstawowe, Watsonie.

PORTUGUESE

Elementar, Watson.

PUNJABI

ਐਲੀਮੈਂਟਰੀ, ਵਾਟਸਨ.

Ailīmaiṇṭarī, Vāṭasana.

ROMANIAN

Elementar, Watson.

RUSSIAN

Элементарно, Уотсон.

Elementarno Vatson.

SAMOAN

Elementary, Watson.

SCOTS GAELIC

Bun-sgoil, Watson.

SERBIAN

Основно, Ватсон.

Osnovno, Vatson.

SLOVAK

Elementary, Watson.

SLOVENIAN

Osnovno, Watson.

SOMALI

Dugsiga hoose, Watson.

SPANISH

Primaria, Watson.

SUNDANESE

SD, Watson.

SWAHILI

Msingi, Watson.

SWEDISH

Elementary, Watson.

TAJIK

Ибтидоӣ, Уотсон.

Ibtidoī, Uotson.

TAMIL

தொடக்க, வாட்சன்.

Toṭakka, Vāṭcaṉ.

TELUGU

ప్రాథమిక, వాట్సన్.

Prāthamika, Vāṭsan.

THAI

ประถม, วัตสัน.

Prathm, Wạt s̄ạn.

TURKISH

İlkokul, Watson.

TURKMEN

Başlangyç, Watson.

UKRAINIAN

Елементарний, Уотсон.

Elementarnyy, Uot·son.

UZBEK

Boshlang'ich, Uotson.

VIETNAMESE

Tiểu học, Watson.

VIETNAMESE

Elfennaidd, Watson.

YIDDISH

עלעמענטאַר, וואַצאָן.

Elementar, Vatson.

ZULU

Okuyisisekelo, Watson.

❸❺ My brain died.

AFRIKAANS

My brein het gesterf.

ALBANIAN

Truri më vdiq.

AMHARIC

አንጎሌ ሞተ።

Anigolē mote.

ARABIC

مات عقلي.

Mat eaqli.

ARMENIAN

Իմ ուղեղը մահացավ:

Ugheghs mahats'av.

AZERBAIJANI

Beynim öldü.

BASQUE

Garuna hil zitzaidan.

BELARUSIAN

Мой мозг памёр.

Moj mozh pamior.

BOSNIAN

Umro mi je mozak.

BULGARIAN

Мозъкът ми умря..

Mozŭkŭt mi umrya.

BURMESE

ငါ့ ဦး နှောက်သေသွားပြီ။

Ngar u nhaout say swarrpye.

CATALAN

Em va morir el cervell.

CEBUANO

Namatay akong utok.

MANDARIN CHINESE

我的大腦死了。

Wǒ de dànǎo sǐle.

CORSICAN

U mo cervellu hè mortu.

CROATIAN

Umro mi je mozak.

CZECH

Můj mozek zemřel.

DANISH

Min hjerne døde.

DUTCH

Mijn hersenen stierven.

ESPERANTO

Mia cerbo mortis.

ESTONIAN

Mu aju suri.

FILIPINO

Namatay ang utak ko.

FINNISH

Aivoni kuolivat.

FRENCH

Mon cerveau est mort.

GALICIAN

O meu cerebro morreu.

GEORGIAN

Πέθανε ο εγκέφαλός μου.

Chemi t'vini mok'vda.

GERMAN

Mein gehirn ist gestorben.

GREEK

ჩემი ტვინი მოკვდა

Péthane o enkéfalós mou.

HAITIAN CREOLE

Sèvo mwen te mouri.

HAUSA

Kwakwalwata ta mutu.

HAWAIIAN

Ua make koʻu lolo.

HINDI

मेरा दिमाग मर गया।

Mera dimaag mar gaya.

HMONG

Kuv lub paj hlwb tuag.

HUNGARIAN

Meghalt az agyam.

ICELANDIC

Heilinn minn dó.

IGBO

Ụbụrụ m nwụrụ.

INDONESIAN

Otak saya mati.

IRISH

Fuair m'inchinn bás.

ITALIAN

Il mio cervello è morto.

JAPANESE

私の脳は死んだ。

Watashi no nō wa shinda.

JAVANESE

Otakku mati.

KANNADA

ನನ್ನ ಮೆದುಳು ಸತ್ತುಹೋಯಿತು.

Nanna meduḷu sattuhōyitu.

KAZAKH

Менің миым өлді.

Meniñ miım öldi.

KINYARWANDA

Ubwonko bwanjye bwarapfuye.

KOREAN

내 뇌가 죽었다.

Nae noega jug-eossda.

KURDISH

Mejiyê min mir.

KYRGYZ

Менин мээм өлдү.

Menin meem öldü.

LATVIAN

Manas smadzenes nomira.

LITHUANIAN

Mano smegenys mirė.

LUXEMBOURGISH

Mäi gehir as gestuerwen.

MACEDONIAN

Мојот мозок умре.

Mojot mozok umre.

MALAGASY

Maty ny atidohako.

MALAY

Otak saya mati.

MALTESE

Moħħi miet.

MAORI

Ka mate taku roro.

MARATHI

माझा मेंदू मेला.

Mājhā mēndū mēlā.

MONGOLIAN

Миний тархи үхсэн.

Minii tarkhi ükhsen.

NEPALI

मेरो मस्तिष्क मरेको छ।

Mērō mastiṣka marēkō cha.

NORWEGIAN

Hjernen min døde.

NYANJA

Ubongo wanga unamwalira.

POLISH

Mój mózg umarł.

PORTUGUESE

Meu cérebro morreu.

PUNJABI

ਮੇਰਾ ਦਿਮਾਗ ਮਰ ਗਿਆ.

Mērā dimāga mara gi'ā.

ROMANIAN

Creierul meu a murit.

RUSSIAN

Мой мозг умер.

Moy mozg umer.

SAMOAN

Ua oti lo'u fai'ai.

SCOTS GAELIC

Bhàsaich m 'eanchainn.

SERBIAN

Умро ми је мозак.

Umro mi je mozak.

SLOVAK

Zomrel mi mozog.

SLOVENIAN

Odmrli so mi možgani.

SOMALI

Maskaxdaydii ayaa dhimatay.

SPANISH

Mi cerebro murió.

SUNDANESE

Otak kuring maot.

SWAHILI

Ubongo wangu ulikufa.

SWEDISH

Min hjärna dog.

TAJIK

Мағзи ман мурд.

Maqzi man murd.

TAMIL

என் மூளை இறந்துவிட்டது.

En̲ mūḷai ir̲antuviṭṭatu.

TELUGU

నా మెదడు చనిపోయింది.

Nā medaḍu canipōyindi.

THAI

สมองของฉันตาย

S̄mxng k̄hxng c̄hạn tāy.

TURKISH

Beynim öldü.

TURKMEN

Beýnim öldi.

UKRAINIAN

Мій мозок помер.

Miy mozok pomer.

UZBEK

Mening miyam o'ldi.

VIETNAMESE

Bộ não của tôi đã chết.

VIETNAMESE

Bu farw fy ymennydd.

YIDDISH

מײַן מאַרך איז געשטאָרבן.

Mayn markh iz geshtarbn.

ZULU

Ingqondo yami yafa.

36 Epic!

AFRIKAANS

Epies!

ALBANIAN

Epik!

AMHARIC

ድንቅ!

Dinik'i!

ARABIC

ملحمة!

Almalham!

ARMENIAN

Էպոս!

Epikakan!

AZERBAIJANI

Epik!

BASQUE

Epikoa!

BELARUSIAN

Эпічнае!

Epapieja!

BOSNIAN

Epski!

BULGARIAN

Епично!

Epichno!

BURMESE

မော်ကွန်း!

Mawkwann!

CATALAN

Èpica!

CEBUANO

Epiko!

MANDARIN CHINESE

史詩！

Shǐshī!

CORSICAN

Epica!

CROATIAN

Epski!

CZECH

Epické!

DANISH

Episk!

DUTCH

Episch!

ESPERANTO

Epopea!

ESTONIAN

Eepiline!

FILIPINO

Epiko!

FINNISH

Eeppinen!

FRENCH

Épique!

GALICIAN

Épico!

GEORGIAN

ეპიკური!

Ep'ik'uri!

GERMAN

Epos!

GREEK

Επος!

Epos!

HAITIAN CREOLE

Sezon!

HAUSA

Almara!

HAWAIIAN

Epic!

HINDI

महाकाव्य!

Mahaakaavy!

HMONG

Siab tawv!

HUNGARIAN

Epikus!

ICELANDIC

Epískt!

IGBO

Dike!

INDONESIAN

Epik!

IRISH

Eipiciúil!

ITALIAN

Epico!

JAPANESE

すごい！

Sugoi!

JAVANESE

Epik!

KANNADA

ಮಹಾಕಾವ್ಯ!

Mahākāvya!

KAZAKH

Эпос!

Épos!

KINYARWANDA

Intwari!

KOREAN

서사시!

Seosasi!

KURDISH

Epîk!

KYRGYZ

Эпикалык!

Epikalık!

LATVIAN

Episks!

LITHUANIAN

Epinis!

LUXEMBOURGISH

Epesch!

MACEDONIAN

Епска!

Epska!

MALAGASY

Lehibe!

MALAY

Epik!

MALTESE

Epika!

MAORI

Toa!

MARATHI

महाकाव्य!

Mahākāvya!

MONGOLIAN

Эпик!

Epik!

NEPALI

महाकाव्य!

Mahākāvya!

NORWEGIAN

Episk!

POLISH

Epicki!

PORTUGUESE

Épico!

PUNJABI

ਮਹਾਂਕਾਵਿ!

Mahāṅkāvi!

ROMANIAN

Epic!

RUSSIAN

Эпично!

Epichno!

SAMOAN

Toa!

SCOTS GAELIC

Epic!

SERBIAN

Еп!

Ep!

SLOVAK

Epické!

SLOVENIAN

Epsko!

SOMALI

Tacaddi!

SPANISH

¡Épico!

SUNDANESE

Epik!

SWAHILI

Kishujaa!

SWEDISH

Episk!

TAJIK

Эпикӣ!

Epikī!

TAMIL

காவியம்!

Kāviyam!

TELUGU

పురాణ!

Purāṇa!

THAI

มหากาพย์!

mh̄ā kāphy̒!

TURKISH

Epik!

TURKMEN

Epiki!

UKRAINIAN

Епопея!

Epopeya!

UZBEK

Epik!

VIETNAMESE

Sử thi!

VIETNAMESE

Epig!

YIDDISH

עפּיש!

Epish!

ZULU

Yeqhawe!

37 Join the club.

AFRIKAANS

Sluit aan by die klub.

ALBANIAN

Bashkohu me klubin.

AMHARIC

ክለቡን ይቀላቀሉ።

Kilebuni yik'elak'elu.

ARABIC

انضم إلى النادي.

Andama 'iilaa alnaadi.

ARMENIAN

Միացեք ակումբին:

Miats'ir akumbin.

AZERBAIJANI

Kluba qoşulun.

BASQUE

Sartu klubera.

BELARUSIAN

Далучайся да клуба.

Dalučajciesia da kluba.

BOSNIAN

Pridruži se klubu.

BULGARIAN

Присъединете се към клуба.

Prisŭedini se kŭm kluba.

BURMESE

ကလပ်ကိုဆက်သွယ်ပါ။

Kalaut ko saatswal par.

CATALAN

Uneix-te al club.

CEBUANO

Apil sa grupo.

MANDARIN CHINESE

加入俱樂部。

Jiārù jùlèbù.

CORSICAN

Unisciti à u club.

CROATIAN

Pridružite se klubu.

CZECH

Přidejte se do klubu.

DANISH

Velkommen i klubben.

DUTCH

Word lid van de club.

ESPERANTO

Aliĝu al la klubo.

ESTONIAN

Ühine klubiga.

FILIPINO

Sumali sa club.

FINNISH

Liity kerhoon.

FRENCH

Joindre le club.

GALICIAN

Únete ao club.

GEORGIAN

გაწევრიანდით კლუბში

Gats'evriandit k'lubshi.

GERMAN

Tritt in den klub ein.

GREEK

Γίνετε μέλος του συλλόγου.

Gínete mélos tou syllógou.

HAITIAN CREOLE

Antre nan klib la.

HAUSA

Shiga kulob din.

HAWAIIAN

Hui pū i ka hui.

HINDI

संघ में शामिल हों।

Sangh mein shaamil hon.

HMONG

Koom nrog lub club.

HUNGARIAN

Csatlakozni a klubba.

ICELANDIC

Gangtu í klúbbinn.

IGBO

Jikọọ klọb ahụ.

INDONESIAN

Gabung ke klub.

IRISH

Bí ar an gclub.

ITALIAN

Entra nel club.

JAPANESE

クラブに加入する。

Kurabu ni kanyū suru.

JAVANESE

Melu klub.

KANNADA

ಕ್ಲಬ್‌ಗೆ ಸೇರಿ.

Klabge sēri.

KAZAKH

Клубқа қосылыңыз.

Klwbqa qosılıñız.

KINYARWANDA

Injira muri club.

KOREAN

동아리에 가입하다.

Dong-alie gaibhada.

KURDISH

Tevlî klûbê bibin.

KYRGYZ

Клубга кошулуңуз.

Klubga koşuluŋuz.

LATVIAN

Pievienojies klubam.

LITHUANIAN

Prisijungti prie klubo.

LUXEMBOURGISH

Maacht mat beim club.

MACEDONIAN

Придружи се на Клубот.

Pridruži se na klubot.

MALAGASY

Midira amin'ny klioba.

MALAY

Sertailah kelab.

MALTESE

Ingħaqad mal-klabb.

MAORI

Whakauru atu ki te karapu.

MARATHI

क्लबमध्ये सामील व्हा.

Klabamadhyē sāmīla vhā.

MONGOLIAN

Клубт элсэх.

Klubt elsekh.

NEPALI

क्लबमा सामेल हुनुहोस्।

Klabamā sāmēla hunuhōs.

NORWEGIAN

Bli med i klubben.

NYANJA

Lowani nawo kalabu.

POLISH

Dołączyć do klubu.

PORTUGUESE

Junte-se ao clube.

PUNJABI

ਕਲੱਬ ਵਿੱਚ ਸ਼ਾਮਲ ਹੋਵੋ.

Kalaba vica śāmala hōvō.

ROMANIAN

Înscrie-te în club.

RUSSIAN

Вступить в клуб.

Vstupit' v klub.

SAMOAN

Auai i le kalapu.

SCOTS GAELIC

Thig còmhla ris a 'chlub.

SERBIAN

Придружити клубу.

Pridružiti klubu.

SLOVAK

Pridaj sa do klubu.

SLOVENIAN

Pridruži se klubu.

SOMALI

Ku biir kooxda.

SPANISH

Únete al club.

SUNDANESE

Gabung sareng klub.

SWAHILI

Jiunge na kilabu.

SWEDISH

Gå med i klubben.

TAJIK

Ба клуб ҳамроҳ шавед.

Ba klub hamroh şaved.

TAMIL

குழுவில் இணையுங்கள்.

Kuḻuvil iṇaiyuṅkaḷ.

TELUGU

క్లబ్‌లో చేరండి.

Klablō cēraṇḍi.

THAI

เข้าร่วมคลับ.

K̄hêā r̀wm khlạb.

TURKISH

Kulübe katıl.

TURKMEN

Kluba goşulyň.

UKRAINIAN

Приєднатися до клубу.

Pryyednatysya do klubu.

UZBEK

Klubga qo'shiling.

VIETNAMESE

Tham gia câu lạc bộ.

VIETNAMESE

Ymunwch â'r clwb.

YIDDISH

פֿאַרבינדן דעם קלוב.

Farbindn dem klub.

ZULU

Joyina iklabhu.

38 Is that a tornado?

AFRIKAANS

Is dit ‘n tornado?

ALBANIAN

A është kjo një tornado?

AMHARIC

ያ አውሎ ንፋስ ነው?

Ya āwilo nifasi newi?

ARABIC

هل هذا اعصار؟

Hal hadha ‘iiesaru?

ARMENIAN

Արդյո՞ք դա տորնադո է:

Da tornado e?

AZERBAIJANI

Bu bir tornado?

BASQUE

Hori tornado bat da?

BELARUSIAN

Гэта смерч?

Heta tarnada?

BOSNIAN

Je li to tornado?

BULGARIAN

Това торнадо ли е?

Tova tornado li e?

BURMESE

အဲဒါလေဆင်နှာမောင်းလား။

Aelldar laysainnharmaungg larr?

CATALAN

És això un tornado?

CEBUANO

Usa ba kana buhawi?

MANDARIN CHINESE

那是龍捲風嗎？

Nà shì lóngjuǎnfēng ma?

CORSICAN

Hè una tornata?

CROATIAN

Je li to tornado?

CZECH

Je to tornádo?

DANISH

Er det en tornado?

DUTCH

Is dat een tornado?

ESPERANTO

Ĉu tio estas tornado?

ESTONIAN

Kas see on tornaado?

FILIPINO

Buhawi ba yan?

FINNISH

Onko se tornado?

FRENCH

C’est une tornade?

GALICIAN

¿É un tornado?

GEORGIAN

ეს ტორნადოა?

Es t’ornadoa?

GERMAN

Ist das ein tornado?

GREEK

Είναι ανεμοστρόβιλος?

Eínai anemostróvilos?

HAITIAN CREOLE

Èske se yon tònad?

HAUSA

Wannan hadari ne?

HAWAIIAN

He puahiohio anei kēlā?

HINDI

क्या वह बवंडर है?

Kya vah bavandar hai?

HMONG

Puas yog cua daj cua dub?

HUNGARIAN

Ez tornádó?

ICELANDIC

Er það hvirfilbylur?

IGBO

Nke ahụ ọ bụ oké ifufe?

INDONESIAN

Apakah itu angin puting beliung?

IRISH

An tornado é sin?

ITALIAN

È un tornado?

JAPANESE

それは竜巻ですか？

Sore wa tatsumakidesu ka?

JAVANESE

Apa kuwi puting beliung?

KANNADA

ಅದು ಸುಂಟರಗಾಳಿಯೇ?

Adu suṇṭaragāḷiyē?

KAZAKH

Бұл торнадо ма?

Bul tornado ma?

KINYARWANDA

Iyo ni tornado?

KOREAN

토네이도인가?

Toneidoinga?

KURDISH

Ma ew tofan e?

KYRGYZ

Бул торнадобу?

Bul tornadobu?

LATVIAN

Vai tas ir tornado?

LITHUANIAN

Ar tai viesulas?

LUXEMBOURGISH

As dat en tornado?

MACEDONIAN

Дали е тоа торнадо?

Dali e toa tornado?

MALAGASY

Rivo-doza ve izany?

MALAY

Adakah itu puting beliung?

MALTESE

Dan huwa tornado?

MAORI

He awhiowhio tera?

MARATHI

तो चक्रीवादळ आहे का?

Tō cakrīvādaḷa āhē kā?

MONGOLIAN

Энэ хар салхи мөн үү?

Ene khar salkhi mön üü?

NEPALI

के त्यो टोर्नाडो हो?

Kē tyō ṭōrnāḍō hō?

NORWEGIAN

Er det en tornado?

NYANJA

Kodi ndiye mkuntho?

POLISH

Czy to tornado?

PORTUGUESE

Isso é um tornado?

PUNJABI

ਕੀ ਇਹ ਬਵੰਡਰ ਹੈ?

Kī iha bavaḍara hai?

ROMANIAN

Este o tornadă?

RUSSIAN

Это торнадо?

Eto tornado?

SAMOAN

O se asiosio lena?

SCOTS GAELIC

An e iomghaoth a tha sin?

SERBIAN

Је ли то торнадо?

Je li to tornado?

SLOVAK

Je to tornádo?

SLOVENIAN

Je to tornado?

SOMALI

Ma duufaan baa?

SPANISH

¿Eso es un tornado?

SUNDANESE

Naha éta puting beliung?

SWAHILI

Je! Hiyo ni kimbunga?

SWEDISH

Är det en tornado?

TAJIK

Оё ин гирдбод аст?

Ojo in girdвod ast?

TAMIL

அது ஒரு சூறாவளியா?

Atu oru cūṟāvaḷiyā?

TELUGU

అది సుడిగాలిలా?

Adi suḍigālilā?

THAI

นั่นคือพายุทอร์นาโด?

Nạn khụ̄x phāyu thxr̒nādo?

TURKISH

Bu bir kasırga mı?

TURKMEN

Bu tornado?

UKRAINIAN

Це торнадо?

Tse tornado?

UZBEK

Bu bo'ronmi?

VIETNAMESE

Đó có phải là một cơn lốc xoáy?

VIETNAMESE

Ai corwynt yw hwnnw?

YIDDISH

?איז דאָס אַ טאָרנאַדאָ

Iz dos a tornado?

ZULU

Ingabe leso isiphepho?

39 Made you look.

AFRIKAANS

Het jou laat kyk.

ALBANIAN

Të bëri të dukesh.

AMHARIC

እንድትመለከቱ አደረጋችሁ።

Iniditimeleketu āderegachihu.

ARABIC

جعلك تبدو.

Jaelak tabdu.

ARMENIAN

Ստիպեց քեզ տեսք տալ:

Stipets'k'ez tesk' tal.

AZERBAIJANI

Səni görməyə məcbur etdi.

BASQUE

Begiratu zaitu.

BELARUSIAN

Прымусіў вас выглядаць.

Prymusiŭ vas vyhliadać.

BOSNIAN

Učinio si da izgledaš.

BULGARIAN

Накара те да изглеждаш.

Nakara te da izglezhdash.

BURMESE

မင်းကိုကြည့်ဖြစ်အောင်လုပ်ခဲ့တယ်။

Mainn ko kyany hpyitaaung lotehkaetaal.

CATALAN

T'ha fet mirar.

CEBUANO

Gipatan-aw nimo.

MANDARIN CHINESE

讓你看。

Ràng nǐ kàn.

CORSICAN

Ti hà fattu fighjà.

CROATIAN

Učinio da izgleda.

CZECH

Přiměl jsi se podívat.

DANISH

Fik dig til at kigge.

DUTCH

Heb je laten kijken.

ESPERANTO

Aspektigis vin.

ESTONIAN

Pani vaatama.

FILIPINO

Nagpatingin sa iyo.

FINNISH

Sai sinut näyttämään.

FRENCH

T'a fait regarder.

GALICIAN

Fíxoche mirar.

GEORGIAN

გაგიჩინე მზერა.

Gagichine mzera.

GERMAN

Hat dich aussehen lassen.

GREEK

Σε έκανε να φαίνεσαι.

Se ékane na faínesai.

HAITIAN CREOLE

Fè ou gade.

HAUSA

Ya sanya ku duba.

HAWAIIAN

Ua nānā ʻoe.

HINDI

देखो तुम्हें बना दिया।

Dekho tumhen bana diya.

HMONG

Ua rau koj saib.

HUNGARIAN

Megnézte.

ICELANDIC

Fékk þig til að líta.

IGBO

Mee ka ị lee anya.

INDONESIAN

Membuatmu terlihat.

IRISH

Rinne tú breathnú.

ITALIAN

Ti ho fatto sembrare.

JAPANESE

あなたを見てもらいました。

Anata o mite moraimashita.

JAVANESE

Nggawe sampeyan katon.

KANNADA

ನಿಮ್ಮನ್ನು ನೋಡುವಂತೆ ಮಾಡಿದೆ.

Nim'mannu nōḍuvante māḍide.

KAZAKH

Сізге қарауға мәжбүр етті.

Sizge qarawğa mäjbür etti.

KINYARWANDA

Yaguteye kureba.

KOREAN

당신을 보게 만들었습니다.

Dangsin-eul boge mandeul-eossseubnida.

KURDISH

Te kir ku xuya bike.

KYRGYZ

Сени кароого мажбур кылды.

Seni karoogo majbur kıldı.

LATVIAN

Lika izskatīties.

LITHUANIAN

Privertė atrodyti.

LUXEMBOURGISH

Huet Iech ausgesinn.

MACEDONIAN

Ве натера да изгледате.

Ve natera da izgledate.

MALAGASY

Nahatonga anao hijery.

MALAY

Membuat anda kelihatan.

MALTESE

Għamilt tħares.

MAORI

I titiro koe ki te ahua.

MARATHI

तुला पहावयास लावले.

Tulā pahāvayāsa lāvalē.

MONGOLIAN

Чамайг харагдуулсан.

Chamaig kharagduulsan.

NEPALI

तिमीलाई नजर लगायो।

Timīlā'ī najara lagāyō.

NORWEGIAN

Fikk deg til å se.

POLISH

Spowodowało, że wyglądasz.

PORTUGUESE

Fez você olhar.

PUNJABI

ਤੁਹਾਨੂੰ ਦਿੱਖ ਦਿੱਤੀ.

Tuhānū dikha ditī.

ROMANIAN

Te-a făcut să arăți.

RUSSIAN

Заставил посмотреть.

Zastavil posmotret'.

SAMOAN

Fa'aali lau vaai.

SCOTS GAELIC

Thug thu ort coimhead.

SERBIAN

Учинио си да изгледаш.

Učinio si da izgledaš.

SLOVAK

Prinútil ťa vyzerať.

SLOVENIAN

Naredil si pogled.

SOMALI

Ku eegtay.

SPANISH

Te hizo mirar.

SUNDANESE

Dijantenkeun anjeun katingali.

SWAHILI

Imekufanya uangalie.

SWEDISH

Fik dig att se.

TAJIK

Шуморо водор сохт.

Şumoro vodor soxt.

TAMIL

உன்னை பார்க்கவைத்தது.

U<u>nn</u>ai pārkkavaittatu.

TELUGU

మిమ్మల్ని చూసేలా
చేసింది.

Mim'malni cūsēlā cēsindi.

THAI

ทำให้คุณดู

Thảh̄ı̂ khuṇ dū.

TURKISH

Sağladım.

TURKMEN

Görünmäge mejbur etdi.

UKRAINIAN

Змусив вас виглядати.

Zmusyv vas vyhlyadaty.

UZBEK

Sizni qarashga majbur qildi.

VIETNAMESE

Làm cho bạn nhìn.

VIETNAMESE

Wedi gwneud ichi edrych.

YIDDISH

געמאכט איר קוקן.

Gemakht ir kukn.

ZULU

Kukwenze wabheka.

40 Are we lost?

AFRIKAANS

Is ons verlore?

ALBANIAN

Jemi te humbur?

AMHARIC

ጠፍተናል ወይ?

T'efitenali weyi?

ARABIC

هل خسرنا؟

Hal khasirna?

ARMENIAN

Կորած ենք?

Korats yenk'?

AZERBAIJANI

İtirdikmi?

BASQUE

Galduta al gaude?

BELARUSIAN

Мы згубіліся?

My zhubilisia?

BOSNIAN

Jesmo li se izgubili?

BULGARIAN

Изгубени ли сме?

Izgubeni li sme?

BURMESE

ငါတို့လမ်းပျောက်နေလား။

Ngarthoet lam pyawwatnay larr?

CATALAN

Estem perduts?

CEBUANO

Nawala na ta?

MANDARIN CHINESE

我們迷路了嗎？

Wǒmen mílùle ma?

CORSICAN

Simu persi?

CROATIAN

Jesmo li se izgubili?

CZECH

Jsme ztraceni?

DANISH

Er vi tabt?

DUTCH

Zijn we verdwaald?

ESPERANTO

Ĉu ni estas perditaj?

ESTONIAN

Kas oleme eksinud?

FILIPINO

Naligaw ba tayo?

FINNISH

Olemmeko eksyneet?

FRENCH

Sommes-nous perdu?

GALICIAN

Estamos perdidos?

GEORGIAN

დავიკარგეთ?

Davik'arget?

GERMAN

Sind wir verloren?

GREEK

Χαθήκαμε?

Chathíkame?

HAITIAN CREOLE

Èske nou pèdi?

HAUSA

Shin mun bata?

HAWAIIAN

Ua nalo anei mākou?

HINDI

क्या हम हार गए हैं?

Kya ham haar gae hain?

HMONG

Puas yog peb poob?

HUNGARIAN

Elvesztünk?

ICELANDIC

Erum við týnd?

IGBO

Anyị furu efu?

INDONESIAN

Apakah kita tersesat?

IRISH

An bhfuil muid caillte?

ITALIAN

Ci siamo persi?

JAPANESE

私たちは迷子になっていますか？

Watashitachiha maigo ni natte imasu ka?

JAVANESE

Apa kita kesasar?

KANNADA

ನಾವು ಕಳೆದು ಹೋಗಿದ್ದೇವೆಯೇ?

Nāvu kaḷedu hōgiddēveyē?

KAZAKH

Біз адасып қалдық па?

Biz adasıp qaldıq pa?

KINYARWANDA

Twarazimiye?

KOREAN

우리는 길을 잃었습니까?

Ulineun gil-eul ilh-eossseubnikka?

KURDISH

Ma em winda ne?

KYRGYZ

Адашып калдыкпы?

Adaşıp kaldıkpı?

LATVIAN

Vai esam apmaldījušies?

LITHUANIAN

Ar mes pasiklydę?

LUXEMBOURGISH

Sinn mir verluer?

MACEDONIAN

Дали сме изгубени?

Dali sme izgubeni?

MALAGASY

Very ve isika?

MALAY

Adakah kita tersesat?

MALTESE

Aħna mitlufin?

MAORI

Kua ngaro tatou?

MARATHI

आपण हरलो आहोत का?

Āpaṇa haralō āhōta kā?

MONGOLIAN

Бид алдагдсан уу?

Bid aldagdsan uu?

NEPALI

के हामी हराएका छौं?

Kē hāmī harā'ēkā chauṁ?

NORWEGIAN

Er vi tapt?

POLISH

Czy jesteśmy zgubieni?

PORTUGUESE

Estamos perdidos?

PUNJABI

ਕੀ ਅਸੀਂ ਗੁੰਮ ਹੋ ਗਏ ਹਾਂ?

Kī asīṁ guma hō ga'ē hāṁ?

ROMANIAN

Suntem pierduti?

RUSSIAN

Мы заблудились?

My zabludilis'?

SAMOAN

Ua tatou leiloa?

SCOTS GAELIC

A bheil sinn air chall?

SERBIAN

Јесмо ли се изгубили?

Jesmo li se izgubili?

SLOVAK

Sme stratení?

SLOVENIAN

Ali smo izgubljeni?

SOMALI

Ma lumay?

SPANISH

¿Estamos perdidos?

SUNDANESE

Naha urang leungit?

SWAHILI

Tumepotea?

SWEDISH

Är vi vilse?

TAJIK

Оё мо гум шудаем?

Ojo mo gum şudaem?

TAMIL

நாம் தொலைந்து
விட்டோமா?

Nām tolaintu viṭṭōmā?

TELUGU

మనం ఓడిపోయామా?

Manaṁ ōḍipōyāmā?

THAI

เราหลงทาง?

reā h̄lng thāng?

TURKISH

Kayıp mı olduk?

TURKMEN

Biz ýitdikmi?

UKRAINIAN

Ми пропали?

My propaly?

UZBEK

Adashdikmi?

VIETNAMESE

Có phải chúng ta đã lạc rồi
không?

VIETNAMESE

Ydyn ni ar goll?

YIDDISH

זענען מיר פאַרפאַלן?

Zenen mir farfaln?

ZULU

Silahlekile?

41 The sky is falling!

AFRIKAANS

Die hemel val!

ALBANIAN

Qielli po bie!

AMHARIC

ሰማዩ እየወደቀ ነው!

Semayu iyewedek'e newi!

ARABIC

السماء تقع!

Alsama' taqeu!

ARMENIAN

Երկինքը ընկնում է:

Yerkink'y ynknum e!

AZERBAIJANI

Göy düşür!

BASQUE

Zerua erortzen ari da!

BELARUSIAN

Неба падае!

Nieba padaje!

BOSNIAN

Nebo pada!

BULGARIAN

Небето пада!

Nebeto pada!

BURMESE

ကောင်းကင်ကကျနေတယ်!

Kaunggkain k kya naytaal!

CATALAN

El cel cau!

CEBUANO

Ang langit nahulog!

MANDARIN CHINESE

天要塌了！

Tiān yào tāle!

CORSICAN

U celu casca!

CROATIAN

Nebo pada!

CZECH

Nebe padá!

DANISH

Himlen falder!

DUTCH

De hemel valt!

ESPERANTO

La ĉielo falas!

ESTONIAN

Taevas langeb!

FILIPINO

Bumabagsak ang kalangitan!

FINNISH

Taivas putoaa!

FRENCH

Le ciel tombe!

GALICIAN

O ceo está caendo!

GEORGIAN

ცა იშლება!

Tsa ishleba!

GERMAN

Der himmel fällt!

GREEK

Πέφτει ο ουρανός!

Péftei o ouranós!

HAITIAN CREOLE

Syèl la tonbe!

HAUSA

Sama tana fadowa!

HAWAIIAN

Ke helele‘i nei ka lani!

HINDI

आसमान गिर रहा है!

Aasamaan gir raha hai!

HMONG

Ntuj poob lawm!

HUNGARIAN

Az ég leesik!

ICELANDIC

Himinninn er að detta!

IGBO

Eluigwe na -ada!

INDONESIAN

Langit berjatuhan!

IRISH

Tá an spéir ag titim!

ITALIAN

Il cielo sta cadendo!

JAPANESE

空が落ちてきます！

Sora ga ochite kimasu!

JAVANESE

Langite lagi tiba!

KANNADA

ಆಕಾಶ ಕುಸಿಯುತ್ತಿದೆ!

Ākāśa kusiyuttide!

KAZAKH

Аспан құлап жатыр!

Aspan qulap jatır!

KINYARWANDA

Ijuru riragwa!

KOREAN

하늘이 무너지고 있다!

Haneul-i muneojigo issda!

KURDISH

Ezman dadikeve!

KYRGYZ

Асман түшүп жатат!

Asman tüşüp jatat!

LATVIAN

Debesis krīt!

LITHUANIAN

Dangus krinta!

LUXEMBOURGISH

Den himmel fällt!

MACEDONIAN

Небото паѓа!

Neboto paǵa!

MALAGASY

Milatsaka ny lanitra!

MALAY

Langit jatuh!

MALTESE

Is-sema qed taqa!

MAORI

Kei te taka te rangi!

MARATHI

आकाश कोसळत आहे!

Ākāśa kōsaḷata āhē!

MONGOLIAN

Тэнгэр унаж байна!

Tenger unaj baina!

NEPALI

आकाश खस्दै छ!

Ākāśa khasdai cha!

NORWEGIAN

Himmelen faller!

POLISH

Niebo spada!

PORTUGUESE

O céu está caindo!

PUNJABI

ਅਸਮਾਨ ਡਿੱਗ ਰਿਹਾ ਹੈ!

Asamāna ḍiga rihā hai!

ROMANIAN

Cerul cade!

RUSSIAN

Небо падает!

Nebo padayet!

SAMOAN

Ua pa'u le lagi!

SCOTS GAELIC

Tha an speur a 'tuiteam!

SERBIAN

Небо пада!

Nebo pada!

SLOVAK

Obloha padá!

SLOVENIAN

Nebo pada!

SOMALI

Cirka ayaa soo dhacaya!

SPANISH

¡El cielo se está cayendo!

SUNDANESE

Langit ragrag!

SWAHILI

Anga linaanguka!

SWEDISH

Himlen faller!

TAJIK

Осмон фурӯ меравад!

Osmon furū meravad!

TAMIL

வானம் விழுகிறது!

Vāṉam viḻukiṟatu!

TELUGU

ఆకాశం పడిపోతోంది!

Ākāśaṁ paḍipōtōndi!

THAI

ฟ้าถล่ม!

F̂ā t̄hl̀m!

TURKISH

Gökyüzü düşüyor!

TURKMEN

Asman ýykylýar!

UKRAINIAN

Небо падає!

Nebo padaye!

UZBEK

Osmon tushmoqda!

VIETNAMESE

Bầu trời đang sập xuống!

VIETNAMESE

Mae'r awyr yn cwympo!

YIDDISH

דער הימל פאלט!

Der himl falt!

ZULU

Izulu liyawa!

42 Who clogged the toilet?

AFRIKAANS

Wie het die toilet verstop?

ALBANIAN

Kush e bllokoi tualetin?

AMHARIC

ሽንት ቤቱን ማን ዘጋቶታል?

Shiniti bētuni mani zegitotali?

ARABIC

من الذي تسبب في انسداد المرحاض؟

Man aladhi tasabab fi ansidad almirhadi?

ARMENIAN

Ո՞վ է խցանել զուգարանը:

Vov e khts'anel zugarany?

AZERBAIJANI

Tualeti kim bağladı?

BASQUE

Nork itxi zuen komuna?

BELARUSIAN

Хто забіў туалет?

Chto zabiŭ tualiet?

BOSNIAN

Ko je začepio toalet?

BULGARIAN

Кой запуши тоалетната?

Koĭ zapushi toaletnata?

BURMESE

အိမ်သာကိုဘယ်သူကပိတ်ဆို့ခဲ့တာလဲ။

Aainsar ko bhaalsuuk pateshoet hkae tarlell?

CATALAN

Qui va tapar el vàter?

CEBUANO

Kinsa ang nagbabag sa kasilyas?

MANDARIN CHINESE

誰堵了馬桶？

Shuí dǔle mǎtǒng?

CORSICAN

Quale hè chì hà intuppatu u bagnu?

CROATIAN

Tko je začepio WC?

CZECH

Kdo ucpal záchod?

DANISH

Hvem tilstoppede toilettet?

DUTCH

Wie heeft de wc verstopt?

ESPERANTO

Kiu ŝtopis la necesejon?

ESTONIAN

Kes ummistas tualeti?

FILIPINO

Sino ang nagbara sa banyo?

FINNISH

Kuka tukki wc: n?

FRENCH

Qui a bouché les toilettes?

GALICIAN

Quen tapou o retrete?

GEORGIAN

ვინ ჩაკეტა ტუალეტი?

Vin chak'et'a t'ualet'i?

GERMAN

Wer hat die toilette verstopft?

GREEK

Ποιος έκλεισε την τουαλέτα;

Poios ékleise tin toualéta?

HAITIAN CREOLE

Ki moun ki bouche twalèt la?

HAUSA

Wanene ya toshe bandaki?

HAWAIIAN

Na wai i keʻakeʻa i ka lua?

HINDI

शौचालय किसने बंद किया?

Shauchaalay kisane band kiya?

HMONG

Leej twg txhaws qhov quav?

HUNGARIAN

Ki tömte el a vécét?

ICELANDIC

Hver stíflaði salernið?

IGBO

Kedu onye kpochiri ụlọ mposi?

INDONESIAN

Siapa yang menyumbat toilet?

IRISH

Cé a chlog an leithreas?

ITALIAN

Chi ha intasato il wc?

JAPANESE

誰がトイレを詰まらせたのですか？

Dare ga toire o tsumara seta nodesu ka?

JAVANESE

Sapa sing mblok toilet?

KANNADA

ಶೌಚಾಲಯವನ್ನು ಮುಚ್ಚಿಟ್ಟವರು ಯಾರು?

Śaucālayavannu mucciṭṭavaru yāru?

KAZAKH

Дәретхананы кім жауып тастады?

Däretxananı kim jawıp tastadı?

KINYARWANDA

Ninde wafunze umusarani?

KOREAN

누가 화장실을 막았습니까?

Nuga hwajangsil-eul mag-assseubnikka?

KURDISH

Kê tuwalet girtiye?

KYRGYZ

Даараткананы ким жаап койгон?

Daaratkananı kim jaap koygon?

LATVIAN

Kas aizsērēja tualeti?

LITHUANIAN

Kas užkimšo tualetą?

LUXEMBOURGISH

Wie verstoppt d'toilette?

MACEDONIAN

Кој го затнал тоалетот?

Koj go zatnal toaletot?

MALAGASY

Iza no nanentsina ny kabine?

MALAY

Siapa yang menyumbat tandas?

MALTESE

Min sadd it-tojlit?

MAORI

Na wai i aukati i te wharepaku?

MARATHI

शौचालय कोणी अडवले?

Śaucālaya kōṇī aḍavalē?

MONGOLIAN

Ариун цэврийн өрөөг хэн бөглөсөн бэ?

Ariun tsevriin öröög khen böglösön be?

NEPALI

शौचालय कसले बन्द गर्यो?

Śaucālaya kasalē banda garyō?

NORWEGIAN

Hvem tetter toalettet?

POLISH

Kto zatkał toaletę?

PORTUGUESE

Quem entupiu o banheiro?

PUNJABI

ਟਾਇਲਟ ਨੂੰ ਕਿਸ ਨੇ ਬੰਦ ਕੀਤਾ?

Ṭā'ilaṭa nū kisa nē bada kītā?

ROMANIAN

Cine a înfundat toaleta?

RUSSIAN

Кто забил унитаз?

Kto zabil unitaz?

SAMOAN

O ai na punitia le faleuila?

SCOTS GAELIC

Cò clogged an taigh beag?

SERBIAN

Ко је зачепио тоалет?

Ko je začepio toalet?

SLOVAK

Kto upchal toaletu?

SLOVENIAN

Kdo je zamašil stranišče?

SOMALI

Yaa musqusha xiray?

SPANISH

¿Quién obstruyó el inodoro?

SUNDANESE

Saha anu ngahalangan jamban?

SWAHILI

Nani aliyeziba choo?

SWEDISH

Vem täppte till toaletten?

TAJIK

Кӣ ҳоҷатхонаро пӯшидааст?

Kī hoçatxonaro pūşidaast?

TAMIL

கழிப்பறையை அடைத்தது யார்?

Kal̲ippar̲aiyai aṭaittatu yār?

TELUGU

మరుగుదొడ్డిని ఎవరు అడ్డుకున్నారు?

Marugudoḍḍini evaru aḍḍukunnāru?

THAI

ใครอุดตันห้องน้ำ?

Khır xud tạn h̄xngn̂ả?

TURKISH

Tuvaleti kim tıkadı?

TURKMEN

Hajathanany kim ýapdy?

UKRAINIAN

Хто засмітив унітаз?

Khto zasmityv unitaz?

UZBEK

Kim hojatxonani yopib qo'ydi?

VIETNAMESE

Ai làm tắc bồn cầu?

VIETNAMESE

Pwy rwystrodd y toiled?

YIDDISH

ווער האט פארמאכט די טוילעט?

Ver hat farmakht di toylet?

ZULU

Ngubani owayevale ithoyilethi?

43 Not it!

AFRIKAANS

Nie dit nie!

ALBANIAN

Jo atë!

AMHARIC

አይደለም!

Ayidelemi!

ARABIC

!ليس ذلك

Lays dhalika!

ARMENIAN

Ոչ այն!

Voch' ayn!

AZERBAIJANI

O deyil!

BASQUE

Ez!

BELARUSIAN

Не гэта!

Nie heta!

BOSNIAN

Nije to!

BULGARIAN

Не това!

Ne tova!

BURMESE

မဟုတ်ဘူးလား!

Mahotebhuularr!

CATALAN

No, no!

CEBUANO

Dili kini!

MANDARIN CHINESE

不是！

Bùshì!

CORSICAN

Micca micca!

CROATIAN

Nije to!

CZECH

To ne!

DANISH

Ikke det!

DUTCH

Niet het!

ESPERANTO

Ne ĝi!

ESTONIAN

Mitte seda!

FILIPINO

Hindi naman!

FINNISH

Ei se!

FRENCH

Pas!

GALICIAN

Non!

GEORGIAN

არ არის!

Ar aris!

GERMAN

Nicht das!

GREEK

Οχι αυτό!

Ochi aftó!

HAITIAN CREOLE

Se pa li!

HAUSA

Ba shi ba!

HAWAIIAN

ʻAʻole ia!

HINDI

यह नहीं!

Yah nahin!

HMONG

Tsis yog!

HUNGARIAN

Nem az!

ICELANDIC

Ekki það!

IGBO

Ọ bụghị ya!

INDONESIAN

Bukan itu!

IRISH

Nach ea!

ITALIAN

Non è vero!

JAPANESE

そうじゃない！

Sō janai!

JAVANESE

Dudu!

KANNADA

ಅಲ್ಲ!

Alla!

KAZAKH

Олай емес!

Olay emes!

KINYARWANDA

Ntabwo aribyo!

KOREAN

그거 아니야!

Geugeo aniya!

KURDISH

Ne ew!

KYRGYZ

Ал эмес!

Al emes!

LATVIAN

Ne tā!

LITHUANIAN

Ne tai!

LUXEMBOURGISH

Net et!

MACEDONIAN

Не тоа!

Ne toa!

MALAGASY

Tsia!

MALAY

Bukan itu!

MALTESE

Mhux!

MAORI

Kao!

MARATHI

ते नाही!

Tē nāhī!

MONGOLIAN

Тийм биш!

Tiim bish!

NEPALI

हैन!

Haina!

NORWEGIAN

Ikke det!

POLISH

Nie to!

PORTUGUESE

Não Isso!

PUNJABI

ਇਹ ਨਹੀਂ!

Iha nahīṁ!

ROMANIAN

Nu asta!

RUSSIAN

Не то!

Ne to!

SAMOAN

Leai!

SCOTS GAELIC

Nach e!

SERBIAN

Не!

Ne!

SLOVAK

Nie to!

SLOVENIAN

Ne to!

SOMALI

Ma aha!

SPANISH

¡No es eso!

SUNDANESE

Henteu éta!

SWAHILI

Sio hivyo!

SWEDISH

Inte det!

TAJIK

На он!

Na on!

TAMIL

அது இல்லை!

Atu illai!

TELUGU

అది కాదు!

Adi kādu!

THAI

ไม่ใช่มัน!

Mị̀chì mạn!

TURKISH

Bu değil!

TURKMEN

Notok!

UKRAINIAN

Не це!

Ne tse!

UZBEK

Bu emas!

VIETNAMESE

Không phải nó!

VIETNAMESE

Nid ydyw!

YIDDISH

ניט עס!

Nit es!

ZULU

Hhayi bo!

44 Be my guest.

AFRIKAANS

Wees my gas.

ALBANIAN

Bëhu mysafiri im.

AMHARIC

እንግዳዬ ሁን.

Inigidayī huni.

ARABIC

كن ضيفي.

Kun dayfi.

ARMENIAN

Իմ հիւրս եղիր.

Im hiwrs yeghir.

AZERBAIJANI

Qonağım ol.

BASQUE

Izan zaitez nire gonbidatua.

BELARUSIAN

Будзь маім госцем.

Budź maim hosciem.

BOSNIAN

Budi moj gost.

BULGARIAN

Бъди мой гост.

Bŭdi moĭ gost.

BURMESE

ငါ့ဧည့်သည်ဖြစ်ပါစေ။

Ngar e ny sai hpyitparhcay .

CATALAN

Sigues el meu convidat.

CEBUANO

Pag bisita ko.

MANDARIN CHINESE

別客氣。

Bié kèqì.

CORSICAN

Esse u mo invitatu.

CROATIAN

Budi moj gost.

CZECH

Buď mým hostem.

DANISH

Du er velkommen.

DUTCH

Wees mijn gast.

ESPERANTO

Estu mia gasto.

ESTONIAN

Ole lahke.

FILIPINO

Maging bisita kita.

FINNISH

Ole vieraani.

FRENCH

Soit mon invité.

GALICIAN

Sé o meu convidado.

GEORGIAN

იყავი ჩემი სტუმარი.

Iq'avi chemi st'umari.

GERMAN

Sei mein gast.

GREEK

Γίνε καλεσμένος μου.

Gíne kalesménos mou.

HAITIAN CREOLE

Fè envite mwen.

HAUSA

Kasance bako na.

HAWAIIAN

E lilo i malihini iaʻu.

HINDI

मेरे मेहमान हो।

Mere mehamaan ho.

HMONG

Ua kuv tus qhua.

HUNGARIAN

Légy a vendégem.

ICELANDIC

Gjörðu svo vel.

IGBO

Bụrụ onye ọbịa m.

INDONESIAN

Jadilah tamu saya.

IRISH

Bí i mo aoi.

ITALIAN

Essere mio ospite.

JAPANESE

私のゲストになりなさい。

Watashi no gesuto ni nari nasai.

JAVANESE

Dadi tamu ku.

KANNADA

ನನ್ನ ಅತಿಥಿಗಳಾಗಿ.

Nanna atithigaḷāgi.

KAZAKH

Менің қонағым болу.

Meniñ qonağım bolw.

KINYARWANDA

Ba umushyitsi wanjye.

KOREAN

사양하지 마세요.

sayanghaji maseyo.

KURDISH

Bibe mêvanê min.

KYRGYZ

Менин коногум бол.

Menin konogum bol.

LATVIAN

Esi mans viesis.

LITHUANIAN

Būk mano svečias.

LUXEMBOURGISH

Sidd mäi Gaascht.

MACEDONIAN

Биди ми гостин.

Bidi mi gostin.

MALAGASY

Tongava vahiniko.

MALAY

Jadilah tetamu saya.

MALTESE

Kun il-mistieden tiegħi.

MAORI

Hei manuhiri ahau.

MARATHI

माझे पाहुणे व्हा.

Mājhē pāhuṇē vhā.

MONGOLIAN

Миний зочин болоорой.

Minii zochin bolooroi.

NEPALI

मेरो पाहुना बन्नुहोस्।

Mērō pāhunā bannuhōs.

NORWEGIAN

Vær min gjest.

POLISH

Bądź moim gościem.

PORTUGUESE

Seja meu convidado.

PUNJABI

ਮੇਰੇ ਮਹਿਮਾਨ ਬਣੋ.

Mērē mahimāna baṇō.

ROMANIAN

Fii invitatul meu.

RUSSIAN

Будь моим гостем.

Bud' moim gostem.

SAMOAN

Avea ma a'u malo

SCOTS GAELIC

Bi nad aoigh agam.

SERBIAN

Буди мој гост.

Budi moj gost.

SLOVAK

Buď mojím hosťom.

SLOVENIAN

Bodi moj gost.

SOMALI

Marti ii noqo.

SPANISH

Sé mi invitado.

SUNDANESE

Janten tamu abdi.

SWAHILI

Kuwa mgeni wangu.

SWEDISH

Varsågod.

TAJIK

Меҳмони ман бошед.

Mehmoni man boşed.

TAMIL

எனது விருந்தாளியாக இரு.

Eṉatu viruntāḷiyāka iru.

TELUGU

నా అతిథిగా ఉండండి.

Nā atithigā uṇḍaṇḍi.

THAI

ด้วยความยินดี.

D̂wy khwām yindī.

TURKISH

Misafirim ol.

TURKMEN

Myhmanym bol.

UKRAINIAN

Будь моїм гостем.

Bud' moyim hostem.

UZBEK

Mening mehmonim bo'ling.

VIETNAMESE

Cứ tự nhiên.

VIETNAMESE

Byddwch yn westai i mi.

YIDDISH

זיי מיין גאַסט.

Zey meyn gast.

ZULU

Yiba isivakashi sami.

45 I do not like green eggs and ham.

AFRIKAANS

Ek hou nie van groen eiers en ham nie.

ALBANIAN

Nuk më pëlqejnë vezët jeshile dhe proshuta.

AMHARIC

አረንጓዴ እንቁላሎችን እና ካም አልወድም።

Arenigwadē inik'ulalochini ina kami āliwedimi.

ARABIC

.انا لا احب البيض الاخضر و الخنزير

Ana la ahib albayd alakhdir w alkhinziru.

ARMENIAN

Ես չեմ սիրում կանաչ ձու և խոզապուխտ:

Yes ch'em sirum kanach' dzu yev khozapukht.

AZERBAIJANI

Yaşıl yumurta və vetçina sevmirəm.

BASQUE

Ez ditut arrautza eta urdaiazpiko berdeak gustatzen.

BELARUSIAN

Я не люблю зялёныя яйкі і вяндліну.

Ja nie liubliu zialionyja jajki i viandlinu.

BOSNIAN

Ne volim zelena jaja i šunku.

BULGARIAN

Не обичам зелени яйца и шунка.

Ne obicham zeleni yaĭtsa i shunka.

BURMESE

ကြက်ဥအစိမ်းနဲ့ဝက်ပေါင်ခြောက်မကြိုက်ဘူး။

Kyaatu aahcaim nae waat paung hkyawwat makyaitebhuu.

CATALAN

No m'agraden els ous verds i el pernil.

CEBUANO

Dili ko gusto ang berde nga itlog ug ham.

MANDARIN CHINESE

我不喜歡綠雞蛋和火腿。

Wǒ bù xǐhuān lǜ jīdàn hé huǒtuǐ.

CORSICAN

Ùn mi piacenu micca l'ova verde è u prisuttu.

CROATIAN

Ne volim zelena jaja i šunku.

CZECH

Nemám rád zelená vejce a šunku.

DANISH

Jeg kan ikke lide grønne æg og skinke.

DUTCH

Ik hou niet van groene eieren en ham.

ESPERANTO

Mi ne ŝatas verdajn ovojn kaj ŝinkon.

ESTONIAN

Mulle ei meeldi rohelised munad ja sink.

FILIPINO

Ayoko ng mga berdeng itlog at ham.

FINNISH

En pidä vihreistä munista ja kinkusta.

FRENCH

Je n'aime pas les œufs verts et le jambon.

GALICIAN

Non me gustan os ovos e o xamón verdes.

GEORGIAN

მე არ მომწონს მწვანე კვერცხი და ლორი.

Me ar momts'ons mts'vane k'vertskhi da lori.

GERMAN

Ich mag keine grünen eier und schinken.

GREEK

Δεν μου αρέσουν τα πράσινα αυγά και το ζαμπόν.

Den mou arésoun ta prásina avgá kai to zampón.

HAITIAN CREOLE

Mwen pa renmen ze vèt ak janbon.

HAUSA

Ba na son kore kwai da naman alade.

HAWAIIAN

ʻAʻole wau makemake i nā hua ʻōmaʻomaʻo a me ka ham.

HINDI

मुझे हरे अंडे और हैम पसंद नहीं हैं।

Mujhe hare ande aur haim pasand nahin hain.

HMONG

Kuv tsis nyiam qe ntsuab thiab nqaij npua.

HUNGARIAN

Nem szeretem a zöld tojást és a sonkát.

ICELANDIC

Mér líkar ekki við græn egg og skinku.

IGBO

Anaghị m amasị àkwá akwụkwọ ndụ akwụkwọ ndụ na ham.

INDONESIAN

Saya tidak suka telur hijau dan ham.

IRISH

Ní maith liom uibheacha glasa agus liamhás.

ITALIAN

Non mi piacciono le uova verdi e il prosciutto.

JAPANESE

私は緑の卵とハムが好きではありません。

Watashi wa midori no tamago to hamu ga sukide wa arimasen.

JAVANESE

Aku ora seneng endhog ijo lan ham.

KANNADA

ನನಗೆ ಹಸಿರು ಮೊಟ್ಟೆ ಮತ್ತು ಹ್ಯಾಮ್ ಇಷ್ಟವಿಲ್ಲ.

Nanage hasiru moṭṭe mattu hyām iṣṭavilla.

KAZAKH

Маған жасыл жұмыртқа мен ветчина ұнамайды.

Mağan jasıl jumırtqa men vetçïna unamaydı.

KINYARWANDA

Ntabwo nkunda amagi y'icyatsi na ham.

KOREAN

나는 녹색 계란과 햄을 좋아하지 않습니다.

Naneun nogsaeg gyelangwa haem-eul joh-ahaji anhseubnida.

KURDISH

Ez ji hêkên kesk û zozanan hez nakim.

KYRGYZ

Мен жашыл жумуртканы жана ветчинаны жактырбайм.

Men jaşıl jumurtkanı jana vetçinanı jaktırbaym.

LATVIAN

Man nepatīk zaļās olas un šķiņķis.

LITHUANIAN

Nemėgstu žalių kiaušinių ir kumpio.

LUXEMBOURGISH

Ech hu keng gréng eeër a schinken gär.

MACEDONIAN

Не сакам зелени јајца и шунка.

Ne sakam zeleni jajca i šunka.

MALAGASY

Tsy tiako atody maintso sy ham.

MALAY

Saya tidak suka telur hijau dan ham.

MALTESE

Ma nħobbx bajd aħdar u perżut.

MAORI

Kaore au e pai ki nga hua kaakaariki me te ham.

MARATHI

मला हिरवी अंडी आणि हॅम आवडत नाही.

Malā hiravī aṇḍī āṇi hĕma āvaḍata nāhī.

MONGOLIAN

Би ногоон өндөг, хиаманд дургүй.

Bi nogoon öndög, khiamand durgüi.

NEPALI

मलाई हरियो अण्डा र हैम मन पर्दैन।

Malā'ī hariyō aṇḍā ra haima mana pardaina.

NORWEGIAN

Jeg liker ikke grønne egg og skinke.

POLISH

Nie lubię zielonych jajek i szynki.

PORTUGUESE

Não gosto de ovos verdes e presunto.

PUNJABI

ਮੈਨੂੰ ਹਰੇ ਅੰਡੇ ਅਤੇ ਹੈਮ ਪਸੰਦ ਨਹੀਂ ਹਨ.

Mainū harē aḍē atē haima pasada nahīṁ hana.

ROMANIAN

Nu-mi plac ouăle verzi și șunca.

RUSSIAN

Не люблю зеленые яйца и ветчину.

Ne lyublyu zelenyye yaytsa i vetchinu.

SAMOAN

Ou te le fiafia i fuala'au lanumeamata ma ham.

SCOTS GAELIC

Cha toil leam uighean uaine agus hama.

SERBIAN

Не волим зелена јаја и шунку.

Ne volim zelena jaja i šunku.

SLOVAK

Nemám rád zelené vajíčka a šunku.

SLOVENIAN

Ne maram zelenih jajc in šunke.

SOMALI

Ma jecli ukunta cagaaran iyo ham.

SPANISH

No me gustan los huevos verdes con jamón.

SUNDANESE

Abdi henteu resep endog héjo sareng ham.

SWAHILI

Sipendi mayai ya kijani na ham.

SWEDISH

Jag gillar inte gröna ägg och skinka.

TAJIK

Ман тухми сабз ва ветчинаро дӯст намедорам.

Man tuxmi sabz va vetcinaro dūst namedoram.

TAMIL

எனக்கு பச்சை முட்டைகள் மற்றும் ஹாம் பிடிக்காது.

Eṉakku paccai muṭṭaikaḷ maṟṟum hām piṭikkātu.

TELUGU

నాకు పచ్చ గుడ్లు మరియు హామ్ ఇష్టం లేదు.

Nāku pacci guḍlu mariyu hām iṣṭaṁ lēdu.

THAI

ฉันไม่ชอบไข่เขียวและแฮม

C̄hạn mị̀ chxb k̄hị̀ k̄heīyw læa ḥæm

TURKISH

Yeşil yumurta ve jambon sevmiyorum.

TURKMEN

Men ýaşyl ýumurtga we hamam halamok.

UKRAINIAN

Я не люблю зелені яйця та шинку.
Ya ne lyublyu zeleni yaytsya ta shynku.

UZBEK

Menga yashil tuxum va jambon yoqmaydi.

VIETNAMESE

Tôi không thích những quả trứng xanh và thịt hun khói.

VIETNAMESE

Nid wyf yn hoffi wyau gwyrdd a ham.

YIDDISH

איך טאָן ניט ווי גרין עגגס און שינקע.

Ikh ton nit vi grin eggs aun shinke.

ZULU

Angiwathandi amaqanda aluhlaza neham.

46 You cheated.

AFRIKAANS

Jy het bedrieg.

ALBANIAN

Ti mashtrove.

AMHARIC

አጭበርብረሃል።

Ach'iberibirehali.

ARABIC

انت غشيت.

Ant ghshit.

ARMENIAN

Խաբեցիր։

Khabets'ir.

AZERBAIJANI

Aldatdın.

BASQUE

Iruzur egin zenuen.

BELARUSIAN

Вы падманулі.

Vy padmanuli.

BOSNIAN

Varao si.

BULGARIAN

Измами.

Izmami.

BURMESE

မင်းလှည့်စားခဲ့တယ်။

Mainn lha ny hcarr hkaetaal.

CATALAN

Has enganyat.

CEBUANO

Nanikas ka.

MANDARIN CHINESE

你作弊。

Nǐ zuòbì.

CORSICAN

Avete ingannatu.

CROATIAN

Varao si.

CZECH

Podváděl jsi.

DANISH

Du snød.

DUTCH

Je speelde vals.

ESPERANTO

Vi trompis.

ESTONIAN

Sa petsid.

FILIPINO

Nandaya ka.

FINNISH

Petit.

FRENCH

Tu as triché.

GALICIAN

Enganaches.

GEORGIAN

შენ მოიტყუე.

Shen moit'q'ue.

GERMAN

Du hast betrogen.

GREEK

Εκλεψες.

Eklepses.

HAITIAN CREOLE

Ou tronpe.

HAUSA

Kun yi yaudara.

HAWAIIAN

Ua hoʻopunipuni ʻoe.

HINDI

आपने धोखा दिया।

Aapane dhokha diya.

HMONG

Koj dag.

HUNGARIAN

Csaltál.

ICELANDIC

Þú svindlaðir.

IGBO

Ị ghọgburu.

INDONESIAN

Kamu curang.

IRISH

Cheated tú.

ITALIAN

Hai barato.

JAPANESE

あなたはだまされました。

Anata wa damasa remashita.

JAVANESE

Sampeyan ngapusi.

KANNADA

ನೀನು ಮೋಸ ಮಾಡಿದೆ.

Nīnu mōsa māḍide.

KAZAKH

Сіз алдадыңыз.

Siz aldadıñız.

KINYARWANDA

Warashutse.

KOREAN

당신은 속였다.

Dangsin-eun sog-yeossda.

KURDISH

Te xapand.

KYRGYZ

Сен алдадын.

Sen aldadın.

LATVIAN

Jūs krāpāties.

LITHUANIAN

Tu sukčiavai.

LUXEMBOURGISH

Dir hutt gefuddelt.

MACEDONIAN

Вие измамивте.

Vie izmamivte.

MALAGASY

Namitaka ianao.

MALAY

Anda menipu.

MALTESE

Int misruqin.

MAORI

I tinihanga koe.

MARATHI

तू फसवलेस.

Tū phasavalēsa.

MONGOLIAN

Та хуурсан.

Ta khuursan.

NEPALI

तिमीले धोका दियौ।

Timīlē dhōkā diyau.

NORWEGIAN

Du jukset.

POLISH

Oszukiwałeś.

PORTUGUESE

Você trapaceou.

PUNJABI

ਤੁਸੀਂ ਧੋਖਾ ਦਿੱਤਾ.

Tusīṁ dhōkhā ditā.

ROMANIAN

Ai trisat.

RUSSIAN

Ты смухлевал.

Ty smukhleval.

SAMOAN

Ua e olegia.

SCOTS GAELIC

Rinn thu meallta.

SERBIAN

Си варао.
Si varao.

SLOVAK

Podvádzal si.

SLOVENIAN

Varal si.

SOMALI

Waad khiyaamaysay.

SPANISH

Hiciste trampa.

SUNDANESE

Anjeun nipu.

SWAHILI

Umedanganya.

SWEDISH

Du fuskade.

TAJIK

Шумо фиреб кардед.

Şumo fireв karded.

TAMIL

நீங்கள் ஏமாற்றினீர்கள்.

Nīṅkaḷ ēmāṟṟiṉīrkaḷ.

TELUGU

మీరు మోసగించారు.

Mīru mōsagin̄cāru.

THAI

คุณหลอกลวง.

Khuṇ h̄lxklwng.

TURKISH

Aldattın.

TURKMEN

Aldadyň.

UKRAINIAN

Ви обдурили.

Vy obduryly.

UZBEK

Siz aldadingiz.

VIETNAMESE

Bạn lừa.

VIETNAMESE

Fe wnaethoch chi dwyllo.

YIDDISH

איר טשיטיד.

Ir tshitid.

ZULU

Ukhohlisile.

47 Nice pumpkin head.

AFRIKAANS

Dit is 'n lekker pampoenkop.

ALBANIAN

Kjo është një kokë e bukur kungulli.

AMHARIC

ያ ጥሩ ዱባ ራስ ነው።

Ya t'iru duba rasi newi.

ARABIC

هذا رأس قرع جميل.

Hadha ras qare jamil.

ARMENIAN

Դա գեղեցիկ դդումի գլուխ է:

Da geghets'ik ddumi glukh e.

AZERBAIJANI

Bu gözəl balqabaq başıdır.

BASQUE

Hori kalabaza buru polita da.

BELARUSIAN

Гэта прыгожая гарбузовая галоўка.

Heta pryhožaja harbuzovaja haloŭka.

BOSNIAN

To je lijepa glava bundeve.

BULGARIAN

Това е хубава тиквена глава.

Tova e khubava tikvena glava.

BURMESE

အဲဒါကကောင်းတဲ့ရွှေဖရုံသီးခေါင်း။

Aelldark kaunggtae shway hparonesee hkaungg.

CATALAN

És un bon cap de carbassa.

CEBUANO

Maayo kana nga ulo sa kalabasa.

MANDARIN CHINESE

那是一個漂亮的南瓜頭。

Nà shì yīgè piàoliang de nánguā tóu.

CORSICAN

Hè una bella testa di zucca.

CROATIAN

To je lijepa glava bundeve.

CZECH

To je pěkná dýňová hlava.

DANISH

Det er et dejligt græskarhoved.

DUTCH

Dat is een mooie pompoenkop.

ESPERANTO

Tio estas bela kukurba kapo.

ESTONIAN

See on kena kõrvitsapea.

FILIPINO

Iyon ay isang magandang ulo ng kalabasa.

FINNISH

Se on hieno kurpitsan pää.

FRENCH

C'est une belle tête de citrouille.

GALICIAN

Esta é unha boa cabeza de cabaza.

GEORGIAN

ეს არის ლამაზი გოგრის თავი.

Es aris lamazi gogris tavi.

GERMAN

Das ist ein schöner kürbiskopf.

GREEK

Αυτό είναι ένα ωραίο κεφάλι κολοκύθας.

Aftó eínai éna oraío kefáli kolokýthas.

HAITIAN CREOLE

Sa se yon bèl tèt joumou.

HAUSA

Wannan shine kabewa mai kyau.

HAWAIIAN

ʻO ia kahi poʻo ʻumeke maikaʻi kēlā.

HINDI

यह एक अच्छा कद्दू का सिर है।

Yah ek achchha kaddoo ka sir hai.

HMONG

Qhov ntawd yog lub taub taub taub zoo.

HUNGARIAN

Ez egy szép tökfej.

ICELANDIC

Þetta er gott graskerhaus.

IGBO

Nke ahụ bụ isi ugu mara mma.

INDONESIAN

Itu adalah kepala labu yang bagus.

IRISH

Is ceann deas pumpkin é sin.

ITALIAN

È una bella testa di zucca.

JAPANESE

それは素敵なカボチャの頭です。

Sore wa sutekina kabocha no atamadesu.

JAVANESE

Iki sirah waluh sing apik.

KANNADA

ಅದು ಒಳ್ಳೆಯ ಕುಂಬಳಕಾಯಿ ತಲೆ.

Adu oḷḷeya kumbaḷakāyi tale.

KAZAKH

Бұл асқабақтың жақсы басы.

Bul asqabaqtıñ jaqsı bası.

KINYARWANDA

Numutwe mwiza wigihaza.

KOREAN

멋진 호박 머리입니다.

Meosjin hobag meoliibnida.

KURDISH

Ew serê kûçikek xweş e.

KYRGYZ

Бул жакшы ашкабактын башы.

Bul jakşı aşkabaktın başı.

LATVIAN

Tā ir jauka ķirbja galva.

LITHUANIAN

Tai graži moliūgo galva.

LUXEMBOURGISH

Dat as e flotte kürbiskop.

MACEDONIAN

Тоа е убава глава од тиква.

Toa e ubava glava od tikva.

MALAGASY

Loha voatavo tsara izany.

MALAY

Itu adalah kepala labu yang bagus.

MALTESE

Dik hija ras sabiħa tal-qara ħamra.

MAORI

He upoko paukena pai tera.

MARATHI

ते एक छान भोपळ्याचे डोके आहे.

Tē ēka chāna bhōpaḷyācē ḍōkē āhē.

MONGOLIAN

Энэ бол сайхан хулууны толгой юм.

Ene bol saikhan khuluuny tolgoi yum.

NEPALI

त्यो एक राम्रो कद्दू टाउको हो।

Tyō ēka rāmrō kaddū ṭā'ukō hō.

NORWEGIAN

Det er et fint gresskarhode.

POLISH

To fajna dyniowa głowa.

PORTUGUESE

Essa é uma bela cabeça de abóbora.

PUNJABI

ਇਹ ਇੱਕ ਵਧੀਆ ਪੇਠਾ ਸਿਰ ਹੈ.

Iha ika vadhī'ā pēṭhā sira hai.

ROMANIAN

Acesta este un cap frumos de dovleac.

RUSSIAN

Это красивая тыквенная голова.

Eto krasivaya tykvennaya golova.

SAMOAN

Manaia lelei le ulu maukeni.

SCOTS GAELIC

Is e sin ceann pumpkin snog.

SERBIAN

То је лепа глава бундеве.

To je lepa glava bundeve.

SLOVAK

To je pekná tekvicová hlava.

SLOVENIAN

To je lepa bučna glava.

SOMALI

Taasi waa madaxa bocorka fiican.

SPANISH

Esa es una linda cabeza de calabaza.

SUNDANESE

Éta sirah waluh anu saé.

SWAHILI

Hiyo ni kichwa kizuri cha malenge.

SWEDISH

Det är ett fint pumpahuvud.

TAJIK

Ин сари кадуи хуб аст.

In sari kadui xuв ast.

TAMIL

அது ஒரு நல்ல பூசணி தலை.

Atu oru nalla pūcaṇi talai.

TELUGU

అది మంచి గుమ్మడికాయ తల.

Adi mañci gum'maḍikāya tala.

THAI

นั่นคือหัวฟักทองที่ดี

Nạ̀n khụ̄x h̄ạw fạkthxng thī̀ dī

TURKISH

Bu güzel bir balkabağı kafası.

TURKMEN

Gowy kädi kellesi.

UKRAINIAN

Це гарна гарбузова голова.

Tse harna harbuzova holova.

UZBEK

Bu chiroyli qovoq boshi.

VIETNAMESE

Đó là một cái đầu bí ngô đẹp.

VIETNAMESE

Mae hwnnw'n ben pwmpen braf.

YIDDISH

אַז איז אַ פײַן קירבעס קאָפּ.

Az iz a fayn kirbes kop.

ZULU

Leli ikhanda elihle lamathanga.

48 Step on it!

AFRIKAANS

Ry vinniger!

ALBANIAN

Udhëtoni më shpejt!

AMHARIC

በፍጥነት ይንዱ!

Befit'ineti yinidu!

ARABIC

محرك أسرع!

Muharik 'asraeu!

ARMENIAN

Քշեք ավելի արագ:

K'shek' aveli arag!

AZERBAIJANI

Daha sürətli sür!

BASQUE

Gidatu azkarrago!

BELARUSIAN

Едзьце хутчэй!

Jedźcie chutčej!

BOSNIAN

Vozite brže!

BULGARIAN

Шофирайте по -бързо!

Shofiraĭte po -bŭrzo!

BURMESE

မြန်မြန်မောင်း!

Myanmyan maungg!

CATALAN

Condueix més ràpid.

CEBUANO

Paspas ang pagmaneho!

MANDARIN CHINESE

開得更快！

Kāi dé gèng kuài!

CORSICAN

Conduce più veloce!

CROATIAN

Vozite brže!

CZECH

Jezděte rychleji!

DANISH

Kør hurtigere!

DUTCH

Rijd sneller!

ESPERANTO

Veturu pli rapide!

ESTONIAN

Sõida kiiremini!

FILIPINO

Mas mabilis na magmaneho!

FINNISH

Aja nopeammin!

FRENCH

Conduit plus vite!

GALICIAN

Conduce máis rápido.

GEORGIAN

იმოძრავეთ უფრო სწრაფად!

Imodzravet upro sts'rapad!

GERMAN

Fahr schneller!

GREEK

Οδηγήστε πιο γρήγορα!

Odigíste pio grígora!

HAITIAN CREOLE

Kondwi pi vit!

HAUSA

Fitar da sauri!

HAWAIIAN

'Oi aku ka wikiwiki

HINDI

तेजी से ड्राइव करें!

Tejee se draiv karen!

HMONG

Tsav nrawm dua!

HUNGARIAN

Haladjon gyorsabban!

ICELANDIC

Ekið hraðar!

IGBO

Ụgbọala ngwa ngwa!

INDONESIAN

Berkendara lebih cepat!

IRISH

Tiomáint níos gasta!

ITALIAN

Guida più veloce!

JAPANESE

より速く運転してください！

Yori hayaku unten shite kudasai!

JAVANESE

Drive luwih cepet!

KANNADA

ವೇಗವಾಗಿ ಚಾಲನೆ ಮಾಡಿ!

Vēgavāgi cālane māḍi!

KAZAKH

Тезірек айда!

Tezirek ayda!

KINYARWANDA

Twara vuba!

KOREAN

더 빠르게 운전하세요!

Deo ppaleuge unjeonhaseyo!

KURDISH

Zûtir ajot!

KYRGYZ

Тезирээк айдагыла!

Tezireek aydagıla!

LATVIAN

Brauc ātrāk!

LITHUANIAN

Važiuokite greičiau!

LUXEMBOURGISH

Fuert méi séier!

MACEDONIAN

Возете побрзо!

Vozete pobrzo!

MALAGASY

Mandeha haingana kokoa!

MALAY

Pandu lebih laju!

MALTESE

Ssuq aktar malajr!

MAORI

Kia tere te taraiwa!

MARATHI

वेगाने गाडी चालवा!

Vēgānē gāḍī cālavā!

MONGOLIAN

Илүү хурдан жолоодоорой!

Ilüü khurdan joloodooroi!

NEPALI

छिटो चलाउनुहोस्!

Chiṭō calā'unuhōs!

NORWEGIAN

Kjør fortere!

POLISH

Jedź szybciej!

PORTUGUESE

Dirija mais rápido!

PUNJABI

ਤੇਜ਼ ਗੱਡੀ ਚਲਾਓ!

Tēza gaḍī calā'ō!

ROMANIAN

Conduceți mai repede!

RUSSIAN

Езжай быстрее!

Yezzhay bystreye!

SAMOAN

Ave vave atu!

SCOTS GAELIC

Siubhail nas luaithe!

SERBIAN

Возите брже!

Vozite brže!

SLOVAK

Jazdite rýchlejšie!

SLOVENIAN

Vozite hitreje!

SOMALI

Si dhaqso leh u kaxee!

SPANISH

¡Conduce más rápido!

SUNDANESE

Ngajalankeun langkung gancang!

SWAHILI

Endesha kwa kasi!

SWEDISH

Kör snabbare!

TAJIK

Тезтар ронед!

Teztar roned!

TAMIL

வேகமாக ஓட்டு!

Vēkamāka ōṭṭu!

TELUGU

వేగంగా నడపండి!

Vēgaṅgā naḍapaṇḍi!

THAI

ขับเร็วขึ้น!

Khạb rĕw k̄hụ̂n!

TURKISH

Daha hızlı sür!

TURKMEN

Çalt sürüň!

UKRAINIAN

Їдьте швидше!

Yid'te shvydshe!

UZBEK

Tezroq haydang!

VIETNAMESE

Lái xe nhanh hơn!

VIETNAMESE

Gyrrwch yn gyflymach!

YIDDISH

פאָר פאַסטער!

For faster!

ZULU

Shayela ngokushesha!

49 I'm getting nothing for Christmas.

AFRIKAANS

Ek kry niks vir Kersfees nie.

ALBANIAN

Nuk marr asgjë për Krishtlindje.

AMHARIC

ለገና ምንም አላገኝሁም።

Legena minimi ālagenyehumi.

ARABIC

أنا لا أحصل على شيء في عيد الميلاد.

'Ana la 'ahsul ealaa shay' fi eid almilad.

ARMENIAN

Ամանորին ոչինչ չեմ ստանում:

Amanorin voch'inch' ch'em stanum:

AZERBAIJANI

Miladdan heç nə almıram.

BASQUE

Gabonetarako ez dut ezer lortzen.

BELARUSIAN

Я нічога не атрымліваю на Каляды.

Ja ničoha nie atrymlivaju na Kaliady.

BOSNIAN

Ne dobivam ništa za Božić.

BULGARIAN

Не получавам нищо за Коледа.

Ne poluchavam nishto za Koleda.

BURMESE

ခရစ်စမတ်အတွက်ငါဘာမှမရလိုက်ဘူး။

Hkaraithcamaat aatwat ngar bharmham r lite bhuu .

CATALAN

No rebo res per Nadal.

CEBUANO

Wala koy nakuha alang sa Pasko.

MANDARIN CHINESE

聖誕節我什麼也得不到。

Shèngdàn jié wǒ shénme yě dé bù dào.

CORSICAN

Ùn aghju nunda per Natale.

CROATIAN

Za Božić ne dobivam ništa.

CZECH

Na Vánoce nedostanu nic.

DANISH

Jeg får ikke noget til jul.

DUTCH

Ik krijg niets voor Kerstmis.

ESPERANTO

Mi ricevas nenion por Kristnasko.

ESTONIAN

Ma ei saa jõuludeks midagi.

FILIPINO

Wala akong nakukuha para sa Pasko.

FINNISH

En saa jouluksi mitään.

FRENCH

Je ne reçois rien pour Noël.

GALICIAN

Non recibo nada por Nadal.

GEORGIAN

საშობაოდ არაფერს ვიღებ.

Sashobaod arapers vigheb.

GERMAN

Ich bekomme nichts zu Weihnachten.

GREEK

Δεν παίρνω τίποτα για τα Χριστούγεννα.

Den paírno típota gia ta Christoúgenna.

HAITIAN CREOLE

Mwen pap resevwa anyen pou Nwèl la.

HAUSA

Ba na samun komai don Kirsimeti.

HAWAIIAN

ʻAʻole wau e loaʻa i kekahi mea no ka Kalikimaka.

HINDI

मुझे क्रिसमस के लिए कुछ नहीं मिल रहा है।

Mujhe krisamas ke lie kuchh nahin mil raha hai.

HMONG

Kuv tsis tau txais dab tsi rau Christmas.

HUNGARIAN

Karácsonyra nem kapok semmit.

ICELANDIC

Ég fæ ekkert fyrir jólin.

IGBO

Enweghị m ihe ọ bụla maka ekeresimesi.

INDONESIAN

Saya tidak mendapatkan apa-apa untuk Natal.

IRISH

Níl aon rud á fháil agam don Nollaig.

ITALIAN

Non ricevo niente per Natale.

JAPANESE

クリスマスには何も得られません。

Kurisumasuni wa nani mo e raremasen.

JAVANESE

Aku ora entuk apa-apa kanggo Natal.

KANNADA

ನಾನು ಕ್ರಿಸ್‌ಮಸ್‌ಗೆ ಏನನ್ನೂ ಪಡೆಯುತ್ತಿಲ್ಲ.

Nānu krismasge ēnannū paḍeyuttilla.

KAZAKH

Мен Рождествоға ештеңе алмаймын.

Men Rojdestvoğa eşteñe almaymın.

KINYARWANDA

Ntacyo mbona kuri Noheri.

KOREAN

나는 크리스마스에 아무것도 얻지 못한다.

Naneun keuliseumaseue amugeosdo eodji moshanda.

KURDISH

Ez ji bo Sersalê tiştek nastînim.

KYRGYZ

Мен Рождество үчүн эч нерсе албайм.

Men Rojdestvo üçün eç nerse albaym.

LATVIAN

Ziemassvētkos es neko nesaņemu.

LITHUANIAN

Kalėdoms nieko negaunu.

LUXEMBOURGISH

Ech kréien näischt fir Chrëschtdag.

MACEDONIAN

Не добивам ништо за Божиќ.

Ne dobivam ništo za Božiḱ.

MALAGASY

Tsy mahazo na inona na inona aho amin'ny Noely.

MALAY

Saya tidak mendapat apa-apa untuk Krismas.

MALTESE

Ma nieħu xejn għall-Milied.

MAORI

Kei te whiwhi au i tetahi mea mo te Kirihimete.

MARATHI

मला नाताळसाठी काहीच मिळत नाही.

Malā nātāḷasāṭhī kāhīca miḷata nāhī.

MONGOLIAN

Зул сарын баяраар би юу ч авдаггүй.

Zul saryn bayaraar bi yuu ch avdaggüi.

NEPALI

म क्रिसमसको लागी केहि पाउँदिन।

Ma krisamasakō lāgī kēhi pā'um̐dina.

NORWEGIAN

Jeg får ingenting til jul.

POLISH

Na Boże Narodzenie nic nie dostanę.

PORTUGUESE

Não vou ganhar nada no Natal.

PUNJABI

ਮੈਨੂੰ ਕ੍ਰਿਸਮਿਸ ਲਈ ਕੁਝ ਨਹੀਂ ਮਿਲ ਰਿਹਾ.

Mainū krisamisa la'ī kujha nahīṁ mila rihā.

ROMANIAN

Nu primesc nimic de Crăciun.

RUSSIAN

Я ничего не получаю на Рождество.

Ya nichego ne poluchayu na Rozhdestvo.

SAMOAN

E leai se mea ou te mauaina mo le Kerisimasi.

SCOTS GAELIC

Chan eil mi a 'faighinn dad airson na Nollaige.

SERBIAN

Не добијам ништа за Божић.

Ne dobijam ništa za Božić.

SLOVAK

Na Vianoce nedostanem nič.

SLOVENIAN

Za božič ne dobim nič.

SOMALI

Waxba ma helayo Kirismaska.

SPANISH

No voy a recibir nada por Navidad.

SUNDANESE

Kuring meunang nanaon pikeun Natal.

SWAHILI

Sipati chochote kwa Krismasi.

SWEDISH

Jag får ingenting till jul.

TAJIK

Ман барои Мавлуди Исо чизе намегирам.

Man вaroi Mavludi Iso cize namegiram.

TAMIL

நான் கிறிஸ்துமஸுக்கு எதுவும் பெறவில்லை.

Nān ki<u>r</u>istumasukku etuvum pe<u>r</u>avillai.

TELUGU

నేను క్రిస్మస్ కోసం ఏమీ పొందలేను.

Nēnu krismas kōsaṁ ēmī pondalēnu.

THAI

ฉันไม่ได้อะไรเลยสำหรับคริสต์มาส

C̄hạn mị̀ dị̂ xarị ley s̄ảh̄rạb khris̄t̒mās̄

TURKISH

Noel için hiçbir şey almıyorum.

TURKMEN

Ro Christmasdestwo üçin hiç zat alamok.

UKRAINIAN

Я на Різдво нічого не отримую.

Ya na Rizdvo nichoho ne otrymuyu.

UZBEK

Men Rojdestvo uchun hech narsa olmayapman.

VIETNAMESE

Tôi không nhận được gì cho Giáng sinh.

VIETNAMESE

Dwi ddim yn cael dim ar gyfer y Nadolig.

YIDDISH

איך באַקומען גאָרנישט פֿאַר ניטל.

Ikh bakumen gornisht far nitl.

ZULU

Angitholi lutho ngoKhisimusi.

50 Four score and seven years ago . . .

AFRIKAANS

Sewe en veertig jaar gelede . . .

ALBANIAN

Dyzet e shtatë vjet më parë . . .

AMHARIC

ከአርባ ሰባት ዓመታት በፊት።

Ke'āriba sebati 'ametati befīti . . .

ARABIC

قبل سبعة وأربعين عاما.

Qabl sabeat wa'arbaein eaman . . .

ARMENIAN

Քառասուն յոթ տարի առաջ:

K'arrasun yot' tari arraj . . .

AZERBAIJANI

Qırx yeddi il əvvəl . . .

BASQUE

Duela berrogeita zazpi urte . . .

BELARUSIAN

Сорак сем гадоў таму . . .

Sorak siem hadoŭ tamu . . .

BOSNIAN

Prije četrdeset sedam godina . . .

BULGARIAN

Преди четиридесет и седем години . . .

Predi chetirideset i sedem godini . . .

BURMESE

လွန်ခဲ့သောလေးဆယ့်ခုနစ်နှစ်က

Lwanhkaesaw layy s y hkunaitnhaitk . . .

CATALAN

Fa quaranta-set anys . . .

CEBUANO

Kap-atan ug pito ka tuig ang milabay . . .

MANDARIN CHINESE

四十七年前。

Sìshíqī nián qián . . .

CORSICAN

Quarantina di-sette anni fà . . .

CROATIAN

Prije četrdeset sedam godina . . .

CZECH

Před čtyřiceti sedmi lety . . .

DANISH

For fyrre-syv år siden . . .

DUTCH

Zevenenveertig jaar geleden . . .

ESPERANTO

Antaŭ kvardek sep jaroj . . .

ESTONIAN

Nelikümmend seitse aastat tagasi . . .

FILIPINO

Apatnapu't pitong taon na ang nakalilipas . . .

FINNISH

Neljäkymmentäseitsemän vuotta sitten . . .

FRENCH

Il y a quarante-sept ans . . .

GALICIAN

Hai corenta e sete anos . . .

GEORGIAN

ორმოცდაშვიდი წლის წინ . . .

Ormotsdashvidi ts'lis ts'in . . .

GERMAN

Vor siebenundvierzig jahre . . .

GREEK

Σαράντα επτά χρόνια πριν.

Saránta eptá chrónia prin . . .

HAITIAN CREOLE

Karant-sèt ane de sa . . .

HAUSA

Shekaru arba'in da bakwai da suka wuce . . .

HAWAIIAN

Kanaha-kumamāhiku mau makahiki i hala . . .

HINDI

सैंतालीस साल पहले।

Saintaalees saal pahale . . .

HMONG

Plaub caug-xya xyoo dhau los . . .

HUNGARIAN

Negyvenhét évvel ezelőtt . . .

ICELANDIC

Fyrir fjörutíu og sjö árum síðan . . .

IGBO

Afọ iri anọ na asaa gara aga . . .

INDONESIAN

Empat puluh tujuh tahun yang lalu . . .

IRISH

Daichead a seacht mbliana ó shin . . .

ITALIAN

Quarantasette anni fa . . .

JAPANESE

四十七年前

Yon ju nana nen mae . . .

JAVANESE

Patang puluh pitu taun kepungkur . . .

KANNADA

ನಲವತ್ತೇಳು ವರ್ಷಗಳ ಹಿಂದೆ . . .

Nalavattēḷu varṣagaḷa hinde . . .

KAZAKH

Қырық жеті жыл бұрын . . .

Qırıq jeti jıl burın . . .

KINYARWANDA

Imyaka mirongo ine n'irindwi irashize . . .

KOREAN

사십칠년전 . . .

Sasip chill nyeon jeon . . .

KURDISH

Çil û heft sal berê . . .

KYRGYZ

Кырк жети жыл мурун . . .

Kırk jeti jıl murun . . .

LATVIAN

Pirms četrdesmit septiņiem gadiem . . .

LITHUANIAN

Prieš keturiasdešimt septynerius metus . . .

LUXEMBOURGISH

Viru siwwenzeg joer . . .

MACEDONIAN

Пред четириесет и седум години . . .

Pred četirieset i sedum godini . . .

MALAGASY

Fito amby efapolo taona lasa izay . . .

MALAY

Empat puluh tujuh tahun yang lalu . . .

MALTESE

Sebgħa u erbgħin sena ilu . . .

MAORI

Toru tekau ma whitu tau ki muri . . .

MARATHI

सत्तेचाळीस वर्षांपूर्वी

Sattēcāḷīsa varṣāmpūrvī . . .

MONGOLIAN

Дөчин долоон жилийн өмнө . . .

Döchin doloon jiliin ömnö . . .

NEPALI

चालीससातवर्ष पहिले।

Cālīsasātavarṣa pahilē . . .

NORWEGIAN

For førtisju år siden . . .

POLISH

Czterdzieści siedem lat temu . . .

PORTUGUESE

Quarenta e sete anos atrás . . .

PUNJABI

ਚਾਲੀ-ਸੱਤ ਸਾਲ ਪਹਿਲਾਂ

Cālī-sata sāla pahilāṁ . . .

ROMANIAN

Acum patruzeci și șapte de ani . . .

RUSSIAN

Сорок семь лет назад . . .

Sorok sem' let nazad . . .

SAMOAN

Fasefulufitu tausaga talu ai . . .

SCOTS GAELIC

Dà fhichead sa seachd bliadhna air ais . . .

SERBIAN

Пре четрдесет седам година . . .

Pre četrdeset sedam godina . . .

SLOVAK

Pred štyridsiatimi siedmimi rokmi . . .

SLOVENIAN

Pred sedeminštiridesetimi leti . . .

SOMALI

Afartan iyo toddoba sano ka hor . . .

SPANISH

Hace cuarenta y siete años . . .

SUNDANESE

Opat puluh tujuh taun ka pengker . . .

SWAHILI

Miaka arobaini na saba iliyopita . . .

SWEDISH

För fyrtiosju år sedan . . .

TAJIK

Чилу ҳафт сол пеш . . .

Cilu haft sol peş . . .

TAMIL

நாற்பத்தேழு ஆண்டுகளுக்கு முன்பு

Nār̲pattēl̲u āṇṭukaḷukku mun̲pu . . .

TELUGU

నలభై ఏడు సంవత్సరాల క్రితం

Nalabhai ēḍu sanvatsarāla kritaṁ . . .

THAI

สี่สิบเจ็ดปีที่แล้ว

Sī̀ sīb cĕd pī thī̀ læ̂w . . .

TURKISH

Kırk yedi yıl önce . . .

TURKMEN

Kyrk ýedi ýyl ozal . . .

UKRAINIAN

Сорок сім років тому . . .

Sorok sim rokiv tomu . . .

UZBEK

Qirq yetti yil oldin . . .

VIETNAMESE

Bốn mươi bảy năm trước . . .

VIETNAMESE

Pedwar deg saith mlynedd yn ôl . . .

YIDDISH

זיבן און פערציק יאָר צוריק.

Zibn aun fertsik yor tsurik . . .

ZULU

Eminyakeni engamashumi amane nesikhombisa edlule . . .

51 The vampires are here again.

AFRIKAANS

Die vampiere is weer hier.

ALBANIAN

Vampirët janë përsëri këtu.

AMHARIC

ቫምፓየሮች እንደገና እዚህ አሉ።

Vamipayerochi inidegena izīhi ālu.

ARABIC

مصاصو الدماء هنا مرة أخرى.

Masaasu aldima' huna maratan 'ukhraa.

ARMENIAN

Արնախումները կրկին այստեղ են:

Arnakhumnery krkin aystegh yen.

AZERBAIJANI

Vampirlər yenidən buradadır.

BASQUE

Banpiroak hemen dira berriro.

BELARUSIAN

Вампіры зноў тут.

Vampiry znoй tut.

BOSNIAN

Vampiri su ponovo ovde.

BULGARIAN

Вампирите отново са тук.

Vampirite otnovo sa tuk.

BURMESE

သွေးစုပ်ဖုတ်ကောင်တွေဒီမှာရှိနေပြန်တယ်။

Swayhcotehpotekaung tway demhar shinay pyantaal.

CATALAN

Els vampirs tornen a ser aquí.

CEBUANO

Ania na usab ang mga bampira.

MANDARIN CHINESE

吸血鬼又來了。

Xīxuèguǐ yòu láile.

CORSICAN

I vampiri sò quì torna.

CROATIAN

Vampiri su opet ovdje.

CZECH

Upíři jsou zase tady.

DANISH

Vampyrerne er her igen.

DUTCH

De vampiers zijn er weer.

ESPERANTO

La vampiroj estas ĉi tie denove.

ESTONIAN

Vampiirid on jälle siin.

FILIPINO

Nandito na naman ang mga bampira.

FINNISH

Vampyyrit ovat täällä taas.

FRENCH

Les vampires sont de nouveau là.

GALICIAN

Os vampiros están de novo aquí.

GEORGIAN

ვამპირები ისევ აქ არიან.
Vamp'irebi isev ak arian.

GERMAN

Die vampire sind wieder da.

GREEK

Οι βρικόλακες είναι ξανά εδώ.

Oi vrikólakes eínai xaná edó.

HAITIAN CREOLE

Vanpir yo isit la ankò.

HAUSA

Vampires suna nan kuma.

HAWAIIAN

Eia hou nā vampires.

HINDI

पिशाच्च यहाँ फिर से हैं।

Pishaach yahaan phir se hain.

HMONG

Vampires nyob ntawm no dua.

HUNGARIAN

A vámpírok megint itt vannak.

ICELANDIC

Vampírurnar eru hér aftur.

IGBO

Ndị vampires nọ ebe a ọzọ.

INDONESIAN

Vampir ada di sini lagi.

IRISH

Tá na vaimpírí anseo arís.

ITALIAN

I vampiri sono di nuovo qui.

JAPANESE

吸血鬼は再びここにいます。

Kyūketsuki wa futatabi koko ni imasu.

JAVANESE

Vampir ana ing kene maneh.

KANNADA

ಪಿಶಾಚಿಗಳು ಮತ್ತೆ ಇಲ್ಲಿವೆ.

Piśācigaḷu matte illive.

KAZAKH

Вампирлер қайтадан осында.

Vampïrler qaytadan osında.

KINYARWANDA

Vampire irongeye.

KOREAN

뱀파이어가 다시 여기에 있습니다.

Baempaieoga dasi yeogie issseubnida.

KURDISH

Vampîr dîsa li vir in.

KYRGYZ

Вампирлер кайрадан бул жерде.

Vampirler kayradan bul jerde.

LATVIAN

Vampīri atkal ir klāt.

LITHUANIAN

Vampyrai vėl čia.

LUXEMBOURGISH

D'vampiren sinn erëm hei.

MACEDONIAN

Вампирите се повторно тука.

Vampirite se povtorno tuka.

MALAGASY

Tonga eto indray ireo vampira.

MALAY

Vampir ada di sini lagi.

MALTESE

Il-vampiri reġgħu qegħdin hawn.

MAORI

Kei konei ano nga vampira.

MARATHI

व्हँपायर्स पुन्हा येथे आहेत.

Vhampāyarsa punhā yēthē āhēta.

MONGOLIAN

Цус сорогчид дахин энд байна.

Tsus sorogchid dakhin end baina.

NEPALI

पिशाच फेरि यहाँ छन्।

Piśāca phēri yahām̐ chan.

NORWEGIAN

Vampyrene er her igjen.

POLISH

Wampiry znów tu są.

PORTUGUESE

Os vampiros estão aqui novamente.

PUNJABI

ਪਿਸ਼ਾਚ ਦੁਬਾਰਾ ਇੱਥੇ ਹਨ.

Piśāca dubārā ithē hana.

ROMANIAN

Vampirii sunt din nou aici.

RUSSIAN

Вампиры снова здесь.

Vampiry snova zdes'.

SAMOAN

Ua toe omai vampires.

SCOTS GAELIC

Tha na vampires an seo a-rithist.

SERBIAN

Вампири су поново овде.

Vampiri su ponovo ovde.

SLOVAK

Upíri sú opäť tu.

SLOVENIAN

Vampirji so spet tukaj.

SOMALI

Vampires -ka ayaa mar labaad halkan jooga.

SPANISH

Los vampiros están aquí de nuevo.

SUNDANESE

Vampir aya di dieu deui.

SWAHILI

Vampires wako hapa tena.

SWEDISH

Vampyrerna är här igen.

TAJIK

Вампирҳо боз дар ин ҷо ҳастанд.

Vampirho boz dar in ço hastand.

TAMIL

காட்டேரிகள் மீண்டும் இங்கு வந்துள்ளன.

Kāṭṭērikaḷ mīṇṭum iṅku vantuḷḷaṉa.

TELUGU

పిశాచాలు మళ్లీ ఇక్కడ ఉన్నాయి.

Piśācālu maḷlī ikkaḍa unnāyi.

THAI

แวมไพร์มาอีกแล้ว

Wæmphịr̒ mā xīk læ̂w.

TURKISH

Vampirler yine burada.

TURKMEN

Wampirler ýene şu ýerde.

UKRAINIAN

Вампіри знову тут.

Vampiry znovu tut.

UZBEK

Vampirlar yana shu erda.

VIETNAMESE

Ma cà rồng lại ở đây.

VIETNAMESE

Mae'r fampirod yma eto.

YIDDISH

די וואַמפּיירז זענען דאָ ווידער.

Di vampeyrz zenen do vider.

ZULU

Ama-vampire alapha futhi.

52 I'm sure these screws aren't important.

AFRIKAANS

Ek is seker dat hierdie skroewe nie belangrik is nie.

ALBANIAN

Jam i sigurt se këto vida nuk janë të rëndësishme.

AMHARIC

እነዚህ ዊቶች አስፈላጊ እንዳልሆኑ እርግጠኛ ነኝ።

Inezīhi wītochi āsifelagī inidalihonu irigit'enya nenyi.

ARABIC

أنا متأكد من أن هذه البراغي ليست مهمة.

'Ana muta'akid min 'ana hadhih albaraghi laysat muhimatan.

ARMENIAN

Վստահ եմ, որ այս պտուտակները կարևոր չեն:

Vstah yem, vor ays ptutaknery karevor ch'en.

AZERBAIJANI

Əminəm ki, bu vintlər vacib deyil.

BASQUE

Ziur nago torloju hauek ez direla garrantzitsuak.

BELARUSIAN

Я ўпэўнены, што гэтыя шрубы не важныя.

Ja ŭpeŭnieny, što hetyja šruby nie važnyja.

BOSNIAN

Siguran sam da ti vijci nisu važni.

BULGARIAN

Сигурен съм, че тези винтове не са важни.

Siguren sŭm, che tezi vintove ne sa vazhni.

BURMESE

ဒီဝက်အူတွေကအရေးမကြီးဘူးဆို
တာငါသေချာတယ်။

De waat auu twayk aarayymakyeebhuu sotar ngar sayhkyaartaal .

CATALAN

Estic segur que aquests cargols no són importants.

CEBUANO

Sigurado ako nga kini nga mga turnilyo dili hinungdanon.

MANDARIN CHINESE

我相信這些螺絲並不重要。

Wǒ xiāngxìn zhèxiē luósī bìng bù chóng yào.

CORSICAN

Sò sicuru chì sti viti ùn sò micca impurtanti.

CROATIAN

Siguran sam da ti vijci nisu važni.

CZECH

Jsem si jistý, že tyto šrouby nejsou důležité.

DANISH

Jeg er sikker på, at disse skruer ikke er vigtige.

DUTCH

Ik weet zeker dat deze schroeven niet belangrijk zijn.

ESPERANTO

Mi certas, ke ĉi tiuj ŝraŭboj ne gravas.

ESTONIAN

Olen kindel, et need kruvid pole olulised.

FILIPINO

Sigurado akong hindi mahalaga ang mga tornilyo na ito.

FINNISH

Olen varma, että nämä ruuvit eivät ole tärkeitä.

FRENCH

Je suis sûr que ces vis ne sont pas importantes.

GALICIAN

Estou seguro de que estes parafusos non son importantes.

GEORGIAN

დარწმუნებული ვარ, რომ ეს ხრახნები არ არის მნიშვნელოვანი.

Darts'munebuli var, rom es khrakhnebi ar aris mnishvnelovani.

GERMAN

Ich bin sicher, diese schrauben sind nicht wichtig.

GREEK

Είμαι βέβαιος ότι αυτές οι βίδες δεν είναι σημαντικές.

Eímai vévaios óti aftés oi vídes den eínai simantikés.

HAITIAN CREOLE

Mwen si ke vis sa yo pa enpòtan.

HAUSA

Na tabbata waɗannan sukurori ba su da mahimmanci.

HAWAIIAN

ʻIke wau ʻaʻole koʻikoʻi kēia mau ʻāpana.

HINDI

मुझे यकीन है कि ये पेंच महत्वपूर्ण नहीं हैं।

Mujhe yakeen hai ki ye pench mahatvapoorn nahin hain.

HMONG

Kuv paub tseeb tias cov ntsia hlau no tsis tseem ceeb.

HUNGARIAN

Biztos vagyok benne, hogy ezek a csavarok nem fontosak.

ICELANDIC

Ég er viss um að þessar skrúfur eru ekki mikilvægar.

IGBO

Ama m na klọb ndị a adịghị mkpa.

INDONESIAN

Saya yakin sekrup ini tidak penting.

IRISH

Táim cinnte nach bhfuil na scriúnna seo tábhachtach.

ITALIAN

Sono sicuro che queste viti non sono importanti.

JAPANESE

これらのネジは重要ではないと確信しています。

Korera no neji wa jūyōde wa nai to kakushin shite imasu.

JAVANESE

Aku yakin sekrup kasebut ora penting.

KANNADA

ಈ ತಿರುಪುಗಳು ಮುಖ್ಯವಲ್ಲ ಎಂದು ನನಗೆ ಖಾತ್ರಿಯಿದೆ.

Ī tirupugaḷu mukhyavalla endu nanage khātriyide.

KAZAKH

Мен бұл бұрандалардың маңызды емес екеніне сенімдімін.

Men bul burandalardıñ mañızdı emes ekenine senimdimin.

KINYARWANDA

Nzi neza ko iyi miyoboro atari ngombwa.

KOREAN

나는 이 나사가 중요하지 않다고 확신합니다.

Naneun i nasaga jung-yohaji anhdago hwagsinhabnida.

KURDISH

Ez piştrast im ku ev pêl ne girîng in.

KYRGYZ

Бул бурамалар маанилүү эмес экенине ишенем.

Bul buramalar maanilüü emes ekenine işenem.

LATVIAN

Esmu pārliecināts, ka šīm skrūvēm nav nozīmes.

LITHUANIAN

Esu tikras, kad šie varžtai nėra svarbūs.

LUXEMBOURGISH

Ech si sécher datt dës schrauwen net wichteg sinn.

MACEDONIAN

Сигурен сум дека овие завртки не се важни.

Siguren sum deka ovie zavrtki ne se važni.

MALAGASY

Azoko antoka fa tsy zava-dehibe ireo visy ireo.

MALAY

Saya yakin skru ini tidak penting.

MALTESE

Jiena ċert li dawn il-viti mhumiex importanti.

MAORI

Kei te mohio ahau ehara i te mea nui enei kopikopiko.

MARATHI

मला खात्री आहे की हे स्क्रू महत्वाचे नाहीत.

Malā khātrī āhē kī hē skrū mahatvācē nāhīta.

MONGOLIAN

Эдгээр шураг нь чухал биш гэдэгт би итгэлтэй байна.

Edgeer shurag ni chukhal bish gedegt bi itgeltei baina.

NEPALI

म पक्का छु कि यी शिकंजा महत्वपूर्ण छैनन्।

Ma pakkā chu ki yī śikañjā mahatvapūrṇa chainan.

NORWEGIAN

Jeg er sikker på at disse skruene ikke er viktige.

POLISH

Jestem pewien, że te śruby nie są ważne.

PORTUGUESE

Tenho certeza de que esses parafusos não são importantes.

PUNJABI

ਮੈਨੂੰ ਯਕੀਨ ਹੈ ਕਿ ਇਹ ਪੇਚ ਮਹੱਤਵਪੂਰਣ ਨਹੀਂ ਹਨ.

Mainū yakīna hai ki iha pēca mahatavapūraṇa nahīṁ hana.

ROMANIAN

Sunt sigur că aceste șuruburi nu sunt importante.

RUSSIAN

Я уверен, что эти винты не важны.

YA uveren, chto eti vinty ne vazhny.

SAMOAN

Ou te mautinoa e le taua nei faovilivili.

SCOTS GAELIC

Tha mi cinnteach nach eil na sgrìoban sin cudromach.

SERBIAN

Сигуран сам да ови шрафови нису важни.

Siguran sam da ovi šrafovi nisu važni.

SLOVAK

Som si istý, že tieto skrutky nie sú dôležité.

SLOVENIAN

Prepričan sem, da ti vijaki niso pomembni.

SOMALI

Waan hubaa in boolalkani aysan muhiim ahayn.

SPANISH

Estoy seguro de que estos tornillos no son importantes.

SUNDANESE

Kuring yakin sekrup ieu henteu penting.

SWAHILI

Nina hakika hizi screws sio muhimu.

SWEDISH

Jag är säker på att dessa skruvar inte är viktiga.

TAJIK

Ман боварӣ дорам, ки ин винтҳо муҳим нестанд.

Man вovarī doram, ki in vintho muhim nestand.

TAMIL

இந்த திருகுகள் முக்கியமல்ல என்று நான் உறுதியாக நம்புகிறேன்.

Inta tirukukaḷ mukkiyamalla eṉṟu nāṉ uṟutiyāka nampukiṟēṉ.

TELUGU

ఈ మరలు ముఖ్యం కాదని నేను ఖచ్చితంగా అనుకుంటున్నాను.

Ī maralu mukhyaṁ kādani nēnu khaccitaṅgā anukuṇṭunnānu.

THAI

ฉันแน่ใจว่าสกรูเหล่านี้ไม่สำคัญ

Chạn næ̀cı ẁā s̄k rū h̄el̀ā nī̂ mị̀ s̄ảkhạỵ.

TURKISH

Bu vidaların önemli olmadığından eminim.

TURKMEN

Bu nurbatlaryň möhüm däldigine ynanýaryn.

UKRAINIAN

Я впевнений, що ці гвинти не важливі.

Ya vpevnenyy, shcho tsi hvynty ne vazhlyvi.

UZBEK

Ishonchim komilki, bu vintlardek muhim emas.

VIETNAMESE

Tôi chắc chắn rằng những con vít này không quan trọng.

VIETNAMESE

Rwy'n siŵr nad yw'r sgriwiau hyn yn bwysig.

YIDDISH

איך בין זיכער אַז די סקרוז זענען נישט וויכטיק.

Ikh bin zikher az di skruz zenen nisht vikhtik.

ZULU

Nginesiqiniseko sokuthi lezi zikulufo azibalulekile.

53 Fly, you fools!

AFRIKAANS

Vlieg, julle dwase!

ALBANIAN

Fluturoni, ju budallenj!

AMHARIC

ዝንቦች ፣ እናንተ ደደቦች!

Zinibochi, inanite dedebochi!

ARABIC

تطير أيها الحمقى!

Tatir 'ayuha alhamqaa!

ARMENIAN

Թռչե՛ք, հիմարնե՛ր:

T'rrch'ek', himarner!

AZERBAIJANI

Uçun, axmaqlar!

BASQUE

Hegan, tontoak!

BELARUSIAN

Ляціце, дурні!

Liacicie, durni!

BOSNIAN

Letite, budale!

BULGARIAN

Летете, глупаци!

Letete, glupatsi!

BURMESE

ပျံပါ လူမိုက်!

Pyaan par, luumite!

CATALAN

Vola, ximples!

CEBUANO

Lupad, kamong mga buang!

MANDARIN CHINESE

飛吧，笨蛋！

Fēi ba, bèndàn!

CORSICAN

Vola, o scemi!

CROATIAN

Letite vi budale!

CZECH

Leť, blázni!

DANISH

Flyv, du fjolser!

DUTCH

Vlieg, jullie dwazen!

ESPERANTO

Flugu, stultuloj!

ESTONIAN

Lenda, lollid!

FILIPINO

Lumipad, mga tanga!

FINNISH

Lennä, tyhmät!

FRENCH

Volez pauvres fous!

GALICIAN

Voa, parvos!

GEORGIAN

გაფრინდით, სულელებო!

Gaprindit, sulelebo!

GERMAN

Flieht ihr narren!

GREEK

Πετάξτε ανόητοι!

Petáxte anóitoi!

HAITIAN CREOLE

Vole, moun fou!

HAUSA

Tashi, wawaye!

HAWAIIAN

Lele, e ka poʻe lapuwale!

HINDI

फ्लाई यू फूल्स!

Phlaee yoo phools!

HMONG

Ya, koj ruam!

HUNGARIAN

Repüljetek, bolondok!

ICELANDIC

Fljúgið, þið fífl!

IGBO

Ofufe, unu ndi nzuzu!

INDONESIAN

Terbang, bodoh!

IRISH

Cuil, a amadán!

ITALIAN

Volate, sciocchi!

JAPANESE

飛ぶ、あなたはばか！

Tobu, anata wa baka!

JAVANESE

Fly, sampeyan wong bodho!

KANNADA

ಹಾರಿ, ಮೂರ್ಖರೇ!

Hāri, mūrkharē!

KAZAKH

Ұш, ақымақтар!

Uş, aqımaqtar!

KINYARWANDA

Muguruka, mwa bapfu mwe!

KOREAN

날아라, 이 바보들아!

Nal-ala, i babodeul-a!

KURDISH

Bifirin, ey bêhiş!

KYRGYZ

Уч, акмактар!

Uç, akmaktar!

LATVIAN

Lidojiet, muļķi!

LITHUANIAN

Skriskite, kvailiai!

LUXEMBOURGISH

Flitt, dir narren!

MACEDONIAN

Летајте, будали!

Letajte, budali!

MALAGASY

Manidina, ianareo adala!

MALAY

Terbang, bodoh!

MALTESE

Ittajru, iblah!

MAORI

Rere, e nga wairangi!

MARATHI

उड, मूर्खांनो!

Uḍa, mūrkhānnō!

MONGOLIAN

Ялаа, тэнэгүүд ээ!

Yalaa, tenegüüd ee!

NEPALI

उड्नुहोस्, मूर्खहरु!

Uḍnuhōs, mūrkhaharu!

NORWEGIAN

Fly, dumme!

POLISH

Lećcie głupcy!

PORTUGUESE

Voem, seus idiotas!

PUNJABI

ਉੱਡ, ਹੇ ਮੂਰਖੋ!

Uḍa, hē mūrakhō!

ROMANIAN

Zburați, proști!

RUSSIAN

Летите, дураки!

Letite, duraki!

SAMOAN

Lele, outou vale!

SCOTS GAELIC

Fly, amadan thu!

SERBIAN

Летите, будале!

Letite, budale!

SLOVAK

Leť, blázni!

SLOVENIAN

Leti, norci!

SOMALI

Duula, nacasyahow!

SPANISH

¡Largo de aquí, tontos!

SUNDANESE

Ngapung, jelema bodo!

SWAHILI

Kuruka, wapumbavu wewe!

SWEDISH

Flyga, du dårar!

TAJIK

Парвоз кунед, аблаҳон!

Parvoz kuned, авlahon!

TAMIL

பறக்க, முட்டாள்களே!

Parakka, muṭṭāḷkaḷē!

TELUGU

ఎగరండి, మూర్ఖులారా!

Egaraṇḍi, mūrkhulārā!

THAI

บินไปเลย ไอ้พวกโง่!

Bin pị ley xị̂ phwk ngò!

TURKISH

Uçun aptallar!

TURKMEN

Uç, samsyklar!

UKRAINIAN

Літайте, дурні!

Litayte, durni!

UZBEK

Uchib keting, ahmoqlar!

VIETNAMESE

Bay đi bọn ngốc!

VIETNAMESE

Plu, ffyliaid!

YIDDISH

פליען, איר פֿאָאלס!

Flyen, ir fools!

ZULU

Ndiza, nina ziwula!

54 This tastes like sewage.

AFRIKAANS

Dit smaak soos riool.

ALBANIAN

Kjo ka shije të ujërave të zeza.

AMHARIC

ይህ እንደ ፍሳሽ ጣዕም ነው።

Yihi inide fisashi t'a'imi newi.

ARABIC

هذا طعمه مثل مياه الصرف الصحي.

Hadha taemuh mithl miah alsirf alsahi.

ARMENIAN

Սա կեղտաջրերի համ ունի:

Sa keghtajreri ham uni.

AZERBAIJANI

Bu kanalizasiya dadına bənzəyir.

BASQUE

Honek estolderia bezalako zaporea du.

BELARUSIAN

Гэта на смак як сцёкавыя вады.

Heta na smak jak sciokavyja vady.

BOSNIAN

Ovo ima ukus kanalizacije.

BULGARIAN

Това има вкус на канализация.

Tova ima vkus na kanalizatsiya.

BURMESE

ဒီအရသာကမိလ္လာနဲ့တူတယ်။

De aarasar k mil lar nae tuutaal.

CATALAN

Això té gust de clavegueram.

CEBUANO

Kini lami sama sa hugaw.

MANDARIN CHINESE

這嘗起來像污水。

Zhè cháng qǐlái xiàng wūshuǐ.

CORSICAN

Questu hà u gustu di e acque nere.

CROATIAN

Ovo ima okus kanalizacije.

CZECH

To chutná jako odpadní voda.

DANISH

Dette smager som spildevand.

DUTCH

Dit smaakt naar riool.

ESPERANTO

Ĉi tio gustas kiel kloakaĵo.

ESTONIAN

See maitseb nagu kanalisatsioon.

FILIPINO

Ito ay tulad ng dumi sa alkantarilya.

FINNISH

Tämä maistuu jätevedeltä.

FRENCH

Cela a un goût d'égout.

GALICIAN

Isto sabe a augas residuais.

GEORGIAN

ეს გემოვნებას ჰგავს კანალიზაციას.

Es gemovnebas hgavs k'analizatsias.

GERMAN

Das schmeckt nach abwasser.

GREEK

Έχει γεύση λυμάτων.

Échei géfsi lymáton.

HAITIAN CREOLE

Sa a gou tankou dlo egou yo.

HAUSA

Wannan dandana kamar najasa.

HAWAIIAN

'Ono kēia e like me ka humuhumu.

HINDI

इसका स्वाद सीवेज की तरह होता है।

Isaka svaad seevej kee tarah hota hai.

HMONG

Qhov no zoo li dej phwj tuaj.

HUNGARIAN

Ez ízű, mint a szennyvíz.

ICELANDIC

Þetta bragðast eins og skólp.

IGBO

Nke a na -atọ ka nsị nsị.

INDONESIAN

Ini rasanya seperti limbah.

IRISH

Tá sé seo cosúil le séarachas.

ITALIAN

Questo sa di liquame.

JAPANESE

これは下水のような味がします。

Kore wa gesui no yōna aji ga shimasu.

JAVANESE

Rasane kaya limbah.

KANNADA

ಇದು ಚರಂಡಿಯಂತೆ ರುಚಿ ನೋಡುತ್ತದೆ.

Idu caraṇḍiyante ruci nōḍuttade.

KAZAKH

Бұл ағынды суға ұқсайды.

Bul ağındı swğa uqsaydı.

KINYARWANDA

Ibi biryoha nkumwanda.

KOREAN

이것은 하수구 맛입니다.

Igeos-eun hasugu mas-ibnida.

KURDISH

Ev dişibe kanalîzasyonê.

KYRGYZ

Бул агынды суугa окшош.

Bul agındı suuga okşoş.

LATVIAN

Tas garšo pēc notekūdeņiem.

LITHUANIAN

Tai skonis kaip nuotekos.

LUXEMBOURGISH

Dëst schmaacht wéi kläranlag.

MACEDONIAN

Вкусот е како канализација.

Vkusot e kako kanalizacija.

MALAGASY

Toy ny tatatra ny fako.

MALAY

Rasanya seperti kumbahan.

MALTESE

Dan għandu togħma bħal drenaġġ.

MAORI

He reka tenei ki te waikeri.

MARATHI

याची चव सांडपाण्यासारखी असते.

Yācī cava sāṇḍapāṇyāsārakhī asatē.

MONGOLIAN

Энэ нь бохир ус шиг амттай байдаг.

Ene ni bokhir us shig amttai baidag.

NEPALI

यो सीवेज जस्तै स्वाद छ।

Yō sīvēja jastai svāda cha.

NORWEGIAN

Dette smaker kloakk.

POLISH

To smakuje jak ścieki.

PORTUGUESE

Isso tem gosto de esgoto.

PUNJABI

ਇਹ ਸਵਾਦ ਸੀਵਰੇਜ ਵਰਗਾ ਹੈ.

Iha savāda sīvarēja varagā hai.

ROMANIAN

Are gust de canalizare.

RUSSIAN

Это на вкус как сточные воды.

Eto na vkus kak stochnyye vody.

SAMOAN

O lenei e pei o le palapala.

SCOTS GAELIC

Tha seo blasad mar òtrachas.

SERBIAN

Ово има укус канализације.

Ovo ima ukus kanalizacije.

SLOVAK

Toto chutí ako odpadová voda.

SLOVENIAN

Ta ima okus kot kanalizacija.

SOMALI

Tani waxay dhadhamisaa sida bullaacadda.

SPANISH

Esto sabe a aguas residuales.

SUNDANESE

Ieu raos sapertos kokotor.

SWAHILI

Hii inapenda kama maji taka.

SWEDISH

Det smakar avloppsvatten.

TAJIK

Ин таъми канализатсияро дорад.

In ta'mi kanalizatsijaro dorad.

TAMIL

இது கழிவுநீர் போல சுவைக்கிறது.

Itu kaḻivunīr pōla cuvaikkiṟatu.

TELUGU

ఇది మురుగునీటి రుచి.
Idi murugunīṭi ruci.

THAI

รสชาติเหมือนน้ำเสีย

Rŝchāti h̄emụ̄xn n̂ả s̄eīy.

TURKISH

Bu kanalizasyon gibi tadı.

TURKMEN

Bu tagam kanalizasiýa ýalydyr.

UKRAINIAN

На смак це нагадує стічні води.

Na smak tse nahaduye stichni vody.

UZBEK

Bu kanalizatsiyaga o'xshaydi.

VIETNAMESE

Nó có vị như nước thải.

VIETNAMESE

Mae hyn yn blasu fel carthffosiaeth.

YIDDISH

דאס טייסץ ווי אָפּגאַנג.

Das teysts vi opgang.

ZULU

Lokhu kunambitheka njengendle.

55 Can I borrow a cup of sugar?

AFRIKAANS

Kan ek suiker leen?

ALBANIAN

A mund të marr hua pak sheqer?

AMHARIC

ትንሽ ስኳር መበደር እችላለሁን?

Tinishi sikwari mebederi ichilalehuni?

ARABIC

هل يمكنني استعارة بعض السكر؟

Hal yumkinuni astiearat baed alsukri?

ARMENIAN

Կարո՞ղ եմ շաքար վերցնել:

Karogh yem shak'ar verts'nel?

AZERBAIJANI

Bir az şəkər götürə bilərəmmi?

BASQUE

Mailegu al dezaket azukre bat?

BELARUSIAN

Ці можна пазычыць цукру?

Ci možna pazyčyć cukru?

BOSNIAN

Mogu li posuditi malo šećera?

BULGARIAN

Мога ли да взема назаем малко захар?

Moga li da vzema nazaem malko zakhar?

BURMESE

ငါသကြားနည်းနည်းချေးလို့ရမလား။

Ngar s kyarr naeenaee hkyaayy lhoet ramalarr?

CATALAN

Puc demanar prestat sucre?

CEBUANO

Mahimo ba ako manghulam og asukal?

MANDARIN CHINESE

我可以藉點糖嗎？
Wǒ kěyǐ jí diǎn táng ma?

CORSICAN

Possu piglià prestu un zuccheru?

CROATIAN

Mogu li posuditi malo šećera?

CZECH

Mohu si půjčit nějaký cukr?

DANISH

Kan jeg låne noget sukker?

DUTCH

Mag ik wat suiker lenen?

ESPERANTO

Ĉu mi povas prunti iom da sukero?

ESTONIAN

Kas ma saan suhkrut laenata?

FILIPINO

Maaari ba akong mangutang ng asukal?

FINNISH

Voinko lainata sokeria?

FRENCH

Puis-je emprunter du sucre?

GALICIAN

Podo pedir un pouco de azucre?

GEORGIAN

შემიძლია ცოტაოდენი შაქრის სესხება?

Shemidzlia tsot'aodeni shakris seskheba?

GERMAN

Kann ich mir etwas zucker leihen?

GREEK

Μπορώ να δανειστώ λίγη ζάχαρη?

Boró na daneistó lígi záchari?

HAITIAN CREOLE

Èske mwen ka prete kèk sik?

HAUSA

Zan iya aro sukari?

HAWAIIAN

Hiki iaʻu ke hōʻaiʻē i kekahi kō?

HINDI

क्या मुझे थोड़ी चीनी मिल सकती है?

kya mujhe thodee cheenee mil sakatee hai?

HMONG

Kuv puas tuaj yeem qiv qee cov suab thaj?

HUNGARIAN

Kölcsönkérek egy kis cukrot?

ICELANDIC

Má ég fá lánaðan sykur?

IGBO

Enwere m ike ịgbaziri shuga?

INDONESIAN

Bolehkah saya meminjam gula?

IRISH

An féidir liom roinnt siúcra a fháil ar iasacht?

ITALIAN

Posso prendere in prestito dello zucchero?

JAPANESE

砂糖を借りてもいいですか？

Satō o karite mo īdesu ka?

JAVANESE

Apa aku bisa nyilih gula?

KANNADA

ನಾನು ಸ್ವಲ್ಪ ಸಕ್ಕರೆ ಎರವಲು ಪಡೆಯಬಹುದೇ?

Nānu svalpa sakkare eravalu paḍeyabahudē?

KAZAKH

Мен қантқа қарыз аламын ба?

Men qantqa qarız alamın ba?

KINYARWANDA

Nshobora kuguza isukari?

KOREAN

설탕 좀 빌릴 수 있을까요?

Seoltang jom billil su iss-eulkkayo?

KURDISH

Ez dikarim hinek şekir deyn bikim?

KYRGYZ

Мен кант карызга алсам болобу?

Men kant karızga alsam bolobu?

LATVIAN

Vai es varu aizņemties cukuru?

LITHUANIAN

Ar galiu pasiskolinti cukraus?

LUXEMBOURGISH

Kann ech e puer zocker léinen?

MACEDONIAN

Може ли да позајмам малку шеќер?

Može li da pozajmam malku šeḱer?

MALAGASY

Afaka mindrana siramamy ve aho?

MALAY

Bolehkah saya meminjam sedikit gula?

MALTESE

Nista 'nissellef ftit zokkor?

MAORI

Ka taea e au te nama nama huka?

MARATHI

मी थोडी साखर घेऊ शकतो का?

Mī thōḍī sākhara ghē'ū śakatō kā?

MONGOLIAN

Би элсэн чихэр зээлж болох уу?

Bi elsen chikher zeelj bolokh uu?

NEPALI

के म केहि चीनी उधारो गर्न सक्छु?

Kē ma kēhi cīnī udhārō garna sakchu?

NORWEGIAN

Kan jeg låne litt sukker?

POLISH

Czy mogę pożyczyć trochę cukru?

PORTUGUESE

Posso pegar açúcar emprestado?

PUNJABI

ਕੀ ਮੈਂ ਕੁਝ ਖੰਡ ਉਧਾਰ ਲੈ ਸਕਦਾ ਹਾਂ?

Kī maiṁ kujha khaḍa udhāra lai sakadā hāṁ?

ROMANIAN

Pot împrumuta nişte zahăr?

RUSSIAN

Могу я одолжить немного сахара?

Mogu ya odolzhit' nemnogo sakhara?

SAMOAN

Mafai ona ou nonoina sina suka?

SCOTS GAELIC

An urrainn dhomh beagan siùcair fhaighinn air iasad?

SERBIAN

Могу ли позајмити мало шећера?

Mogu li pozajmiti malo šećera?

SLOVAK

Môžem si požičať cukor?

SLOVENIAN

Si lahko izposodim sladkor?

SOMALI

Ma amaahan karaa xoogaa sonkor ah?

SPANISH

¿Me prestas un poco de azúcar?

SUNDANESE

Dupi abdi tiasa nginjeum gula?

SWAHILI

Je! Ninaweza kukopa sukari?

SWEDISH

Kan jag låna lite socker?

TAJIK

Оё ман метавонам каме шакар қарз гирам?

Ojo man metavonam kame şakar qarz giram?

TAMIL

நான் கொஞ்சம் சர்க்கரை கடன் வாங்கலாமா?

Nāṉ koñcam carkkarai kaṭaṉ vāṅkalāmā?

TELUGU

నేను కొంత చక్కెర అప్పు తీసుకోవచ్చా?

Nēnu konta cakkera appu tīsukōvaccā?

THAI

ฉันขอยืมน้ำตาลหน่อยได้ไหม

Chạn k̄hxyụ̄m n̂ảtāl h̄ǹxy dị̂ h̄ịm?

TURKISH

Biraz şeker ödünç alabilir miyim?

TURKMEN

Şeker alyp bilerinmi?

UKRAINIAN

Чи можна позичити цукру?

Chy mozhna pozychyty tsukru?

UZBEK

Bir oz shakar qarz olsam bo'ladimi?

VIETNAMESE

Cho tôi mượn một ít đường được không?

VIETNAMESE

A allaf fenthyg rhywfaint o siwgr?

YIDDISH

קען איך באָרגן צוקער?

ken ikh borgn tsuker?

ZULU

Ngingakwazi ukuboleka ushukela?

56 Old soldiers never die.

AFRIKAANS

Ou soldate sterf nooit.

ALBANIAN

Ushtarët e vjetër nuk vdesin kurrë.

AMHARIC

አሮጌ ወታደሮች በጭራሽ አይሞቱም።

Arogē wetaderochi bech'irashi āyimotumi.

ARABIC

الجنود القدامى لا يموتون أبدا.

Aljunud alqudamaa la yamutun 'abda.

ARMENIAN

Հին զինվորները երբեք չեն մահանում:

Hin zinvornery yerbek' ch'en mahanum.

AZERBAIJANI

Köhnə əsgərlər heç vaxt ölmür.

BASQUE

Soldadu zaharrak ez dira inoiz hiltzen.

BELARUSIAN

Старыя салдаты ніколі не паміраюць.

Staryja saldaty nikoli nie pamirajuć.

BOSNIAN

Stari vojnici nikada ne umiru.

BULGARIAN

Старите войници никога не умират.

Starite voĭnitsi nikoga ne umirat.

BURMESE

စစ်သားဟောင်းတွေဘယ်တော့မှမသေဘူး။

Hcaitsarr haunggtway bhaaltotmha m say bhuu.

CATALAN

Els vells soldats no moren mai.

CEBUANO

Ang mga tigulang nga sundalo dili mamatay.

MANDARIN CHINESE

老兵永不死。

Lǎobīng yǒng bùsǐ.

CORSICAN

I vechji suldati ùn morenu mai.

CROATIAN

Stari vojnici nikada ne umiru.

CZECH

Staří vojáci nikdy nezemřou.

DANISH

Gamle soldater dør aldrig.

DUTCH

Oude soldaten sterven nooit.

ESPERANTO

Maljunaj soldatoj neniam mortas.

ESTONIAN

Vanad sõdurid ei sure kunagi.

FILIPINO

Ang mga matandang sundalo ay hindi namamatay.

FINNISH

Vanhat sotilaat eivät koskaan kuole.

FRENCH

Les vieux soldats ne meurent jamais.

GALICIAN

Os vellos soldados nunca morren.

GEORGIAN

ძველი ჯარისკაცები არასოდეს კვდებიან.

Dzveli jarisk'atsebi arasodes k'vdebian.

GERMAN

Alte soldaten sterben nie.

GREEK

Οι παλιοί στρατιώτες δεν πεθαίνουν ποτέ.

Oi palioí stratiótes den pethaínoun poté.

HAITIAN CREOLE

Ansyen sòlda pa janm mouri.

HAUSA

Tsofaffin sojoji ba sa mutuwa.

HAWAIIAN

ʻAʻole make nā koa kahiko.

HINDI

पुराने सैनिक कभी नहीं मरते।

Puraane sainik kabhee nahin marate.

HMONG

Cov tub rog qub yeej tsis tuag.

HUNGARIAN

Az öreg katonák soha nem halnak meg.

ICELANDIC

Gamlir hermenn deyja aldrei.

IGBO

Ndị agha ochie anaghị anwụ anwụ.

INDONESIAN

Prajurit tua tidak pernah mati.

IRISH

Ní fhaigheann sean-shaighdiúirí bás riamh.

ITALIAN

I vecchi soldati non muoiono mai.

JAPANESE

老兵は死なない。

Rōhei wa shinanai.

JAVANESE

Prajurit tuwa ora bakal mati.

KANNADA

ಹಳೆಯ ಸೈನಿಕರು ಎಂದಿಗೂ ಸಾಯುವುದಿಲ್ಲ.

Haḷeya sainikaru endigū sāyuvudilla.

KAZAKH

Ескі сарбаздар ешқашан өлмейді.

Eski sarbazdar eşqaşan ölmeydi.

KINYARWANDA

Abasirikare bakera ntibigera bapfa.

KOREAN

노병은 절대 죽지 않습니다.

Nobyeong-eun jeoldae jugji anhseubnida.

KURDISH

Leşkerên pîr qet namirin.

KYRGYZ

Эски аскерлер эч качан өлбөйт.

Eski askerler eç kaçan ölböyt.

LATVIAN

Vecie karavīri nekad nemirst.

LITHUANIAN

Seni kareiviai niekada nemiršta.

LUXEMBOURGISH

Al zaldoten stierwen ni.

MACEDONIAN

Старите војници никогаш не умираат.

Starite vojnici nikogaš ne umiraat.

MALAGASY

Miaramila taloha tsy mba maty.

MALAY

Tentera lama tidak pernah mati.

MALTESE

Suldati qodma qatt ma jmutu.

MAORI

Kaore nga hoia tawhito e mate.

MARATHI

जुने सैनिक कधीही मरत नाहीत.

Junē sainika kadhīhī marata nāhīta.

MONGOLIAN

Хуучин цэргүүд хэзээ ч үхдэггүй.

Khuuchin tsergüüd khezee ch ükhdeggüi.

NEPALI

पुराना सिपाहीहरु कहिल्यै मर्दैनन्।

Purānā sipāhīharu kahilyai mardainan.

NORWEGIAN

Gamle soldater dør aldri.

POLISH

Starzy żołnierze nigdy nie umierają.

PORTUGUESE

Os velhos soldados nunca morrem.

PUNJABI

ਪੁਰਾਣੇ ਸਿਪਾਹੀ ਕਦੇ ਨਹੀਂ ਮਰਦੇ.

Purāṇē sipāhī kadē nahīṁ maradē.

ROMANIAN

Soldații vechi nu mor niciodată.

RUSSIAN

Старые солдаты никогда не умирают.

Staryye soldaty nikogda ne umirayut.

SAMOAN

E le feoti lava fitafita tuai.

SCOTS GAELIC

Cha bhàsaich seann shaighdearan gu bràth.

SERBIAN

Стари војници никада не умиру.

Stari vojnici nikada ne umiru.

SLOVAK

Starí vojaci nikdy nezomrú.

SLOVENIAN

Stari vojaki nikoli ne umrejo.

SOMALI

Askartii hore waligood ma dhintaan.

SPANISH

Los viejos soldados nunca mueren.

SUNDANESE

Prajurit sepuh henteu kantos maot.

SWAHILI

Askari wazee hawafi kamwe.

SWEDISH

Gamla soldater dör aldrig.

TAJIK

Сарбозони кӯҳна ҳеҷ гоҳ намемиранд.

Sarbozoni kūhna heç goh namemirand.

TAMIL

பழைய வீரர்கள் ஒருபோதும் இறக்க மாட்டார்கள்.

Pa<u>l</u>aiya vīrarkaḷ orupōtum i<u>r</u>akka māṭṭārkaḷ.

TELUGU

పాత సైనికులు ఎన్నటికీ చనిపోరు.

Pāta sainikulu ennaṭikī canipōru.

THAI

ทหารเก่าไม่มีวันตาย

Thh̄ār kèā mị̀mī wạn tāy.

TURKISH

Eski askerler asla ölmez.

TURKMEN

Garry esgerler hiç haçan ölmeýärler.

UKRAINIAN

Старі солдати ніколи не вмирають.

Stari soldaty nikoly ne vmyrayut'.

UZBEK

Eski askarlar hech qachon o'lmaydi.

VIETNAMESE

Những người lính già không bao giờ chết.

VIETNAMESE

Nid yw hen filwyr byth yn marw.

YIDDISH

אַלטע זעלנער שטאַרבן קיינמאָל ניט.

Alte zelner shtarbn keynmol nit.

ZULU

Amasosha amadala awafi.

57 Do not pass "Go." Do not collect $200.

AFRIKAANS

Moenie "Go" slaag nie.
Versamel nie $200 nie.

ALBANIAN

Mos e kaloni "Go".
Mos mblidhni 200 dollarë.

AMHARIC

"Go" አትለፉ። 200 ዶላር አትሰብስቡ።

"Go" ātilefu. 200 dolari ātisebisibu.

ARABIC

لا تمر بعلامة "Go". لا تجمع 200 دولار.

La tamuru biealamat "Go". La tujmae 200 dular.

ARMENIAN

Մի անցեք "Go": Մի հավաքեք 200 դոլար:

Mi ants'ek' "Go". Mi havak'ek' 200 dolar.

AZERBAIJANI

"Go" keçməyin. 200 dollar yığmayın.

BASQUE

Ez pasatu "Go". Ez bildu 200 $.

BELARUSIAN

Не праходзьце "Go". Не збірайце 200 долараў.

Nie prachodźcie "Go". Nie zbirajcie 200 dolaraŭ.

BOSNIAN

Ne propuštajte "Go".
Ne skupljajte 200 USD.

BULGARIAN

Не преминавайте "Go".
Не събирайте 200 долара.

Ne preminavaĭte "Go". Ne sŭbiraĭte 200 dolara.

BURMESE

"Go" မကျော်ဖြတ်ပါနှင့်။ ဒေါ်လာ ၂၀၀ မစုဆောင်းပါနှင့်။

"Go" m kyawhpyat par nhang. Dawlar 200 m hcusaungg par nhang.

CATALAN

No passi “Go”.
No cobreu 200 dòlars.

CEBUANO

Ayaw pagpasa “Go”.
Ayaw pagkolekta $200.

MANDARIN CHINESE

不要通過"Go"。 不要收 200 美元。

Bùyào tōngguò "Go".
Bùyào shōu 200 měiyuán.

CORSICAN

Ùn passate micca “Go”.
Ùn raccoglie micca $200.

CROATIAN

Ne propuštajte “Go”.
Nemojte skupljati 200 USD.

CZECH

Nepředávejte “Go”.
Nesbírejte 200 $.

DANISH

Bestå ikke “Go”.
Saml ikke $200.

DUTCH

Ga niet voorbij “Go”.
Verzamel geen $200.

ESPERANTO

Ne preterpasu “Go”.
Ne kolektu $200.

ESTONIAN

Ärge läbige “Go”.
Ärge koguge 200 dollarit.

FILIPINO

Huwag pumasa sa “Go”.
Huwag mangolekta ng $200.

FINNISH

Älä ohita “Go”.
Älä kerää 200 dollaria.

FRENCH

Ne passez pas “Go”.
Ne collectez pas 200 $.

GALICIAN

Non aprobes “Go”.
Non cobres 200 $.

GEORGIAN

არ გაიაროთ “Go”. არ შეაგროვოთ 200 დოლარი.

Ar gaiarot "Go".
Ar sheagrovot 200 dolari.

GERMAN

Übergeben sie “Go” nicht.
Sammle keine 200 dollar.

GREEK

Μην περάσετε “Go”.
Μην συλλέγετε 200 $.

Min perásete “Go”.
Min syllégete 200 $.

HAITIAN CREOLE

Pa pase “Go”. Pa kolekte $200.

HAUSA

Kada ku wuce “Go”.
Kada ku tattara $200.

HAWAIIAN

Mai hala “Go”.
Mai hōʻiliʻili i $200.

HINDI

“Go” पास न करें। $200 जमा न करें।

“Go” paas na karen.
$200 jama na karen.

HMONG

Tsis txhob hla “Go”.
Tsis txhob sau $200.

HUNGARIAN

Ne adja át a “Go” gombot.
Ne gyűjts össze 200 dollárt.

ICELANDIC

Ekki standast “Go”.
Ekki safna $200.

IGBO

Agafere “Go”. Anakọtala $200.

INDONESIAN

Jangan lulus “Go”.
Jangan mengumpulkan $200.

IRISH

Ná pas “Go”. Ná bailigh $200.

ITALIAN

Non passare “Go”.
Non raccogliere $200.

JAPANESE

“Go”を渡さないでください。$200を集めないでください。

“Go” o watasanaide kudasai.
$200 o atsumenaide kudasai.

JAVANESE

Aja kliwat “Go”.
Aja nglumpukake $200.

KANNADA

“Go” ಉತ್ತೀರ್ಣರಾಗಬೇಡಿ.
$200 ಸಂಗ್ರಹಿಸಬೇಡಿ.

“Go” uttīrṇarāgabēḍi.
$200 Saṅgrahisabēḍi.

KAZAKH

"Go" өтпеңіз. 200 доллар жинамаңыз.

"Go" ötpeñiz. 200 dollar jïnamañız.

KINYARWANDA

Nturengere "Go".
Ntukusanyirize amadorari 200.

KOREAN

"Go"를 통과하지 마십시오.
200달러를 모으지 마십시오.

"Go"leul tong-gwahaji masibsio. 200dalleoleul mo-euji masibsio.

KURDISH

"Go" derbas nekin.
200 $ berhev nekin.

KYRGYZ

"Go" өтпө. 200 доллар чогултпаңыз.
"Go" ötpö. 200 dollar çogultpaŋız.

LATVIAN

Neiziet "Go".
Nesavāc 200 USD.

LITHUANIAN

Negalima praeiti "Go".
Nesurinkite 200 USD.

LUXEMBOURGISH

Gitt net "Go" laanscht.
Sammelt net $200.

MACEDONIAN

Не поминувај "Go".
Не собирајте 200 долари.

Ne pominuvaj "Go".
Ne sobirajte 200 dolari.

MALAGASY

Aza mandalo "Go".
Aza manangona 200 $.

MALAY

Jangan lulus "Go". Jangan kumpulkan $200.

MALTESE

Tgħaddix "Go". Tiġborx $200.

MAORI

Kaua e paahitia "Go".
Kaua e kohikohi $200.

MARATHI

"Go" पास करू नका.
$200 गोळा करू नका.

"Go" pāsa karū nakā.
$200 Gōḷā karū nakā.

MONGOLIAN

"Go" битгий дамжуулаарай.
200 доллар бүү цуглуул.

*"Go" bitgii damjuulaarai.
200 dollar büü tsugluul.*

NEPALI

पास नगर्नुहोस् "Go"। २०० डलर स
collect्कलन नगर्नुहोस्।

*Pāsa nagarnuhōs "Go".
200 dalara sa collect kalana nagarnuhōs.*

NORWEGIAN

Ikke pass "Go".
Ikke samle $200.

POLISH

Nie przechodź "Go".
Nie zbieraj 200 dolarów.

PORTUGUESE

Não passe "Go".
Não colete $200.

PUNJABI

"ਜੀਓ" ਪਾਸ ਨਾ ਕਰੋ.
$200 ਇਕੱਠੇ ਨਾ ਕਰੋ.

*Jī'ō pāsa nā karō.
$200 Ikaṭhē nā karō.*

ROMANIAN

Nu treceți "Go".
Nu colectați 200 USD.

RUSSIAN

Не проходите "Go".
Не собирайте 200 долларов.

*Ne prokhodite "Go".
Ne sobirayte 200 dollarov.*

SAMOAN

Aua le pasi "Go".
Aua le aoina le $200.

SCOTS GAELIC

Na gabh seachad "Go".
Na cruinnich $200.

SERBIAN

Не пролази "ГО".
Не скупљајте 200 долара.

*Ne prolazi "Go".
Ne skupljajte 200 dolara.*

SLOVAK

Neprejdite "Go".
Nezbierajte 200 dolárov.

SLOVENIAN

Ne gredo mimo "Go".
Ne zberite 200 USD.

SOMALI

Ha dhaafin “Go”.
Ha uruurin $200.

SPANISH

No pase “Go”.
No recolectes $200.

SUNDANESE

Entong lulus “Go”.
Entong ngumpulkeun $200.

SWAHILI

Usipite “Go”.
Usikusanye $200.

SWEDISH

Passera inte “Go”.
Samla inte in $200.

TAJIK

“ГО” -ро нагузаронед.
200 доллар чамъ накунед.

“Go” -ro naguzaroned.
200 dollar çam’ nakuned.

TAMIL

“Go” தேர்ச்சி பெற வேண்டாம். $200 வசூலிக்க வேண்டாம்.

“Go” tērcci peṟa vēṇṭām.
$200 Vacūlikka vēṇṭām.

TELUGU

“Go” పాస్ చేయవద్దు.
$200 వసూలు చేయవద్దు.

“Go” pās cēyavaddu.
$200 Vasūlu cēyavaddu.

THAI

ไม่ผ่าน “Go” อย่าเก็บเงิน 200 เหรียญ

Mị p̄h̀ān “Go”.
Xỳā kĕb ngein 200 h̄erīyỵ

TURKISH

“Go” seçeneğini geçmeyin.
200 dolar toplamayın.

TURKMEN

“Go” geçmäň. 200 $ ýygnamaň.

UKRAINIAN

Не передавайте “Go”.
Не збирайте 200 доларів.

Ne peredavayte “Go”.
Ne zbyrayte 200 dolariv.

UZBEK

“Go” ni o’tkazib yubormang.
200 dollar yig’mang.

VIETNAMESE

Không vượt qua “Go”.
Không thu $200.

VIETNAMESE

Peidiwch â phasio “Go”.
Peidiwch â chasglu $200.

YIDDISH

דו זאלסט נישט פאָרן “Go”. דו זאלסט
נישט קלייַבן $200.

Du zalst nisht forn “Go”.
Du zalst nisht klaybn $200.

ZULU

Ungadluli “Go”.
Musa ukuqoqa u- $200.

58 Who wrote this book?!?

AFRIKAANS

Wie het hierdie boek geskryf?!?

ALBANIAN

Kush e ka shkruar kete liber?!?

AMHARIC

ይህንን መጽሐፍ ማን ፃፈው?!?

Yihinini mets'iḥāfi mani ts'afewi?!?

ARABIC

من كتب هذا الكتاب؟!؟

Min kutub hadha alkitabi?!?

ARMENIAN

Ո՞վ է գրել այս գիրքը

Vo v e grel ays girk'y?!?

AZERBAIJANI

Bu kitabı kim yazdı?!?

BASQUE

Nork idatzi du liburu hau?!?

BELARUSIAN

Хто напісаў гэтую кнігу?!?

Chto napisaŭ hetuju knihu?!?

BOSNIAN

Ko je napisao ovu knjigu?!?

BULGARIAN

Кой е написал тази книга?!?

Koĭ e napisal tazi kniga?!?

BURMESE

ဒီစာအုပ်ကိုဘယ်သူရေးတာလဲ!?

Dehcaraoteko bhaalsuu rayy tarlell?!?

CATALAN

Qui va escriure aquest llibre?!?

CEBUANO

Kinsa ang nagsulat sa kini nga libro?!?

MANDARIN CHINESE

這本書是誰寫的？！？

Zhè běnshū shì shuí xiě de?!?

CORSICAN

Quale hè chì hà scrittu stu libru?!?

CROATIAN

Tko je napisao ovu knjigu?!?

CZECH

Kdo napsal tuto knihu?!?

DANISH

Hvem skrev denne bog?!?

DUTCH

Wie heeft dit boek geschreven?!?

ESPERANTO

Kiu verkis ĉi tiun libron?!?

ESTONIAN

Kes selle raamatu kirjutas?!?

FILIPINO

Sino ang sumulat ng librong ito?!?

FINNISH

Kuka kirjoitti tämän kirjan?!?

FRENCH

Qui a écrit ce livre ?!?

GALICIAN

Quen escribiu este libro?!?

GEORGIAN

ვინ დაწერა ეს წიგნი?!?

Vin dats'era es ts'igni?!?

GERMAN

Wer hat dieses buch geschrieben?!?

GREEK

Ποιος έγραψε αυτό το βιβλίο?!?

Poios égrapse aftó to vivlío?!?

HAITIAN CREOLE

Ki moun ki ekri liv sa a?!?

HAUSA

Wanene ya rubuta wannan littafin?!?

HAWAIIAN

Na wai i kākau i kēia puke?!?

HINDI

यह किताब किसने लिखी है?!?

Yah kitaab kisane likhee hai?!?

HMONG

Leej twg sau phau ntawv no?!?

HUNGARIAN

Ki írta ezt a könyvet?!?

ICELANDIC

Hver skrifaði þessa bók?!?

IGBO

Onye dere akwụkwọ a?!?

INDONESIAN

Siapa yang menulis buku ini?!?

IRISH

Cé a scríobh an leabhar seo?!?

ITALIAN

Chi ha scritto questo libro?!?

JAPANESE

この本を書いたのは誰ですか？！？

Kono-pon o kaita no wa daredesu ka?!?

JAVANESE

Sapa sing nulis buku iki?!?

KANNADA

ಈ ಪುಸ್ತಕವನ್ನು ಬರೆದವರು ಯಾರು

Ī pustakavannu baredavaru yāru?!?

KAZAKH

Бұл кітапты кім жазды?!?

Bul kitaptı kim jazdı?!?

KINYARWANDA

Ninde wanditse iki gitabo?!?

KOREAN

이 책을 쓴 사람은?!?

I chaeg-eul sseun salam-eun?!?

KURDISH

Kê ev pirtûk nivîsandiye?!?

KYRGYZ

Бул китепти ким жазган?!?

Bul kitepti kim jazgan?!?

LATVIAN

Kas uzrakstīja šo grāmatu?!?

LITHUANIAN

Kas parašė šią knygą?!?

LUXEMBOURGISH

Wien huet dëst buch geschriwwen?!?

MACEDONIAN

Кој ја напиша оваа книга?!?

Koj ja napiša ovaa kniga?!?

MALAGASY

Iza no nanoratra an'ity boky ity?!?

MALAY

Siapa yang menulis buku ini?!?

MALTESE

Min kiteb dan il-ktieb?!?

MAORI

Na wai i tuhi tenei pukapuka?!?

MARATHI

हे पुस्तक कोणी लिहिले?!?

Hē pustaka kōṇī lihilē?!?

MONGOLIAN

Энэ номыг хэн бичсэн бэ?!?

Ene nomyg khen bichsen be?!?

NEPALI

यो पुस्तक कसले लेखेको हो?!?

Yō pustaka kasalē lēkhēkō hō?!?

NORWEGIAN

Hvem skrev denne boken?!?

POLISH

Kto napisał tę książkę?!?

PORTUGUESE

Quem escreveu este livro?!?

PUNJABI

ਇਹ ਕਿਤਾਬ ਕਿਸਨੇ ਲਿਖੀ ਹੈ?!?

Iha kitāba kisanē likhī hai?!?

ROMANIAN

Cine a scris această carte?!?

RUSSIAN

Кто написал эту книгу?!?

Kto napisal etu knigu?!?

SAMOAN

O ai na tusia lenei tusi?!?

SCOTS GAELIC

Cò sgrìobh an leabhar seo?!?

SERBIAN

Ко је написао ову књигу?!?

Ko je napisao ovu knjigu?!?

SLOVAK

Kto napísal túto knihu?!?

SLOVENIAN

Kdo je napisal to knjigo?!?

SOMALI

Yaa qoray buuggan?!?

SPANISH

¿Quién escribió este libro?

SUNDANESE

Saha anu nyerat buku ieu?!?

SWAHILI

Nani ameandika kitabu hiki?!?

SWEDISH

Vem skrev den här boken?!?

TAJIK

Ин китобро кӣ навиштааст?!?

In kitoвro kī naviştaast?!?

TAMIL

இந்த புத்தகத்தை எழுதியது யார்?!?

Inta puttakattai eḻutiyatu yār?!?

TELUGU

ఈ పుస్తకాన్ని ఎవరు రాశారు?!?

Ī pustakānni evaru rāśāru?!?

THAI

ใครเป็นคนเขียนหนังสือเล่มนี้?!?

Khır pĕn khn k̄heīyn h̄nạngs̄ụ̄x lèm nī̂?!?

TURKISH

Bu kitabı kim yazdı?!?

TURKMEN

Bu kitaby kim ýazdy?!?

UKRAINIAN

Хто написав цю книгу?!?

Khto napysav tsyu knyhu?!?

UZBEK

Bu kitobni kim yozgan?!?

VIETNAMESE

Ai đã viết cuốn sách này?!?

VIETNAMESE

Pwy ysgrifennodd y llyfr hwn?!?

YIDDISH

ווער האט געשריבן דעם ספר?!?

Ver hat geshribn dem sfr?!?

ZULU

Ngubani obhale le ncwadi?!?

ABOUT BUSHEL & PECK BOOKS

Bushel & Peck Books is a children's publishing house with a special mission. Through our Book-for-Book Promise™, we donate one book to kids in need for every book we sell. Our beautiful books are given to kids through schools, libraries, local neighborhoods, shelters, nonprofits, and also to many selfless organizations that are working hard to make a difference. So thank you for purchasing this book! Because of you, another book will make its way into the hands of a child who needs it most.

NOMINATE A SCHOOL OR ORGANIZATION TO RECEIVE FREE BOOKS

Do you know a school, library, or organization that could use some free books for their kids? We'd love to help! Please fill out the nomination form on our website (see below), and we'll do everything we can to make something happen.

www.bushelandpeckbooks.com/pages/nominate-a-school-or-organization

If you liked this book, please leave a review online at your favorite retailer. Honest reviews spread the word about Bushel & Peck—and help us make better books, too!